W9-BLB-597

SPACE-SAVING
FURNITURE
PROJECTS

SPACE-SAVING FURNITURE PROJECTS

DAVE MACKENZIE

GUILD OF MASTER CRAFTSMAN PUBLICATIONS LTD

Somerset County Library
Bridgewater, NJ 08807

First published 1998 by
Guild of Master Craftsman Publications Ltd,
166 High Street, Lewes,
East Sussex, BN7 1XU

Reprinted 1999

© Dave Mackenzie 1998

ISBN 1 86108 099 9

Photographs by Dave Mackenzie except on
pages 40, 41, 45, 50, 58, 66, 74, 75, 81, 86, 91, 95, 96,
102, 106, 109, 110, 118, 123, 131, 137, 142, 148, 149
and 161, by Chris Skarbon

Black-and-white line drawings by Dave Mackenzie

All rights reserved

The right of Dave Mackenzie to be identified as the author of
this work has been asserted in accordance with the Copyright
Designs and Patents Act 1998, Sections 77 and 78.

No part of this publication may be reproduced, stored in a
retrieval system, or transmitted in any form or by any means
without the prior permission of the publisher and
copyright owner.

This book is sold subject to the condition that all designs are
copyright and are not for commercial reproduction without
the permission of the designer and copyright owner.

The publishers and authors can accept no legal responsibility
for any consequences arising from the application of
information, advice or instructions given in this publication.

Designed by Ian Hunt Design

Typeface: Berkeley

Colour origination by Viscan Graphics (Singapore)

Printed in Great Britain at the University Press, Cambridge

Contents

NOTE

NOTE ON MEASUREMENTS

True and accurate measurements are given in imperial: the metric measurements given are only conversions from these. Throughout the book instances will be found where an imperial measurement has slightly differing metric equivalents as these have been rounded up or down in each case.

NOTE

USING THE PLANS

Dimension lines have been kept to a minimum in order to avoid obscuring the diagrams. If you have any doubts as to which points the lines refer to, simply place a ruler on the arrow head, and follow the line along.

Introduction

W<small>HEN</small> you move into a new home, perhaps for the first time, your furniture and other household essentials are spread around the available space and very often seem lost in the empty rooms. Within a short time all that changes, and even large houses eventually become cluttered with an accumulation of possessions that are essential to making a home comfortable and convenient to live in. This book explains how to make furniture that utilizes the available space wisely and stores many of these objects, to give your home an organized and uncluttered appearance. Some of the projects, such as the shoe cupboard on page 75 place things out of sight although still conveniently to hand, while others, like the wine racks on page 66, display their contents – in this case the bottles, so that the information on the labels can be read at a glance.

If you look around your home, it is reasonably easy to make an audit of the areas that need most attention. Undoubtedly there will be some which require radical solutions, such as a new extension or an extra room in the loft. However, there will also be numerous small ways in which major improvements can be made by the addition of smaller, custom-made items. It is these improvements that this book will help you to achieve.

The projects in this book are all made from wood – in most cases, pine. Some of them require experience, but most need little more than patience, confidence and a few hand tools. If you have not yet gained much woodworking experience, try one of the simpler pieces and save the more difficult ones until you have acquired more expertise.

1 Saving Space

THERE are many reasons for requiring more space, so it is fortunate that there are numerous ingenious ways of providing it.

The old lady who lived in the shoe knew the problem well. There she was, nicely set up in a compact *bijou* boot, and along come the children. The local council will not let her build a loft extension and convert it to a thigh-length boot because she is living in a conservation area. In fact, she does not have the money for an extension – she has to spend all her time trying to find ways simply to make ends meet. No wonder she did not know what to do. Just like the old lady, few of us have enough living space and we require more. Whether this is due to a growing family or a more expansive lifestyle, the problem is the same.

WASTE DISPOSAL

It may be that these difficulties are self-inflicted: most of us are reluctant to throw anything away because it might be required at some time in the future. If you cannot get into the cupboard under the stairs for the piles of all those things that might come in useful one day, it is time to act. Drag them out into the daylight, and if they have not been used for 12 months or more, be ruthless – bin them.

It will help you to get rid of all the old rubbish if you think of it as recycling materials. Most towns have sites for recycling – old newspapers and magazines, bottles, and so on – and will welcome it with open skips. If any of the items are valuable you can sell them at a car boot sale, or take them to your local charity shop instead.

Another advantage of disposing of your unwanted articles is that it will make work around the house simpler and quicker – for example, it doubles the amount of time it takes to vacuum the carpet if you have to find the cleaner under all the junk first! It then becomes easier simply to put the job off until another time. So, if you are prevented from digging the garden because the spade is hidden behind the clutter in the garage, consider building the shelf unit featured on page 161 (unless, of course, you regard a lost spade as a positive advantage).

It is a good idea to start your space-saving campaign in the kitchen, as this is nearly always an area where extra space is required. List everything that needs to be recycled, or, preferably, take unwanted items out of the cupboards and stack them ready for removal. Take an audit of what is left and ask yourself if it will fit into the available space.

CREATING SPACE

If the answer to the above question is no, there are several courses of action you can follow. Build new cupboards, or fit extra shelves into existing ones; make the shelving unit for plates shown on page 58 and put your prized dinner service on display where the rest of the world can appreciate it; make the wine rack on page 67 to hang on the wall and provide more floor space – consider every solution. When you have finished in the kitchen, move into the hall, and so on throughout the house.

Extra shelving can solve some of the problems, but even more space can be saved if your furniture is made so that it takes up less room when not in use. The Shakers knew a thing or two about this and hung their chairs on wooden pegs driven into the wall. Other classic pieces of space-saving furniture are the ironing board and the deck chair, which fold up for storing. I have used the deck chair principle for the paint box project on page 149.

To make extra space, furniture can have more than one function. The hall coat rack on page 86 incorporates a shelf on which to place small items and the garage shelf on page 161 has pegs for garden tools. Or, you can take your furniture for a spin by adding castors so that it can be placed exactly where it is required. The bathroom caddy on page 142 can be pushed up to the side of the bath, with toiletries placed on it, or pushed into the corner out of the way. Furniture that stacks, such as the nest of tables on page 96, also makes efficient use of floor space.

Knock-down furniture must be one of the oldest of all space-saving devices. Medieval tables were made with wedged mortise and tenon joints without glue. In a baronial hall, an extremely large table was needed when guests were being entertained. Some barons (the technophobes) had such tables built permanently inside the hall, and when they moved castles the table had to remain because it was too large to fit through the door. The more technically aware nobility, however, had their tables made so that they knocked down into smaller pieces for removal and storage. I have used exactly the same idea for the floor-standing wine rack shown on page 69.

Finally, having said all this, space-saving furniture must not sacrifice any of its other virtues in favour solely of efficiency in use and storage. It should still be functional and user-friendly, and should harmonize with the rest of the furniture in the house. The space-saving projects in this book have been designed with all these aspects in mind, to create functional pieces that are enjoyable to make and use.

2 Ergonomics

Both fitted and free-standing furniture should be constructed to be as functional and easy to use as possible. To achieve this aim, the component parts must be the right size and the units should be placed in the correct position. For example, a coffee table should be a suitable height for its intended function, while a coat rack should not be fixed up so high that some of the users are unable to reach it easily, or so low down that the coats trail on the floor.

When furniture is constructed, shelving erected or cupboards installed, consideration must be given to the size, shape, weight and mobility of the people for whom it is intended. Unfortunately – from the furnituremaker's point of view – there is a tremendous range of sizes in any group of people. Fortunately, there are several solutions to the problem.

One solution is to design furniture that is adjustable: an ironing board is a good example.

The problem is that this can lead to complicated construction and is not usual for tables and chairs, although some office furniture is made in this way. Another solution is to tailor furniture to individual users, which can create a new set of design and construction problems, but is sometimes done for a person who is very different from the norm. The example that springs to mind here is the customized bed made for a person who is exceptionally tall.

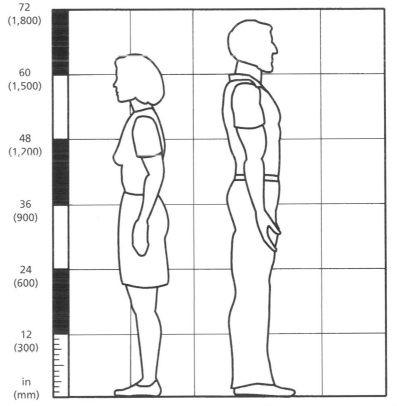

72 (1,800)
60 (1,500)
48 (1,200)
36 (900)
24 (600)
12 (300)
in (mm)

Fig 2.1 Average sizes. Because there is so much variation in size in the adult population, the 'average' man and woman were created.

If you are putting up shelves in your home, you can take into account the individual who will use them most often and tailor their position accordingly. Shelves or cupboards that are hung on the wall in a child's room are a good example, although the positions will have to be changed as the child grows.

The most widely adopted solution to the size problem is to make furniture to a standard set of dimensions that will accommodate an average-sized member of the population (see Fig 2.1). This is the solution I adopted in making the projects in this book. Following the same principle, and the dimensions given in this chapter, will help readers to design their own projects.

ERGONOMICS

The study of the variety of human forms is rather catchily entitled anthropometrics, and its application to design is called ergonomics. They are complex subjects, and in industry some technologists spend their working lives applying these sciences to designing any system with which people interact, including furniture and the fittings for house interiors.

For certain applications, such as the driver's seat in a car, a great deal of work goes into getting the dimensions absolutely right, although after a long journey you might not think so. In domestic furniture this is less critical, but good design will make the difference between a comfortable sitting position and intense irritation.

The important dimensions for various pieces of furniture, based on average sizes, are laid down in international standards. Tables are available which cover all the

BODY SIZES		WOMEN		MEN	
		in	mm	in	mm
A	Stature	63	1,610	69	1,740
B	Elbow height	40	1,005	43	1,090
C	Upward reach	71	1,803	76	1,896
D	Forward reach	24	610	27	686
E	Shoulder height	52	1,310	56	1,425
F	Sitting height	33	850	36	910
G	Sitting elbow height	9	235	10	245
H	Buttock to knee length	22	570	23	595
I	Knee height	20	500	21	545
J	Hip breadth	15	370	14	360
K	Shoulder breadth	16	395	18	465

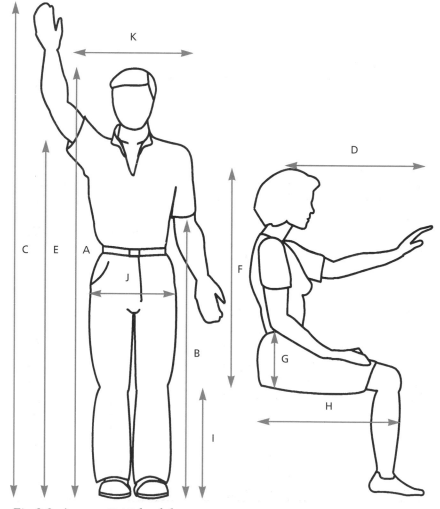

Fig 2.2 *Average British adult measurements.*

important body measurements for the population of Britain. For the purposes of designing systems with which people interact, these tables give three different sizes: average sizes, the smallest sizes after the lowest 5% have been discarded and the largest sizes after the largest 5% have been discarded. A simplified version giving the main body measurements for an average-sized person is shown in Fig 2.2. Tables of dimensions for children are also available.

WORKING SURFACES AND SHELVES FOR STANDING USERS

If a kitchen cupboard or shelf is installed that the cook will access many times during the preparation of a meal, the importance of getting its position correct cannot be overstated (see Fig 2.3). If it is too

high, the cook can stand on tiptoes and stretch for it, but this is not a good idea for although the body will readily adapt to adverse conditions, this very adaptability can lead to stress and injury.

From the standard table, 71in (1,803mm) is the maximum height at which an average-sized woman can reach an object on a shelf. In the kitchen, where space is usually at a premium, this dimension is often ignored when a cupboard is installed. The problem is exacerbated when cupboards are placed above the work surface, as the user cannot stand immediately under the unit but must reach over the work surface as well.

The standard height for a kitchen work surface is 35½in (900mm). A standard height is essential, because dishwashing machines and other appliances are made to fit

under it. When fixing a cupboard above the surface you will therefore have to reach a compromise between providing access to the cupboard (by not fixing it too high) and making sure the working area is unobstructed (by not fixing it too low).

The shower caddy on page 118 is an example of shelving that is fixed to the wall and is unlikely to have an obstruction below it. In addition, as most shower stalls are raised above the floor level, the height at which the shelving is fixed to the wall can reflect this (see Fig 2.4). To get it just right, ask the shortest member of the family to stand in the shower and then fix the shelf where they can reach it without effort.

Some work surfaces are customized for an individual because they are probably the only person who will use them. A good

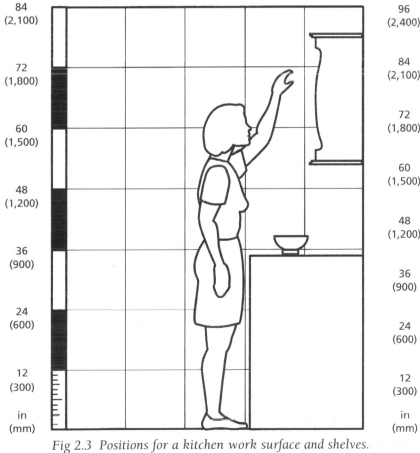

Fig 2.3 Positions for a kitchen work surface and shelves.

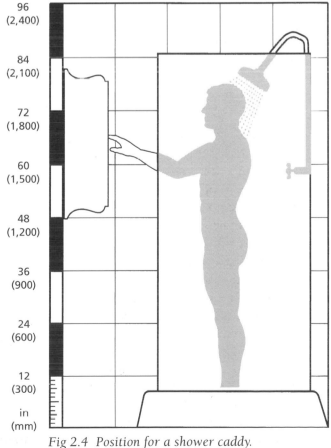

Fig 2.4 Position for a shower caddy.

example of this is the woodworker who makes a bench for their own use. In this case, the person using it must be able to work on the surface and be in a position to exert considerable downward pressure when necessary. A work surface that is too low will cause the individual to stoop, which is uncomfortable if sustained for long periods. The way to gauge the correct height for a woodworking bench is to measure from approximately 9in (29mm) below the elbow to the floor when the user is standing and then make the bench to that height (see Fig 2.5). For tasks where it is not so important to exert downward pressure the bench should be 3in (75mm) higher, which can help the user to avoid stooping.

TABLES AND DESKS FOR SEATED USERS

For a coffee table, the height is the most important dimension; the surface area can vary according to the function for which the table is intended and leg clearance is not a problem, as people do not expect to put their legs under this type of table. The top should be reached easily from a reclining position in an easy chair; a comfortable height is 12in (300mm) plus or minus 2in (50mm) (see Fig 2.6).

A bathroom caddy can be considered as a small table, so the same criteria apply. The top will be reached easily from the bath if the height is equal to that of the bath (see Fig 2.7).

The main dimensions for a dining table are the height, surface area and leg clearance. Whatever its shape, there must be enough room to accommodate the desired number of diners.

A table or desk at which somebody will sit and work requires a different approach, because it will usually be used by one person at a time. For example, the width should not be too great because the user will not be able to reach very far from a sitting position, but if the

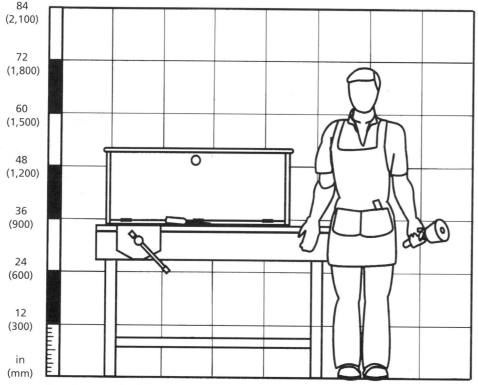

Fig 2.5 Height for a woodworking bench.

Fig 2.6 Height for a coffee table.

table or desk is intended to hold a computer it will require sufficient width for the monitor to be placed behind the keyboard. It is not a good idea to have the monitor offset to one side, as this will eventually stress the user due to the twisted sitting position.

SHELVES, DRAWERS AND CUPBOARD DOORS

Shelves are used in various different pieces of furniture and situations. The principle which governs their position holds true for all the different applications, whether the shelves are on a kitchen wall or in a wardrobe: in general, for the storage of objects that are required frequently, easily reached shelves are used, but for rarely used objects, higher, difficult to reach shelves can be tolerated. In a kitchen, easily accessible cupboard shelves are usually placed about 18in (450mm) above the work surface. These are used to store the sugar, tins of baked beans and other items that are used constantly, whereas the top shelves are reserved for storing Christmas cake decorations and pancake mix. The figures given in Fig 2.2 for upward and forward reach assume that, at the distance given, a person could reach an item on a shelf.

Whether a shelf is at a convenient height depends on the position of the user. A person working in a kitchen is usually standing up, so the shelving is positioned accordingly. The position will not be the same for somebody seated at a desk, where the shelving must be much lower.

When drawers are installed in a table or desk there must be enough room for the user's legs underneath. When they are used in other applications they cannot be placed higher than eye level, unless they have transparent plastic fronts.

When installing furniture such as a shoe cupboard in a hall or passageway, it is important that there is an allowance of at least 33in (838mm) in front of the door when it is opened fully to allow people to walk past it. The same applies to furniture with drawers that open into an area where people need to get past (see Fig 2.8).

CHAIRS

Chair measurements are divided into two sets of data, one for an easy chair and one for a formal chair such as a dining or office chair. If a

| in (mm) | 12 (300) | 24 (600) | 3 (900) | 48 (1,200) | 60 (1,500) |

Fig 2.8 Drawer and cupboard clearance.

chair is intended to be used at a desk for a full working day, it should be adjustable so that it can be customized for a particular person.

When designing a dining chair, the dimensions of the seat and back are important. The height, width and depth of the seat must be considered, while the back must be set at the correct angle and be of the correct height. The seat surface should be substantially flat. The backrest should provide support just below the shoulders in the lumbar region, and if possible, there should be a gap below the backrest so that the buttocks can protrude into it.

The specifications for an easy chair to relax in can vary widely. The height indicated in Fig 2.6 is intended for an average, able-bodied person. An older person would require a higher seat height so that the chair is easy to get out of; this can be achieved if the backrest is less raked.

| 48 (1,200) | 36 (900) | 24 (600) | 12 (300) | in (mm) |

Fig 2.7 Height for a bathroom caddy.

3 Tools

THE tools used to make the projects in this book are a selection that I have collected over a number of years, but they are a personal choice and those used by other woodworkers will differ slightly. If a bandsaw is specified in the instructions for a particular item and you do not happen to have one, it does not mean that the project is impossible to make: there are at least six different ways of cutting a curved shape in a piece of timber and the one you use depends on several factors, not least being the cost. Other considerations are how much time you have available and the pleasure to be gained from the cutting process itself. The tools I choose to use in any given instance depend to some extent on the way I feel and the amount of work to be done. For example, although I own a router I will sometimes cut a rebate using a hand plane simply because it is pleasant to use. However, if I have dozens of rebates to cut then I will choose the router every time.

Tools can be categorized broadly into two groups – hand and power tools – and most woodworkers will have a selection of both kinds. Wonderful results can be produced with hand tools alone (think of Chippendale and Sheraton), but if you do not have a lifetime's experience, a workshop full of craftsmen or unlimited time, power

tools are the next best thing. They speed up the repetitious tasks and can produce items made to fine tolerances. After all, power drills were invented to take care of the boring work.

If you are an inexperienced woodworker, start with a few good-quality hand tools and tackle some of the simpler projects first. As your experience grows you can add new tools as they are needed. When you feel you can justify the expense, invest in some power tools.

HAND TOOLS
MEASURING AND MARKING

The two 'tools' that I always carry in my pocket when woodworking or for any other jobs around the house are an extending steel rule and a pencil. In terms of usefulness, these are closely followed by a try square and a straight-edged steel ruler.

The extending steel rule has a hook on one end of the tape so that you can measure the width of a

Fig 3.1 Measuring and marking tools.

board one-handed. It should also be fitted with a tape lock so that it does not retract unless you want it to. The try square is used for marking lines that are at right angles to the sides of the board and also for checking that an edge is square to the face of the board. The straight-edge is used for drawing straight lines and to check that a board is flat.

The next pair of items required in this category are a mortise gauge, used for scribing pairs of lines parallel to the edge of a board, to mark the position of mortise grooves and tenons, and a marking gauge, which is very similar to a mortise gauge but scribes only a single line. Some mortise gauges have double pins on one side and a single pin on the other, so they can be used for both operations. The length of the stock of these tools governs how far from the edge of a board they will scribe a line. The standard length is about 8in (200mm).

The other marking tools in my collection are a sliding bevel, a marking knife and dividers. The sliding bevel is an adjustable try square that is used to mark lines at an angle. If you are marking a line to guide a saw cut, particularly across the grain, use a marking knife in preference to a pencil as it cuts through some of the fibres on the surface of the wood, which prevents the saw splintering the edge on the up stroke. If you are cutting a sheet of plywood and want to prevent the back face being splintered, score it on both sides with a marking knife. Dividers are adjusted to a set distance and used to mark sizes that you want to repeat several times.

HAND SAWS

A panel saw is used for making straight cuts across the grain on large-sectioned timber or sheets of man-made board. Typically, it will have 10 teeth per 1in (25mm). I use a panel saw with hardened teeth, which means that it cuts extremely well but cannot be sharpened. However, these saws are relatively inexpensive and do not blunt quickly, so are very cost effective.

A tenon saw is a hand saw stiffened with a strip of metal along the back of the blade. This prevents the blade from flexing so that it cuts blade is supported it can be very thin and therefore makes only a narrow kerf. A typical tenon saw is 12in (305mm) long and has 14 teeth per 1in (25mm). These saws are also available with hardened points.

The only other hand saw I use regularly is a coping saw. The blades are extremely thin and also disposable. The saw is used for cutting very tight curves in wood up to 1in (25mm) thick, and for

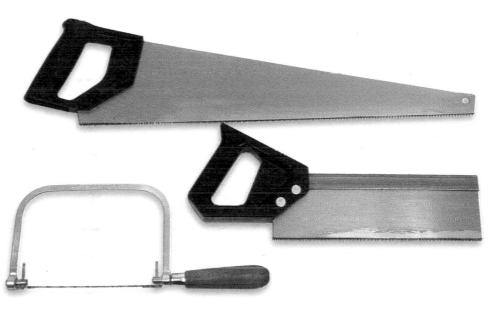

Fig 3.2 Hand saws.

Fig 3.3 Hammers and a carver's mallet.

making closed cutouts in the centre of a piece of timber. To do this, drill a hole in the waste wood in the middle of the cutout. Detach the blade from one end of the saw and thread it through the hole before reconnecting it, then saw around the outline to form a cutout. To remove the saw from the piece of wood, detach the blade from the frame. One of the disadvantages of this saw is that because it is so narrow the blade tends to wander. It therefore helps if both hands are used to control the saw.

HAMMERS

For driving in all but the smallest nails, a medium-weight (about 18oz/500g) claw hammer is an essential piece of equipment. This will not only put nails in but also pull them out. Claw hammers are available with shafts made of wood, steel or plastic.

Cross-peen hammers are used for large nails and small pins. The wedge-shaped head on the back of the hammer is small enough to use on panel pins. I use a small version of the cross-peen hammer for tacks, small nails, upholstery nails and panel pins.

It is not good practice to use a hammer on the handle of a chisel, as even tough plastic handles can be damaged. If hand pressure is not enough, then a wooden mallet is the tool for the job. These come in different shapes and are made from a variety of hardwoods. Those made from beech or lignum-vitae are a good choice.

LATHE TOOLS

For measuring work on the lathe, the minimum tools required are a pair of outside callipers and a ruler.

Turning requires specialized chisels that differ considerably from

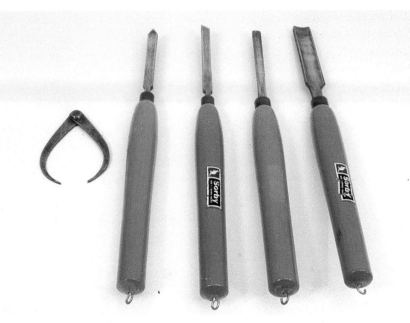

Fig 3.4 Turning tools.

those used for general woodworking. No attempt should be made to use ordinary chisels on a lathe, as this can be dangerous. Lathe chisels are much longer and stronger to give better leverage, which prevents them being torn from your grip. They are available in a couple of different lengths; the longest, at 20in (500mm), are classified as professional tools, while the smaller standard size is approximately 16in (400mm). A basic set of chisels for turning would comprise:

- A roughing-out gouge between ¾in (18mm) and 1½in (38mm) wide, with the end ground flat and the bevel on the outside.
- A spindle gouge between ⅜in (9mm) and ¾in (18mm) wide, with the bevel on the outside and the front ground to a rounded shape.
- A parting tool, which is pointed, with a width of ¼in (6mm), and is used for removing the work from the lathe by cutting away at both ends of the finished piece.
- A skew chisel, which comes in a range of widths between ¾in

(18mm) and 1½in (38mm). The blade is ground on both sides and used for smoothing roughly turned cylinders and for cutting beads.
- A square-ended scraper between ¾in (18mm) and 1¼in (32mm) wide. This has a shallow angle of 10° and is used for fine finishing work or for working on end grain when turning bowls.

When turning a piece of wood on a lathe, chisels will remove large amounts of waste very quickly. For this reason, they require honing frequently and it is a good idea to have your sharpening system (see page 19) situated next to the lathe. Some lathes come with a built-in grinding wheel.

HAND CHISELS AND GOUGES

I find that three bevel-edged chisels with plastic handles are adequate for most jobs. The widths I use are ¼in (6mm), ½in (12mm) and 1in (25mm) and the plastic handles mean they can withstand the occasional blow from a mallet when hand pressure is not enough. Unless they are reinforced with a metal ferrule, wood handles will break if abused in this way.

These chisels are supplemented by 1in (25mm) and ½in (12mm) half-round gouges. They are used for shaping the ends of housings to accommodate shelves that have a rounded front.

PLANES

Hand planes give you more control than a motorized plane. When squaring up rough timber, use a powered hand planer for the initial cuts and then swap to a jackplane to give the final finish and to square up.

A metal jackplane is about 14in (356mm) long and is used for all general-purpose planing.

A block plane is smaller than a jackplane and has the blade set at a more acute angle (20°). This makes it ideal for smoothing end grain.

A small, metal bull-nosed plane is useful for trimming the shoulders of joints and stopped rebates. The blade is set very close to the front of the plane so that it will cut almost up to an obstruction. The blade is equal in width to the body of the plane so that it will trim shoulders.

FILES

The only files I use with any frequency are half-round and round second cut. (Second cut means that the file is medium coarse – somewhere between a rasp and a file with fine teeth.) These are used for smoothing curves after the initial shaping has been made with a rotary rasp and before smoothing with glasspaper. When in use, particularly on resinous pine boards, the files soon become clogged with wood fibres which reduces their efficiency, so they require frequent cleaning with a wire brush.

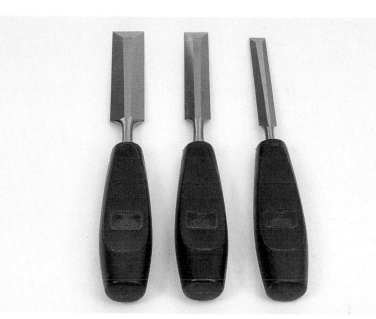

Fig 3.5 Bevel-edged chisels.

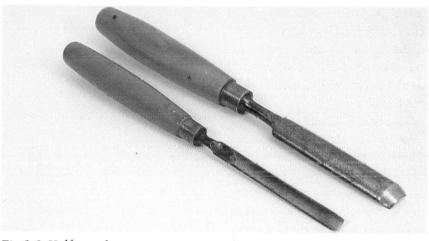

Fig 3.6 Half-round gouges.

Fig 3.7 Hand planes.

Fig 3.8 *Files and a wire brush for cleaning them.*

POWER TOOLS

These can be divided into hand-held and floor-standing tools, both of which are available in a wide variety of different types. The powered hand-held tools used for the projects are a drill, orbital disc sander, router, jigsaw and planer. A lathe and a bandsaw are the two floor-standing tools required.

POWER DRILLS

Most woodworkers, and anyone else who carries out maintenance work around the house, will have a power drill. Drills will make accurate holes not only in wood but also in almost any other material you care to name. How on earth did people make holes in concrete before power drills were invented? A power drill will not only do this but will also put in and remove wood screws effortlessly.

I have two power drills: one driven directly by mains electricity, for the tougher jobs and for use in a drill stand, and a second, lightweight drill with a rechargeable battery, that is much more portable and ideal for hand drilling and putting in screws. These two drills have made some of my hand tools very nearly redundant. My hand drill, brace and bit, and screwdrivers now gather dust on the shelves in the workshop. I have not used a brace and bit since dinosaurs ruled the earth.

The chuck size controls the size of bit shank that the drill will accept: a ½in (12mm) chuck will accept a ½in (12mm) bit. The exception to this is that some bits are available with reduced shanks. For example, a bit that drills a ¾in (18mm) hole will fit into a chuck with a capacity of ½in (12mm). For a mains-powered drill, a chuck size of ⅜in or ½in (10mm or 12mm) is about right; for a battery-powered drill, this will be ⅜in (10mm).

DRILL BITS

To achieve the best results, you will need to use the correct bit for the job. I find the following bits essential.

- Twist bits are used for general-purpose drilling in wood or metal.
- Dowel bits are good for locating a hole accurately because of the sharp point on the top of the bit.
- Spade bits will drill large holes in wood very quickly and have the advantage of being inexpensive.

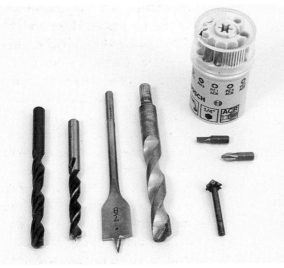

Fig 3.9 *A selection of drill bits.*

Fig 3.10 *Hole saws.*

The only problem is that they can wander off line.

- To make a large hole in wood up to 1in (25mm) thick you can use a hole saw. These are available as a number of individual saw bits or as a set of rings of varying diameter that fit a common holder.
- Masonry bits look a little like twist bits but have toughened metal inserted into the tip for cutting into brick, concrete and so on.
- A countersinking bit is required for enlarging the top of a screw hole, so that the screw head can be sunk into the wood with its top flush with the surface.

- A small selection of screwdriver bits that fit the various types of screw heads will save time on projects that use lots of screws.

Do not overload the drill when drilling large holes in tough materials, but keep it spinning without letting it drop in speed. This will preserve both the drill and the bits.

DRILL STAND AND FLEXIBLE DRIVE

These are two of the 'must have' attachments for a mains-powered drill.

A vertical stand attachment will increase your drill's usefulness and accuracy. Dowels or screws are not so effective and are often unsightly if they slope – and it is almost impossible to hold the drill at 90° to the work surface without the assistance of a stand. The stand can also be used to hold the drill while it drives other attachments. A drum sander is a good example: although you can use a drill with a drum sander attached freehand and take the tool to the work, it would be cumbersome and difficult to control. If the drum and drill are held in a stand and the workpiece is fed on to the drum, it is much easier to control.

For traditional designs I often use serpentine shapes, which are smoothed with a drum sander, flap wheel or small rotary rasps. The flap wheel and rasps are most effective if they are used in conjunction with a flexible drive attached to the drill in the stand.

SANDERS

Several different types of sander are available, each of which has different qualities to recommend it – a belt sander, for example, will remove lots of wood very quickly, while an orbital sander will give a fine finish. If your budget will not stretch to more than one type, I would recommend that you purchase an orbital disc sander. These sanders differ from random orbital sanders in that the discs rotate as well as vibrate. They are easy to use and produce a fine finish but also work relatively quickly. For general-purpose work, the type that has a round rubber disc fitted with Velcro for changing the abrasive paper quickly is ideal. Orbital disc sanders produce a fine, virtually scratch-free surface on the wood. Even so, for the very best results a light hand sanding with glasspaper will give a professional finish.

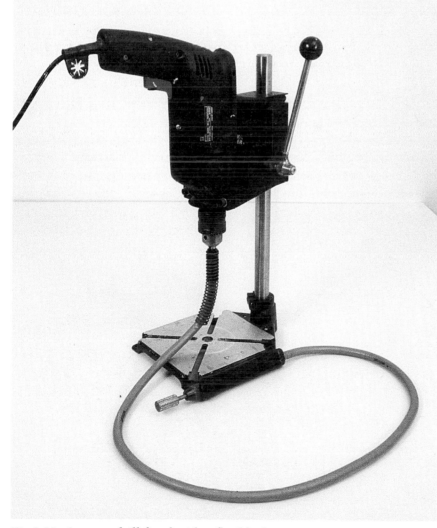

Fig 3.11 A power drill fitted with a flexible drive.

One of the problems with a disc sander is that because it has a round pad it cannot be used in tight corners. To overcome this limitation, a sander with a triangular-shaped pad can be useful.

For smoothing the concave curves used on traditional-style items, such as the telephone shelf on page 81, a drum sander and flap wheel are useful tools. A drum sander is a dense foam drum that has an abrasive belt from a belt sander stretched around the circumference. The foam drum has an arbor attached so that it can be fitted to a power drill. To change the abrasive belt, simply squeeze the foam. Drum sanders are available in different sizes, but one with a diameter of 6in (152mm) is suitable for all the projects in this book.

Flap wheels are made from lots of small rectangles of abrasive cloth that are glued to an arbor, which is fitted into a power drill. They are packed closely together so that they form an abrasive cylinder that shrinks as it is used and the ends of the flaps erode. Lots of different sizes and grades of abrasive are available.

ROUTER

A router is a tool rated highly desirable by professional woodworkers and most serious amateurs. It will shape, groove, rebate, cut joints, bore holes and cut complex mouldings. When used with a sharp cutter it gives accurate cuts with a fine finish, and it has largely replaced many of the rebating and grooving planes commonly used a few years ago.

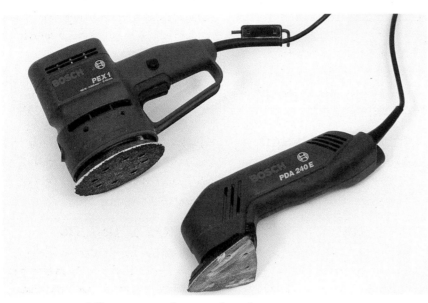

Fig 3.12 Two different types of powered sander.

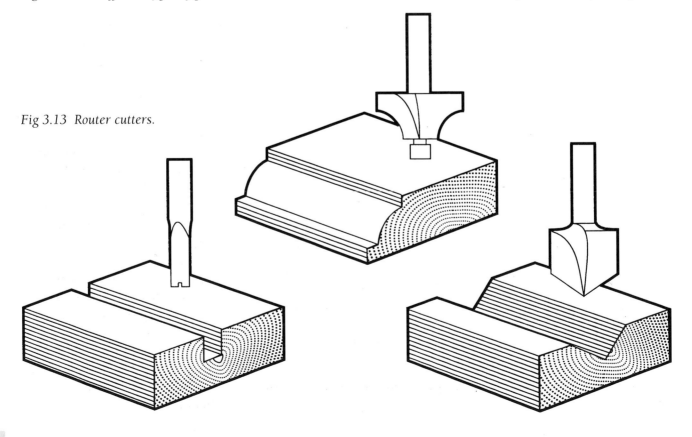

Fig 3.13 Router cutters.

One of the disadvantages is that the cutters are expensive, but if the router is not overloaded – so that the cutters do not get too hot – they should last for a reasonable length of time, particularly if used for cutting softwoods such as pine. Some cutters can be re-sharpened.

Routers are available in two types: plunge routers, and those where the depth of the cutter is fixed at the correct depth for the work in hand. Plunge routers are the most widely used. With these, the depth of the cutter is pre-set but will only reach this depth when downward pressure is applied. The technique is to start the cutter spinning, place the router in position to cut and then push it forwards and downwards until the cutter starts to cut. This makes it easy to get a smooth start when, for example, a groove is being cut, but more importantly it enables the cutter to be lifted clear of the groove at the end of a cut.

A router is used freehand to follow a line or, more commonly, with a fence to guide it parallel to an edge. It can also be fitted into a router table in an upside-down position so that it works like a spindle moulder.

CUTTERS

The very best router cutters are tipped with tungsten carbide. These last longer but when they do need sharpening it must be done professionally.

The projects in this book use $\frac{1}{4}$in (6mm) and $\frac{3}{8}$in (10mm) straight cutters, a 'V' grooving cutter and a beading cutter.

PORTABLE POWERED PLANER

A powered hand planer is a useful addition to a tool collection if you prepare lots of timber from sawn planks instead of purchasing it ready-planed. I often use pine that is recycled from old house timbers, roof joists and floorboards, and a powered planer is ideal for turning what appears to be useless material into desirable timber, which is often of better quality than that sold as new. A powered planer will prevent you suffering from planer's elbow, the non-sporting equivalent of tennis elbow.

The important dimension to look for is the maximum depth of cut. Planers usually come with a blade width of $3\frac{1}{4}$in (82mm), which can be adjusted fairly precisely to remove wood up to a depth of $\frac{1}{16}$in (2mm) at one pass, although small planes have a maximum $\frac{1}{32}$in (1mm) depth of cut for a single pass.

Most planers can be fitted with a fence that will allow them to be used for planing rebates. In some cases this fence can be angled so that the plane will cut chamfers or sloping rebates.

POWERED JIGSAW

A jigsaw has a thin, narrow blade that is held and driven from one end only. This makes it ideal for cutting out enclosed shapes in the centre of a piece of wood, including curves with a small radius. To cut out curved shapes in the centre of a piece of timber as, for example, in the bathroom corner cabinet on page 110, drill a hole to start the cut, push the blade through the hole and then make the cutouts.

Jigsaws are available with variable speeds and angles of cut. Various blades are available for different tasks, including very narrow blades that will cut tighter curves and blades for cutting metal and plastic.

The maximum thickness of wood a jigsaw will cut through depends on how powerful the saw is and on the type of wood being cut, but most modern jigsaws will cut through 1in (25mm) of softwood without any problems and some through considerably more than this.

Fig 3.14 A traditional wooden plane compared with the modern powered equivalent.

A jigsaw can be used freehand or with a fence so that it cuts parallel to an edge. Some fences also have a facility for cutting circles. On most saws, the base plate can be angled so that the saw will cut bevels. When using a jigsaw make sure that the wood is held down with cramps, as the saw will tend to vibrate.

BANDSAW

The bandsaw is one of the most frequently used and versatile power tools I possess. It will cut through pieces of timber 6in (150mm) thick or shave slices as thin as veneer from the end of a piece of wood. It can be fitted with blades of various widths from $\frac{1}{4}$in (6mm) to $\frac{5}{8}$in (15mm). The narrow blades are used for cutting small-radius curves while the widest are for making straight cuts. The saws are available in two- or three-wheel types. The blade runs on the wheels, which are hidden inside the case. The more expensive saws usually have two wheels.

If adjusted properly with the blade guards in place, a bandsaw is inherently safer than a circular saw and not as scary to use. This is because it will not kick back the timber being sawn towards the user.

The critical sizes in the specification for a bandsaw are the maximum thickness it will cut and the distance from the blade to the body of the saw. This distance controls the maximum width of material that can be cut.

LATHE

Several of the projects in this book require access to a lathe. Lathes come in a variety of sizes, from those that are driven by an electric drill to large floor-standing machines designed for professionals. For hobbyists, the bench-mounted lathe is usually preferable.

Fig 3.15 A powered jigsaw.

Fig 3.16 A bandsaw.

Fig 3.17 A lathe.

When buying a lathe, the important dimensions to consider are the distance between the centres, which governs the length of the wood that can be fitted on to the lathe, and the height of the pivots above the lathe bed. This controls the thickness of any piece of wood being mounted between the centres, and is known as the swing of the lathe. If a lathe has an outside faceplate or the head of the lathe can be swivelled through 90° or 180°, the diameter of bowl that can be made will not be limited by the swing of the lathe.

A means of varying the speed of the lathe is necessary for different operations or for turning work of various sizes or in different materials. For example, square-sectioned wood is turned to a cylinder at a slow speed but the final sanding is done with the lathe running much faster.

SHARPENING SYSTEMS

It cannot be emphasized enough that well sharpened tools are essential for good results. Having said that, I have to admit that I find sharpening tools about as exciting as ironing shirts.

In an ideal world, all tools would be sharpened at the end of the work session before they are polished and tucked up in their centrally heated, double-glazed toolbox. If

Fig 3.18 A tool sharpening system.

you find, as I do, that life is too short for this, simply sharpen your tools when they are not cutting effectively and put a good, powered sharpening system high on your list of desirable tools. I have a motorized whetstone sharpener with a slowly rotating stone wheel on one side for grinding. This is lubricated with water so that the cutting edge being ground will not overheat. On the other side is a leather-covered stropping wheel, which is used in conjunction with a polishing paste for producing a fine cutting edge after the tool has been ground to the correct angle.

If sharpening tools is, for you, an essential part of the woodworking experience, you can get equally good results using a honing guide and good quality sharpening stones – it just takes longer. Craftsmen who have been sharpening tools for many years can sharpen a plane iron on an oilstone without a honing guide and produce an edge that will shave the hairs from their arms, but to achieve a good result by this method takes plenty of practice.

Rectangular-shaped oilstones are used for hand sharpening. A naturally occurring stone called Arkansas stone is the best but it is expensive. Synthetic stones, available in different grades, are an effective substitute. Small, shaped stones called slipstones are used for honing gouges with bevels on the inside.

It is a sad fact that when your parents admonished you with the warning that 'bad workmen always blame their tools', they got it wrong. Even craftsmen cannot do a good job with inferior quality or badly sharpened tools. It pays to buy the best you can afford and keep them sharp.

WOODWORKING VICE

You will find it very difficult to make any of the projects in this book without some means of holding the work steady while you use both hands to control the tools. The ideal situation is to have a designated area to work in and a woodworker's bench fitted with a vice. Unfortunately, this is not always possible, but a good compromise is a portable 'workmate', which consists of a folding trestle stand with a large vice fitted to the top.

Your vice should be of the type designed specifically for woodworking and if it is made of metal the jaws should be padded with pieces of wood so that it does not mark the workpiece. The distance between the two jaws when they are fully open specifies the size – in most cases, the bigger the better. One feature of some larger vices that can save a lot of time is a quick-release mechanism which allows the vice to be opened and closed speedily.

CRAMPS

One of the most notable features of a professional woodworker's premises is the number of cramps hung on the wall. Some will be new while others will look as if they have been used every day for the last 50 years – which they probably have. Although there are many variations, the two basic types are 'G' cramps and sash cramps.

'G' cramps are categorized by the maximum distance to which the jaws will open. They are available

Fig 3.19 A bench-mounted vice.

in a huge range of sizes, but for general work you can start with a couple of 6in (152mm) cramps and add to them when required – not *if*, because there will always be a stage when you need more cramps than you have available.

Sash cramps are used to hold together large items such as cupboards or bookcases when they have just been glued. They are categorized by length and are available from 12in (300mm) up to 72in (1,830mm) in length and beyond.

DOWELLING JIG

Dowels are a quick and accurate way of forming a strong joint between pieces of wood. To be effective, the holes for the dowels must be drilled in precisely the correct position (see page 25). There are several devices available to accomplish this, but the one I prefer is a dowelling jig. This is a strongly made tool that comprises a fixed plate at the end of two long rails upon which the drill guides slide. The guides incorporate a

fence for positioning the holes a specific distance from the edge of the work. Long rails can be obtained for joining wide boards.

ABRASIVES

For the final finish or for a quick smoothing job that is too small to warrant blowing the dust from a powered sander, I augment my array of mechanical abrasive devices with a cork block and sheets of glasspaper.

Glasspaper is a generic term that covers a range of different abrasives mounted on different substrates. Glasspaper itself is the one with a pale yellow appearance that is bottom of the range as regards longevity. For preference use aluminium oxide paper, which will last much longer. It is available in a range of grit sizes, with the smallest number representing the coarsest grit. I generally use medium-grade paper followed by fine, and then finish off with fine-grade steel wool.

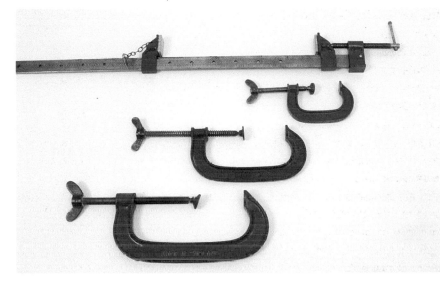

Fig 3.20 *Sash cramp and 'G' cramps.*

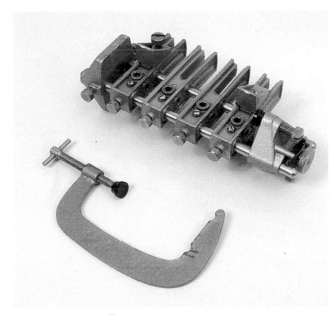

Fig 3.21 *A dowelling jig.*

Fig 3.22 *Woodworking abrasives.*

4 Fixings and Fittings

Fixings and fittings are the essential pieces of hardware required for attaching, joining, hinging, hanging and holding things together. Some, such as nails and screws, are found in every workshop, while others are more specialized and will be purchased for a particular job.

All the fixings and fittings required for the projects in this book are described in the following pages, and information is given on where and how to use them.

FIXING TO WALLS

Many space-saving ideas rely on putting possessions into a cupboard or placing them on shelves that are hung on the wall, which of course saves floor space.

If you were a lumberjack and lived in a log cabin it would not be difficult to hang your possessions on the wall: you would simply bang a nail or wooden peg into the logs from which the wall was constructed and the problem would be solved. For the rest of us, it is not that simple. The first task is to find out what sort of wall you have on the interior. If the wall sounds hollow when it is rapped with the knuckles, there is a good chance it is a hollow wall made from a wooden frame covered with plasterboard. If it sounds solid, it might be made from brick or blocks with a plaster covering, or it might be a mixture of

all three. If your house was built pre-1940 and the outside is brick, then the interior wall will probably also be of brick. In later houses such walls might be of brick or blocks, while many modern houses have partition walls made from wood frames and plasterboard, with outside walls of plaster on blocks.

MASONRY WALLS

MASONRY PLUGS AND SCREWS

For light or medium weights to be hung on to brick, concrete or block walls, plastic wall plugs are used. These are fitted into a hole drilled into the wall, and when the screw is driven into the plug it forces it to expand and grip tightly. For the best results, obtain the correct size of plug for the corresponding screw size, and use the correct size of drill

bit as well. Information about the size of the screws and drill bits to be used is usually given on the packaging containing the plugs.

To drill a brick, concrete or block wall requires a power drill with a masonry bit that is the same size as the plug. Select your plug so that it is slightly longer than the part of the screw that will fit into the wall: this is the screw length minus the thickness of the item to be fixed to the wall. Some plugs will take larger diameters than the screws specified – up to three sizes larger in some cases. If the wall is of concrete or some of the tougher types of brick, the drill will need a hammer-action setting. If a large-diameter hole is required for a heavy-duty expanding bolt (see below), drilling several holes with masonry bits of progressively bigger diameters can make the task easier. Make sure that

Fig 4.1 Masonry screws and plastic wall plugs.

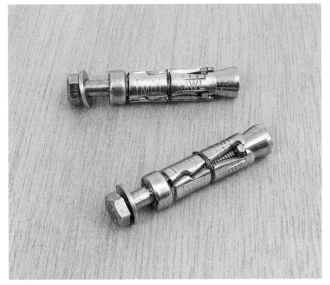

Fig 4.2 *Heavy-duty expanding wall bolts.*

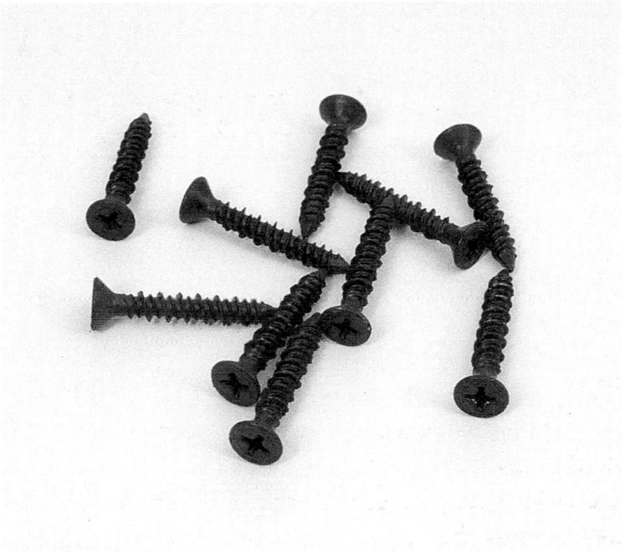

Fig 4.3 *Self-tapping screws for fixing in brick.*

the drill does not overheat, as this will ruin the tip. Drill slowly, and if necessary withdraw the bit occasionally and quench it in water. Before you start drilling, make sure you will not drill into any concealed cables or water pipes.

Mark the position of the hole on the wall with a pencil and drill a hole in that position with the drill held perpendicular to the surface of the wall. Make sure the hole is deep enough for the entire plug to fit into it. Clean out any dust from the hole. Place the plug in the hole until only the raised edge on the end is left protruding. It may be necessary to tap the plug home with a hammer.

Slot the screw through the hole in the item to be fixed and place it in position on the wall. Locate the screw in the plug and tighten it fully. Always fit normal wood screws into plastic plugs: self-tapping screws or screws intended for particleboard will cut the insides of the plastic plugs and will not be secure.

If you are drilling a hole in plaster-covered masonry, the plaster will not be strong enough to hold the item. Ensure that you drill right through it into the masonry behind.

EXPANDING BOLTS

These bolts are used for heavy loads that are to be hung on brick, concrete and hard masonry walls. They are available in a huge range of sizes and are extremely strong. Drill a hole which will accommodate the expanding part of the bolt, place the bolt through the item and into the hole, and when the nut is tightened a wedge will be pulled between the two parts inside the wall and they will expand to make a rock-solid fixing point.

SELF-TAPPING MASONRY SCREWS

These are hardened steel screws that will fix light loads to a wall without requiring plastic wall plugs. Drill a pilot hole that is slightly longer than the screw length, position the item, and when you tighten the screw in the hole it will cut its own thread. Masonry screws will hold reliably in brick, dense blocks and concrete.

STUDDED CAVITY WALLS

Many modern houses do not have brick or block walls dividing the rooms but are partitioned with

studded walls. These are wood frames, typically of 3 x 2in (70 x 50mm) sectioned timber, that are covered on both sides with plasterboard, hardboard or other thin composite boards, leaving a cavity in the centre. The cavity is sometimes filled with insulating material. Drilling a hole to fix one of the expanding or spring toggles that are used on these walls requires some care.

First mark the position of the screw with a cross on the wall. You now need to establish whether the hole is going to penetrate the covering board into the cavity or whether you are drilling into an area where the covering has a batten or lath behind it, which is part of the frame underneath. The way to do this is to drill a small-diameter pilot hole: the resistance the drill meets will give you the required information. If you drill through the board into the wood frame underneath, an ordinary wood screw will be adequate providing it is long enough to reach the wood batten. If the pilot hole indicates that there is cavity behind the hole, use a sharp drill to make the hole large enough to accommodate the cavity-wall fixing device that you have chosen. When drilling this hole do not press too hard, particularly in plasterboard, as this may cause some breakaway when the drill penetrates the back of the board.

SELF-TAPPING PLASTERBOARD FIXINGS

These fixings are made of metal or plastic and are used for hanging relatively lightweight cabinets and fixtures. No drill is required: simply break the surface with a screwdriver, screw the plug into the plasterboard and fit the screw through the item and into the plug.

Fig 4.4 *Self-tapping plasterboard plugs and screws.*

PLASTERBOARD TOGGLES

For use on hollow plasterboard walls where access is available from one side only, these fixings are suitable for hanging light or medium-weight cabinets. Drill a hole the same diameter as the toggle just below the flange. Insert the screw into the fixing, compress the 'wings' and push the fixing into the hole. Tap the fixing flush with the surface. Position the item and tighten the screw until secure.

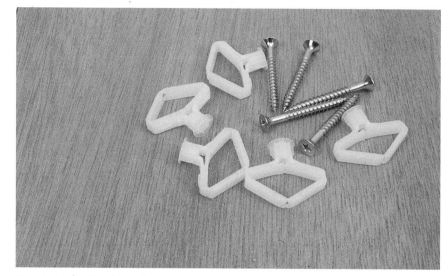

Fig 4.5 *Plastic plasterboard toggles and screws.*

SPRING TOGGLE

These fixings are for use on stud walls, laths and plaster, hollow ceilings and so on. Drill a hole wide enough for you to insert the toggle with the wings compressed. Insert the screw through the fixture and into the fitting; compress the wings and push the fitting into the hole. When through the wall covering, the wings will spring apart. Tighten the screw.

Fig 4.6 *Metal spring toggles and screws.*

PROBLEM WALLS

EXPANDING RUBBER PLUGS

These fixings are made for hanging items on to unknown or problem walls; for example, they will work in stud walls made of plasterboard, hardboard or chipboard. They are also useful for framed walls that do not have a large enough cavity in the centre to take one of the other types of plasterboard toggle.

In solid materials, such as thick chipboard, drill a hole that is the same diameter as the rubber plug and as deep as the plug is long. The plugs will work equally well in regular, smooth holes or irregular ones. Insert the plug, position the fixture and tighten the screw.

For hollow walls, drill a hole through the covering material and insert the plug completely. Position the item, then slot the screw into the centre of the plug and tighten.

JOINING WOOD

There are many fittings available for joining wood. Which ones you use depends on your skills, the tools available and what is appropriate for the job. For the projects in this book I have chosen the most suitable method for each one. Where a wood joint is made, it is described in the project instructions. Techniques that are used repeatedly are described here.

DOWELS

Dowels are wooden pegs that are used to join two pieces of timber together. They are made from hardwood and are usually available in two diameters: ¼in (6mm) and ⅜in (9mm). The length can vary according to the thickness of the timber to be joined, but dowels would not usually be used in wood that is less than ½in (12mm) thick.

Fig 4.7 *Expanding rubber plugs and screws for fixings in problem materials.*

Fig 1.8 *Wooden dowels.*

Dowels can be used for reinforcing butted joints in place of mortise and tenon or housing joints, but are most commonly employed when edge-jointing planks to form a wider plank.

To make a neat, strong joint it is important that the holes in the two pieces of wood line up. The holes for the dowels must be drilled accurately in both pieces of wood: they must not only be in the correct position but must also be perpendicular to the surface of the wood. It is usual to use a dowelling jig to accomplish this (see page 21), but if you do not have one the holes can be lined up using a marking gauge and rule. When drilling the holes, it can help the accuracy if a special dowel bit is used. This is a wood bit with a sharp central point rather than a gently sloping one which prevents the bit from wandering when the hole is started.

Dowels can be purchased ready-made or can be cut to size from lengths of hardwood dowelling. In both cases, the dowels must have grooves cut along their length to allow surplus glue to escape from the hole. Otherwise, when the glue is placed in the hole and the dowel is pushed into it, the dowel may be such a tight fit that the glue becomes trapped in the base of the hole and prevents the dowel from penetrating it fully.

Generally, dowel joints are made so that the dowel is completely concealed within the timber (see Fig 4.9). This requires accurately drilled holes and is achieved most easily with a dowelling jig. Alternatively, dowels can be used to make a 90° butt joint in two boards, when they are not concealed (Fig 4.9). This method requires far less accuracy: apply glue to the two boards, clamp them together and then drill the dowel holes with a dowel bit through both pieces of wood. Tap each dowel into place, and when the glue has dried, plane the protruding end flush with the surface of the wood. Leave the joint clamped while it dries.

SCREWS

Screws are a simple and effective way of joining two pieces of wood together, especially if the join is glued as well. Whenever possible avoid screwing into the end grain, as this will not hold the screw effectively. Always use the correct size of screw for the job.

Wood screws are available in a huge range of sizes and make a secure anchor point. When fixing a shelf or cabinet to a solid wood wall, a screw is the best fitting for the job. If you are trying to fix an object to a

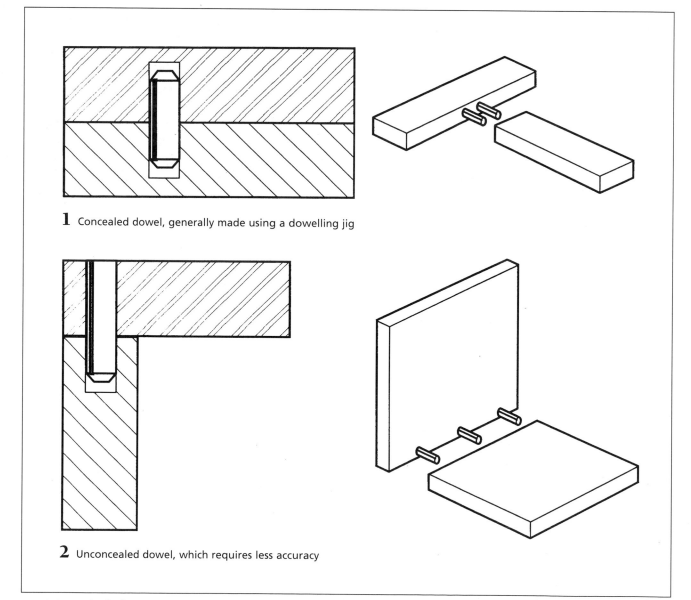

1 Concealed dowel, generally made using a dowelling jig

2 Unconcealed dowel, which requires less accuracy

Fig 4.9 Methods for using dowels.

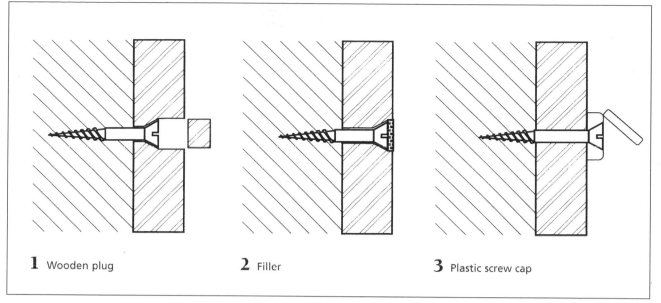

1 Wooden plug   **2** Filler   **3** Plastic screw cap

Fig 4.10 Concealing screw heads.

hollow stud wall and the laths can be located, the screws can be fixed through the plasterboard covering and into the wood lath.

The method is simple: mark the position for the screw, drill a pilot hole and screw it in. If fixing into softwood, the pilot hole should be approximately half the diameter of the screw shank.

CONCEALING SCREW HEADS
To make a neat job, the screw heads are concealed after they have been fitted. There are many ways of doing this – the method you choose will depend on whether the fixture is permanent or whether you will require access to the screw head on subsequent occassions.

FILLER If a screw joint is made in a piece of furniture it is unlikely that you will ever need to take it apart again, so here it is appropriate to conceal the screw head permanently.

Drill the screw hole and then use a countersinking bit to increase its diameter so that the screw can sink below the surface of the wood. Once the screw is secure, push filler into

the hole so that it is raised slightly above the surface. When the filler is dry, use glasspaper to smooth it until it is flush with the surface of the wood (see Fig 4.10).

If the wood is to be varnished, use filler that matches the colour of the wood as closely as possible. If it is to be painted, white cellulose filler is the best choice.

HINGED PLASTIC SCREW CAPS
Items such as the knife racks on page 41 are fixed to the wall with screws, but it is not a good idea to cover the screw heads with filler

because some time in the future you may wish to move the rack to a different location.

There are many solutions to this problem, but one of the neatest is to use hinged plastic caps (see Fig 4.11). These conceal the screw heads, but the lid can be flipped out of the way to get at them when necessary.

Drill the screw hole in the item but do not countersink it. Thread the plastic screw cap on to the screw and secure the item to the wall. Cover the screw head with the plastic lid (see Fig 4.10).

Fig 4.11 White plastic, hinged screw caps.

WOODEN PLUGS Concealing screw heads with plugs made from the same wood as the item is an alternative to using plastic screw caps (see Fig 4.10). You would use plugs when the item is varnished and you want to conceal the screw heads completely.

Drill the screw hole and then use a ½in (12mm) bit in the drill to enlarge the hole to a depth of ¼in (6mm) to accommodate a plug. There are two ways of making a plug to fit the hole. One is to cut a ¼in (6mm) length from a piece of ½in (12mm) dowel. If the item is made from pine, use pine dowel; unfortunately, it is not always possible to purchase dowels to match all the types of wood you might use. Fit the screw, then glue the dowel plug and tap it into place until the top of it is flush with the surface of the wood.

The second method is to cut the plug from a spare piece of wood using a ½in (12mm) plug cutter. This special tool is used in a drill and cuts a neat cylinder of wood to the required diameter. The advantage of this method is that you will always be able to match the wood exactly from offcuts produced when the item was made.

As before, widen the screw hole at the top with a ½in (12mm) drill.

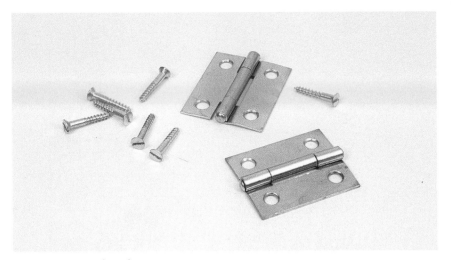

Fig 4.12 Brass butt hinges.

Fit the plug cutter to the drill and make a plug in a spare piece of wood where the grain matches the item to be fixed. Glue the plug into place and use glasspaper to smooth it until it is flush with the surface of the wood.

CABINET FITTINGS

HINGES

Butt hinges and single cranked hinges are the only types used for the projects in this book. Butt hinges (see Fig 4.12) are generally used when a door is hung, be it a door for a small cupboard or the front door of the house. They are not the easiest hinges to fit but they are effective and relatively cheap.

Single cranked hinges, sometimes called 'easy-on hinges' (see Fig 4.13), are (as the name implies) simpler to fit accurately. They are available in a variety of sizes, which is important because the size of the crank must be smaller than the thickness of the wood to which the hinge is being fixed.

MAGNETIC CATCHES

The doors on the cabinets in this book are held in place with magnetic catches. These are simple to fit and work well: a plastic box holding the magnet is fitted to the inside of the cabinet and a steel plate is fixed to the door. The catches are available in several sizes for different applications.

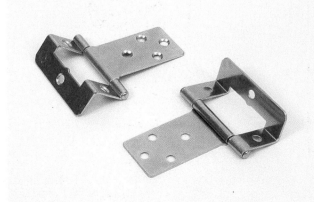

Fig 4.13 Single cranked ('easy-on') hinges.

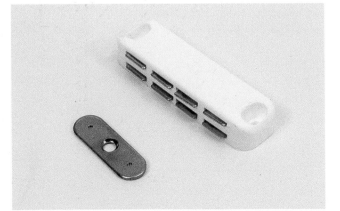

Fig 4.14 A magnetic catch.

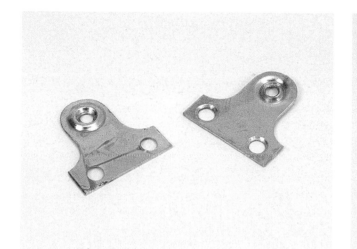

Fig 4.15 Mirror plates.

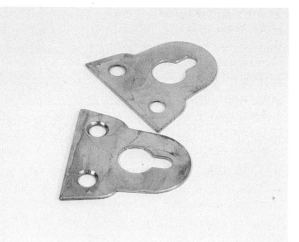

Fig 4.16 Keyhole plates.

MIRROR PLATES

These fittings are used to fix lightweight cabinets flush to the wall. They consist of small, flat metal plates that are screwed to the back of the cabinet so that they protrude from the top or side. The protruding part has a screw hole, which is used for the screw that fixes the cabinet to the wall. The plates are usually used in pairs.

KEYHOLE PLATES

One of the problems with mirror plates is that they are not totally concealed. A keyhole plate is similar but when fitted is completely hidden. The cabinet must have a thick, solid wood back in order to house these fittings, which are generally used in pairs.

Drill two ½in (12mm) holes, approximately ⅜in (9mm) deep, in the back of the cabinet, and fit the plates over the holes. Fix two screws in the wall where the cabinet is to be hung, ensuring that they are exactly the same distance apart as the keyhole plates. Place the plates over the screws and slide the cabinet down, so that the screws are in the narrow part of the keyhole with the screw heads inside the recesses of the wood (see Fig 4.17).

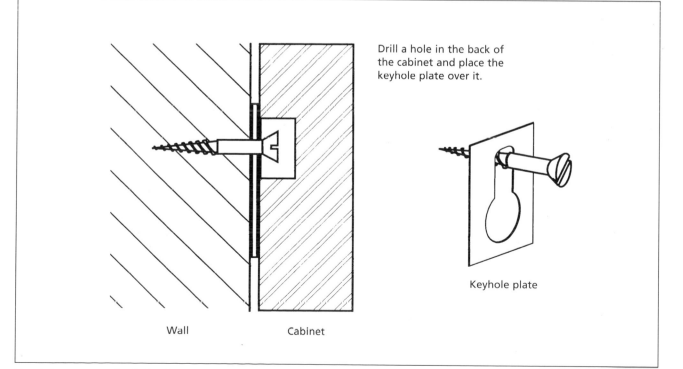

Drill a hole in the back of the cabinet and place the keyhole plate over it.

Wall

Cabinet

Keyhole plate

Fig 4.17 Using a keyhole plate.

PICTURE TURNS

These are pieces of flat, leaf-shaped metal that are used on the backs of picture frames to hold the picture in place. However, they are also a good way to hold a mirror in the rebate on the back of a cupboard door frame. Picture turns are held in place with a screw that is not inserted fully but left so that the leaf-shaped metal can swivel (see Fig 4.19). This allows the mirror to be removed easily if required.

PVA (POLYVINYL ACETATE) ADHESIVE

This adhesive is easily recognised by its white, creamy appearance. It is water-soluble before it dries and has very little odour. It is also easy to apply and dries so that it holds after about one hour, although this can vary according to the ambient temperature.

PVA adhesive remains plastic for two or three days. This can be an advantage, as slight mistakes can be corrected during this time. For example, a carcass that is not exactly square can be corrected by placing a sash cramp across the long diagonal and tightening it. If this is left in place for 24 hours it will make good the mistake.

PVA adhesive has a long shelf life, is comparatively cheap and can be obtained for both indoor and outdoor applications.

Fig 4.18 Picture turns.

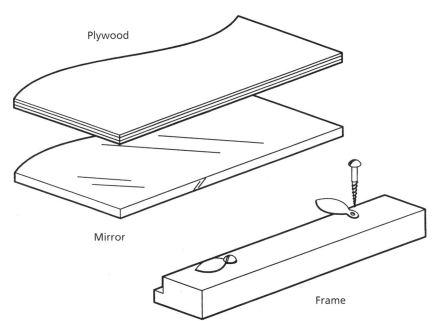

Fig 4.19 Using picture turns.

PLASTIC CORNER BLOCKS

Plastic corner blocks are available in many shapes and sizes but essentially they are all designed to join two pieces of timber together at 90° to each other. A typical application is joining the corners of a box or cabinet together. When used in this situation they are easy to fit but tend to protrude into the inside of the cabinet, which can be a disadvantage. For the projects in this book, corner blocks can be used to fix a shelf or cabinet to the wall as an alternative to using mirror plates.

Fig 4.20 Plastic corner blocks.

5 Finishing

It is said that a fine finish can improve even a mundane piece of furniture dramatically. In recent years, however, there has been a move away from the high gloss finishes to a waxed or oiled look that can be described as matt with a deep glow and this is not as distracting to the eye as a gloss finish. I would therefore recommend that you make your projects with as much care as possible and think of the finish as merely putting the icing on the cake – do not rely on it to work miracles. All the projects in this book are finished with wax or varnish rather than paint so that the beauty of the wood grain can be seen clearly.

FILLING

As wood is a natural material, the surface will be far from perfect. Planed pine purchased from a DIY store should be inspected carefully for loose knots, rough patches where the grain has been torn by the planer, holes, cracks and resin pockets. If the timber is good enough to use, any minor blemishes will need to be repaired either before or after construction of the project. Repair any large gaps or holes by plugging with a piece of wood of a similar colour. Where a loose knot has dropped out, either drill a round hole that encompasses the flaw or cut a rectangular hole, so that it is

easy to shape a plug that will fit into it. It is also possible that, after construction, there may be gaps in your joints, caused not by bad workmanship but by the wood shrinking.

If plugs are made from the same material there will be no problem with colour matching, even after the varnish has been applied.

Small holes are repaired with filler. This can be purchased in colours intended to match the wood you are using. The difficulty with this is apparent if you look closely at a piece of pine board: it is not just one colour but many, ranging from light straw to mid-brown. So, although it is possible to obtain filler to match many types of wood it is prudent to test them first, to find one that is correct for the particular piece you are making. Fill a small hole, allow the filler to dry, apply some varnish and if the colour matches you are clear to proceed.

If the colour match is unacceptable, you can make your own filler using sawdust collected from a powered sander or saw that has been used for cutting the wood, mixed with PVA adhesive. Place a large blob of glue on a clean plastic lid or container, add sawdust and stir until a paste with a creamy consistency is created. Use this to fill the gaps.

Whether you use proprietary filler or a home-made version, the

procedure for applying it is the same. Clean out the gap or hole if necessary and push the filler into the hole with a flat-ended knife until it stands proud of the surface. When it is dry, smooth with glasspaper until the filler is level with the surface of the wood.

Resin pockets should be cleaned out by either cutting the area away or swabbing with white spirit and then filling. To repair areas of torn grain that are not too deep, reduce down the surrounding wood with a power sander until the area is smooth. If the tears are very deep, the wood will require re-planing.

SANDING

When the project is complete, smooth the entire surface with an orbital disc sander using a medium-grade abrasive disc. Follow this with a fine disc to remove any scratches or marks left by the medium-grade disc. Then, using a fine-grade glasspaper on a cork block, hand sand to a fine finish. This is done in the direction of the grain, starting at one end and pushing the sawdust in front of the block. The sawdust and any spent abrasive are thereby removed as work proceeds. Use your fingertips to detect any rough areas or hold the workpiece at an oblique angle to a strong light so that they show up.

VARNISHING

For varnishing you will need some good quality bristle brushes in various sizes and a roll of masking tape with which to mask off any areas of the work that do not require painting.

If you are using polyurethane varnish, you will need to clean the brushes in white spirit; if acrylic, you can use water.

Make sure you follow any safety directions given on the packaging. Apply the varnish with a bristle brush in the direction of the grain, then leave for the varnish to dry and the smell to disperse. This first application will have the effect of swelling the pores of the wood, which raises the grain and makes

the surface of the wood feel rough again. Use a pad of fine-grade steel wool to rub over the surface until it feels smooth to the touch. Ensure that the work area is free from dust and apply a second coat of varnish. This time, when it dries, the surface will be smooth. If the surface is likely to receive a lot of wear, a third coat is a good idea. After a week or so, polish with a good quality wax furniture polish.

TYPES OF FINISH
CLEAR VARNISH

All clear varnishes are available in a matt, satin or gloss surface finish. Matt varnish is gloss varnish with small particles suspended in it to produce a surface that does not

shine. To ensure this effect is achieved, the varnish must be stirred before it is used.

The projects in this book use matt polyurethane or emulsion varnishes. Polyurethane is a spirit-based varnish made from synthetic resins. It can be thinned with white spirit, which is also used to clean the brushes after use. Polyurethane is used where a tough finish is required.

Emulsion varnishes are made from acrylics and are water-soluble before they are applied and dry out. They do not seem to give off as many fumes as polyurethane, are usually quick drying and the brushes can be cleaned with water. In the tin the varnish has a milky appearance but when applied it dries to a clear, hard surface. Emulsion varnish is often used on top of other paint finishes to protect them.

CLEAR WATERPROOFING SOLUTION

This is not a varnish but a thin solution that soaks into the wood to form a waterproof barrier just below the surface. It should be applied with a brush and left to dry for a couple of weeks. The solution can be used on its own or, for extra protection, the item can be varnished or painted afterwards.

WOOD-COLOURED VARNISH

Both emulsion (acrylic) and polyurethane varnishes are available in a wide range of colours that match the appearance of various woods. Under the right circumstances these are very effective; however, if, for example, you paint pine with mahogany-coloured varnish, it might be the correct colour but the character and

Fig 5.1 Varnishing accessories.

grain of the wood will still be and look like pine. Coloured varnishes are therefore most effective if used to enrich the colour of the same wood type. For example, a hardwood door made from one of the mahogany look-a-like materials might appear pale and uninteresting, but an application of the appropriate varnish will transform it into something spectacular.

COLOURED BRUSHING WAX

I particularly like the appearance of pine after it has been exposed to the light for a number of years. However, as 10 years is really too long to wait to obtain the desirable deep golden brown colour, the next best thing is to use an antique pine brushing wax which gives instant results.

Once the project has been smoothed with glasspaper, apply the wax with a brush and leave it to dry for 20 minutes; do not be tempted to leave it any longer as it will become difficult to polish off. When the wax is applied it has a streaky appearance, but when polished the streaks disappear. Now polish off the surplus wax with a soft, lint-free cloth. For a darker appearance, apply a second coat. Finally, apply some wax furniture polish.

COLOURED GLAZE

To simulate the colours of other types of wood when finishing pine, a wide range of wood dyes and coloured varnishes are available. Specialist paint suppliers also offer bright colours such as red, green and blue to paint on the wood which still leave the grain showing through.

All these coloured dyes and glazes will produce good results if simply brushed on to the wood (see Fig 5.4).

Fig 5.2 Coloured brushing wax and neutral wax furniture polish.

Fig 5.3 Transparent coloured glazes.

Fig 5.4 Pine board finished with a blue glaze.

In one respect there is an advantage over clear varnish, for very often a single coat will achieve the desired effect, although you may still need to apply a coat of matt varnish over the top to protect the surface.

However, for a more dramatic effect that accentuates the grain, the wood can be distressed with a wire brush before painting. To do this, hold the wood firmly on the bench and with a stiff wire brush vigorously abuse the surface in the direction of the grain. Doing this will remove the surface of the wood, taking more from the soft areas between the darker-coloured growth rings and making these more receptive to the coloured stain.

Apply the wood stain liberally with a brush and, before it has time to dry, wipe across the surface with a lint-free rag to remove the surplus. When dry, apply a coat of matt varnish.

Figure 5.5 shows a piece of pine finished using the above technique in conjunction with coloured wood glaze. Figure 5.6 shows the same technique used with mahogany wood stain.

LIMING

This is a traditional technique that was used in the past to give an interesting effect on, for example, oak panelling. It works best on woods that have large pores, such as oak. Lime, a white, chalky substance, was rubbed into the pores to give a colour contrast with the natural colour of the rest of the timber. Modern liming methods use liming wax or white emulsion paint instead of lime itself.

Fig 5.5 *Pine board that has been distressed before painting with a blue glaze.*

Fig 5.6 *Pine board that has been distressed before painting with mahogany-coloured dye.*

PSEUDO-LIMING

To obtain the same visual effect as liming on pine furniture, I use a mixture of the wire brushing technique described above and white emulsion paint. This gives the bleached-out effect that you get when pine has been scrubbed with soap and water for a number of years, as on a farmhouse kitchen tabletop or a piece of driftwood (see Fig 5.7).

The method is as follows. Erode the surface of the pine with a wire brush used vigorously in the direction of the grain. Dilute some white emulsion paint, roughly 1:1 with water, to make a thin solution and brush this over the surface, ensuring that all the pores of the wood are penetrated. Before the solution dries, wipe off the surplus from the surface with a slightly damp cloth. This will clean the paint off the raised parts of the grain, which are the hardest and the darkest in colour, leaving lots of paint in the hollows. It also has the effect of raising the grain, so when it is dry, rub the surface lightly with some fine glasspaper. Follow this with two applications of polyurethane varnish, which will give a smooth surface and also darken the wood where there is no white emulsion.

A coloured variation of this can be obtained if the wood is dyed first. Erode the surface of the pine with a stiff wire brush as before. Paint on the coloured dye, but this time do not wipe away the surplus – instead, allow it to dry. Paint over the surface with white emulsion paint diluted as before, and wipe off any surplus paint vigorously with a lint-free cloth. The finished effect can be seen in Fig 5.8.

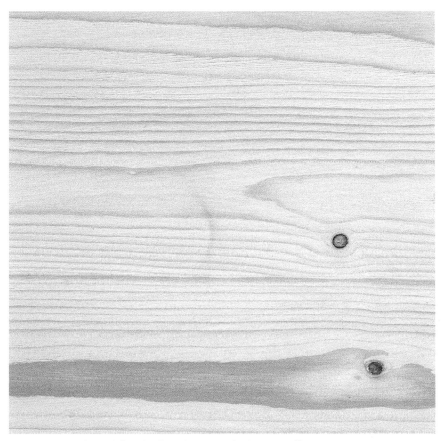

Fig 5.7 Pine board finished with a pseudo-liming effect.

Fig 5.8 Liming over a green glaze.

6 Safety

Woodworking tools and machines can be dangerous. Commercial workshops must comply with rigorous health and safety regulations, and also appoint a person in each department to ensure that safety rules are not flaunted and that all hazardous substances are regulated. We should be just as rigorous when working at home. Be diligent and ensure that fire, fumes, flying dust particles and cutting tools do not cause you harm.

SAFETY EQUIPMENT

NOTE

IMPORTANT

Always read the manufacturer's instructions before using any safety equipment.

EYE PROTECTION

Your eyes need to be protected against wood chips and other flying objects in the workshop. There are three main types of protection: spectacles with side shields, goggles and visors. Protective spectacles are convenient to use; goggles are safer and can be worn over prescription spectacles but are less convenient. Visors and face screens that protect the whole face are excellent and can also be used over spectacles.

NOTE

GENERAL SAFETY RULES

1 Maintain an orderly workplace. Accidents can occur when there is clutter in the way.

2 Do not allow children to use tools, and make sure the tools are out of reach when they are stored.

3 Only work where there is adequate lighting and ventilation.

4 Do not use blunt tools: they are far more likely to cause an accident.

5 Leave all doorways unobstructed and, if you have a choice, provide a doorway at both ends of the workshop. This is for escaping quickly if there is a fire or other hazard, but it is also useful for moving large pieces of furniture in and out of the workshop.

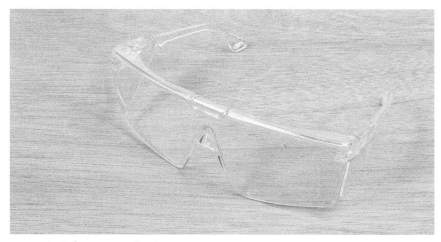

Fig 6.1 Safety spectacles.

All eye protectors should comply with British Standard BS2092 or European Standard EN166, which means that they are made of high-impact plastic. They are also graded for the degree of protection they will afford against the impact of flying particles. In a woodworking environment they should be at least grade 2 or, even better, grade 1. Eye protectors must be comfortable to wear for long periods and should be held firmly in place so that they do not drop off when you bend forward.

EAR PROTECTION

Ear protectors should comply with the safety requirements laid down in European Community Directive 89/686 or BS6344-1. The type I use have an SNR (Simplified Noise Reduction) of 25dB and are based on the attenuation of continuous noise, as met with in the workshop, not pulsed noise such as gunshots.

DUST COLLECTORS

Do not allow dust to accumulate, because it is harmful when inhaled and is also a fire hazard. Always clean up after each work session.

Due to the proliferation of power tools, dust is now a health hazard in the workshop for both professionals and the weekend amateur. The amount of dust in the atmosphere can have an adverse effect on the health of woodworkers. Some of the more exotic rainforest woods are toxic and their dust should not be inhaled under any circumstances.

Working on the premise that it is not healthy to inhale any dust, one of the best ways to avoid this is to collect it when and where it is produced, using a dust collector attached to the power tool. The small dust bags that are supplied with hand sanders are not very efficient, so use a suction cleaner. There are basically two types.

The first type is the industrial version of the domestic vacuum cleaner, which is suitable for collecting sawdust and small chippings but will become clogged by larger shavings (see Fig 6.3). These are known as HVLV (high velocity/low volume) cleaners. In general, they have a small-diameter tube that will connect to many

Fig 6.2 Ear protectors.

portable power tools such as routers and orbital sanders. As the nozzle is situated close to the cutting heads, they will collect most of the airborne dust. The dust storage capacity of this sort of collector is normally less than that of the LVHV type described below. One criticism of these units in that when connected to portable power tools they hinder their use.

The second type of cleaner is usually much larger, with a 4in (100mm) diameter collecting tube. These are low-volume dust and shavings collectors, known in the trade as LVHV (low velocity/high volume), and are intended for use with floor-standing pieces of equipment such as table saws and planer-thicknessers. They will collect all the chips and wood shavings but

Fig 6.3 An industrial vacuum cleaner.

Fig 6.4 A disposable dust mask.

Fig 6.5 A filter-type respirator.

not all the very fine dust particles that are produced. They also have large collecting bags that can be used to discharge into plastic bags ready for disposal.

There are versions of both types of collector that will switch on automatically when the tool is powered up, and both can be used for general tidying up of the workshop.

DUST MASKS

There are some jobs where it is not practical to use a dust collector. Hand sanding, for example, produces very fine dust, as does sweeping up the workshop floor. On these occasions a dust mask is ideal. These masks are known more professionally as half-face respirators, because they cover both the mouth and the nose. They are not a substitute for collecting the dust as it is produced but are a useful additional safety item.

There are two basic types of mask: those that are thrown away when they clog up and those for which the filters are replaceable. The disposable types should be discarded after approximately six working hours or when they appear to be clogged up with dust. The filter types should have the filter

replaced when it is discoloured.

If you intend to use a respirator regularly, the filter-type masks are far better. They usually have a moulded rubber face mask that fits comfortably and can be worn for long periods without discomfort. All respirators get wet on the inside with condensation, particularly in a cold workshop, and I find that the disposable types can become soggy and be unpleasant to wear after half an hour. The better quality filter-type masks have a valve which lets out the condensation so that it is not such a problem.

The filter-type masks have different filters available to suit the job you are working on. As well as for protection against wood dust, they can be worn to combat vapours from solvents, paints and varnishes. Some masks have one large filter housing in the front while others have two filters positioned at the sides. I find that the single filter in the front restricts my view of the workpiece and the double filter is far better.

You should try to obtain an approved mask: in Britain, by the Health and Safety Executive which gives the identification code EN149, denoting the European Standard. It might also have the letters FFP

(fitting, face piece and particles), followed by 1, 2 or 3. A number 1 is the least effective filter and should not be used for continuous periods longer than one hour; for longer periods a number 2 is best, and for hardwoods use a number 3.

> ### NOTE
>
> ### FIRE SAFETY
>
> **1** Do not allow large quantities of dust and shavings to accumulate. Fine wood dust floating in the air can be explosive.
>
> **2** Do not keep rags soaked in oil, varnish or paint solvents in rubbish sacks or boxes in the workshop. Put them in a metal container with a lid, as they can burst into flames spontaneously.
>
> **3** Have a fire extinguisher and large fire bucket handy in the workshop and fit a smoke alarm.
>
> Further detailed fire safety advice can be obtained from your local fire station.

FIRST AID KIT

A first aid kit should be available in every workshop. It should contain sticking plasters, crêpe bandages, rectangular bandages, small bandages, a pair of scissors, a salve for small burns, antiseptic cream, an eye bath, tweezers for splinters and barrier creams that are useful when using glue.

PAINTS AND VARNISHES

Many lacquers, paints and varnishes are based on strong solvents which are potentially hazardous if the user is not protected (see notes on Dust Masks on page 38). Solvents evaporate rapidly, so a respirator with the appropriate filter will prevent inhalation.

Acrylic varnishes and emulsion paints are water-soluble when in liquid form. Brushes used to apply them are cleaned in water and in some cases the paints can also be thinned with water. In general, therefore, they are less hazardous to use and do not smell as strongly as solvent-based paints and varnishes. Polyurethane, yacht varnish and gloss paints are solvent based. Always follow the manufacturer's recommendations (printed on the tin) regarding their use.

If you are concerned about the safety of a substance you intend to use, the manufacturer is required by law to provide you with the details of what it contains and how hazardous it is. This information is contained in a technical data sheet. Simply write off and ask for the COSHH (Control of Substances Hazardous to Health) sheet for their product.

NOTE

POWER TOOL SAFETY

Power tools, both hand-held and floor-standing, provide a quick and convenient way of carrying out many woodworking jobs. However, a number of general rules must be observed if they are to be used safely.

1 Do not expose power tools to wet conditions – do *not* use them in the rain.

2 Ensure that the light is adequate and you can see clearly what you are doing.

3 Do not allow children to play in the area in which you are working.

4 Do not overload the tools, as this will cause wear to the motor and cutting edge due to overheating.

5 Use the correct tool for the job. For example, do not try to use a jigsaw to cut through wood that is too thick.

6 Wear suitable protective clothing and ensure that it is not loose-fitting. If you have long hair, make sure it is tied out of the way or secured under a hat.

7 Wear protective goggles.

8 Wear ear protectors. A small router can generate 85dB, which can damage hearing if prolonged.

9 When using any tool that generates dust and is not connected to a dust extractor, wear a dust mask. The small dust bags supplied with some sanders are not adequate and a mask will be required.

10 Do not carry a power tool by its cable or pull the plug out of the wall by pulling the cable.

11 Maintain power tools by following the manufacturer's instructions. Keep the cutting edges sharp and check the equipment for damage regularly. This not only makes the tools safer, it also prolongs their life.

12 Always use both hands to control a power tool. Secure the workpiece with a clamp. Drape the cable over one shoulder so that it does not get in the way and snag.

13 Always follow the manufacturer's safety instructions.

14 Never remove safety guards.

15 If you have free-standing equipment such as a lathe, ensure that the red stop button is placed in a conspicuous position and that you can reach it when operating the machine.

THE KITCHEN

THE KITCHEN IS THE ONE AREA IN THE HOUSE WHERE YOU CAN ABSOLUTELY GUARANTEE YOU WILL NOT HAVE ENOUGH SPACE. WHEN YOU MOVE INTO A NEW HOUSE, INVARIABLY THE KITCHEN IS FURNISHED WITH CUPBOARDS AND SHELVES. THIS IS JUST AS WELL, BECAUSE KITCHENS ARE NOT USUALLY VERY LARGE COMPARED WITH, FOR EXAMPLE, A LIVING ROOM, YET WE EXPECT TO STORE MORE PIECES OF EQUIPMENT AND OTHER ITEMS THAN IN ALMOST ANY OTHER ROOM IN THE HOUSE. BECAUSE OF THIS, SAVING SPACE IS CRITICALLY IMPORTANT. AT THE SAME TIME, HOWEVER, SOME OF THE EQUIPMENT MUST BE IMMEDIATELY TO HAND. SMALL ADDITIONS, SUCH AS KNIFE AND MUG RACKS, CAN MAKE A BIG DIFFERENCE AS THESE ITEMS WILL NOT THEN BE LEFT TO CLUTTER THE WORK SURFACES BUT ARE ALWAYS HANDY.

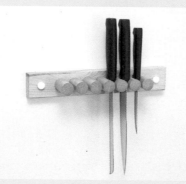

7

Knife Racks

DESIGN 1
DEGREE OF DIFFICULTY: EASY
TIME TO MAKE: 4 HOURS

DESIGN 2
DEGREE OF DIFFICULTY: EASY
TIME TO MAKE: 4 HOURS

T‍HERE is no need to search for your kitchen knives if you make either of these two knife racks. They are designed to hang on the wall just an arm's length from the work surface and so will be readily to hand. Both racks are fixed to the wall with wood screws, the heads of which are concealed with plastic caps, and both will hold half a dozen carving or other food preparation knives, but they could easily be made larger if required.

CUTTING LIST

DESIGN 1

Front (1)	Pine	14 x 2 x ¾in (356 x 51 x 18mm)
Back (1)	Pine	14 x 2 x ¾in (356 x 51 x 18mm)
Spacers (2)	Plywood	2 x 1½ x ¼in (51 x 38 x 6mm)

ALSO REQUIRED:

Plastic screw caps (2)		

DESIGN 2

Back (1)	Pine	12 x 2 x ¾in (305 x 51 x 18mm)
Knife holders (7)	Ramin dowel	2 x 1in diameter (51 x 25mm diameter)

ALSO REQUIRED:

Plastic screw caps (2)		

DESIGN 1

This is the simpler of the two racks and can be made from small pieces of pine left over from other projects.

CONSTRUCTION

1 Mark out and cut the rectangular shapes for the front and back and use a template to draw the curves on the ends: I used a tin containing wood filler, but any cylindrical or circular object that has a diameter of 2in (51mm) would suffice. Cut the curves with a jigsaw but at this stage do not smooth them.

2 Cut the two spacers from a suitable piece of ¼in (6mm) plywood.

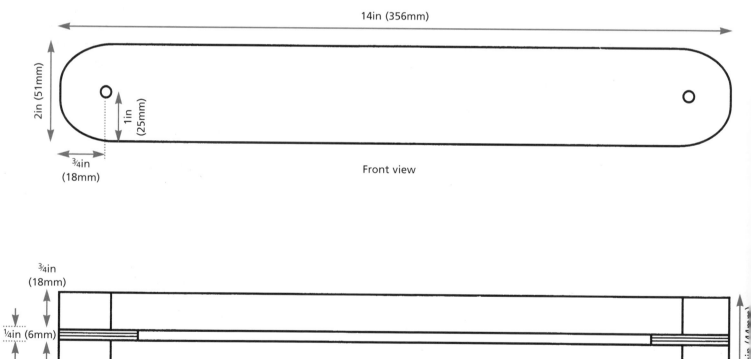

Fig 7.1 Front and top views with dimensions.

Fig 7.2 Construction.

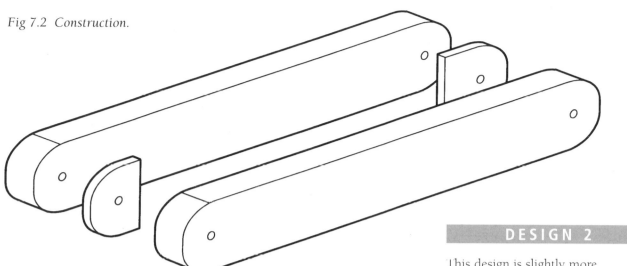

ASSEMBLY AND FINISHING

1 Glue all the pieces together and clamp the assembly until set with 'G' cramps.

2 Smooth the rounded edges of the assembled pieces with files and then use glasspaper to achieve an acceptable finish. If you have one, a disc or drum sander will speed up this part of the process.

3 Drill holes in the ends of the rack for the screws to fix it to the wall but do not countersink them.

4 To finish, apply three coats of polyurethane varnish and use plastic screw caps to conceal the screw heads when the rack is fixed to the wall.

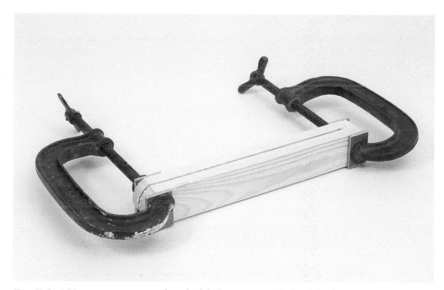

Fig 7.3 'G' cramps are used to hold the pieces while the glue sets.

DESIGN 2

This design is slightly more complicated. For safety reasons, kitchen knives should be stored in this rack with the sharp edges facing the wall.

CONSTRUCTION

1 Cut the back plate to size from a piece of ¾in (18mm) pine and bevel the edges of the front face slightly with a plane. Use a pair of dividers to mark the positions of the screw holes for the dowels and for fixing the rack to the wall. Pierce the surface with a gimlet to ensure that it is easy to start the bit accurately, then drill the holes. On the back of the back plate, countersink the holes for the screws that will fix the 1in (25mm) dowels to it, so that the rack will fit flush to the wall.

2 Cut several lengths of dowel and carefully smooth the end grain with glasspaper. To ensure that the dowels will be perpendicular to the back plate when fixed into place, the ends must be square. In the centre of one end of each dowel, drill a ⅛in (3mm) diameter hole for the fixing screws. Although these screws will be fixed into the end grain of the dowel they will have sufficient strength, as the dowels are also glued and the knives are not very heavy.

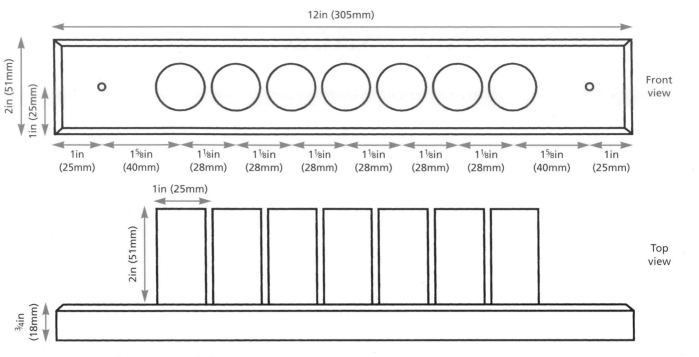

12in (305mm)

2in (51mm)

1in (25mm)

Front view

1in (25mm) | 1⅝in (40mm) | 1⅛in (28mm) | 1⅛in (28mm) | 1⅛in (28mm) | 1⅛in (28mm) | 1⅛in (28mm) | 1⅛in (28mm) | 1⅝in (40mm) | 1in (25mm)

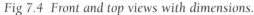

1in (25mm)

2in (51mm)

¾in (18mm)

Top view

Fig 7.4 *Front and top views with dimensions.*

ASSEMBLY AND FINISHING

1 Glue and screw the dowels to the back plate (see Fig 7.6) and wipe off any surplus glue with a damp cloth. If your screw holes are not in the exact centre of all the dowels, the distance between each pair of dowels might not be exactly the same. This can be rectified if the offending dowels are rotated slightly before the glue dries.

2 Use a disc or drum sander to ensure that all the dowels are the same height and line up accurately.

3 Apply three coats of polyurethane varnish and use plastic screw caps to conceal the screw heads when the rack is fixed to the wall.

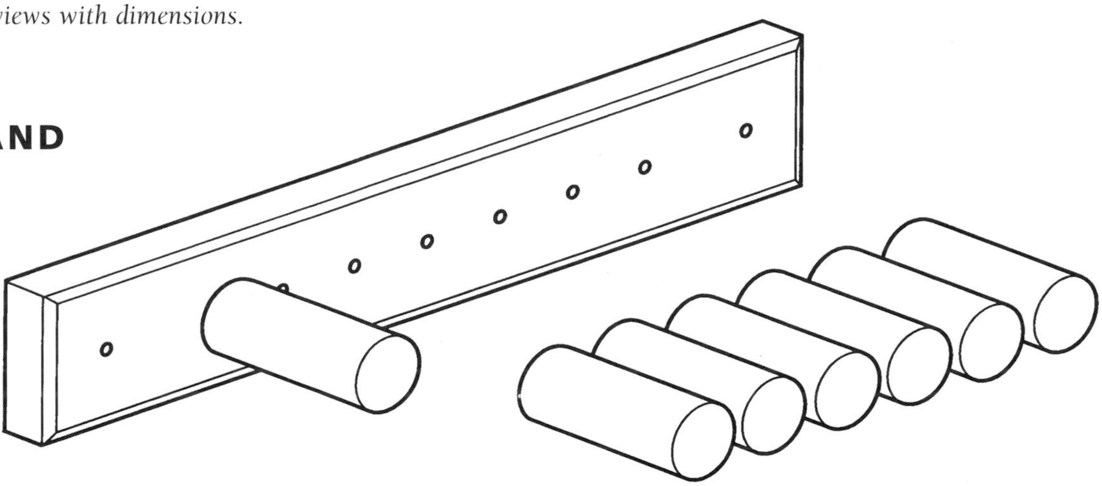

Fig 7.5 *Construction.*

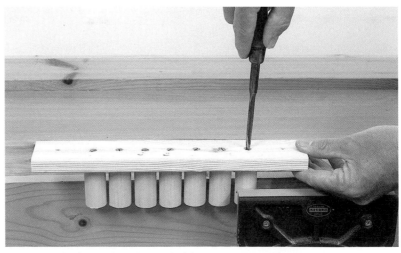

Fig 7.6 *The large dowels are held in position with glue and screws.*

Mug Rack

DEGREE OF DIFFICULTY: EASY
TIME TO MAKE: 8 HOURS

Before the advent of dishwashing machines, most people had a small amount of crockery which they washed up each time it had been used. Because dishwashing machines are usually switched on only when they are full, most of us now have extra crockery. In my house, this applies particularly to mugs – where we used to manage with a couple, we now have half a dozen. There is therefore a need to store them without taking up valuable cupboard space.

This mug rack is made from pine and although it is simple to construct it does require access to a lathe. If a lathe is not available, ⅜in (9mm) hardwood dowel could be used for the pegs, as the knob on the end is for decoration only – the mugs will not slide off the pegs as they are sloped to prevent this.

CUTTING LIST		
Back (1)	Pine	28½ x 3¾ x ¾in (724 x 95 x 18mm)
Pegs (6)	Pine	5⅝ x ¾ x ¾in (143 x 18 x 18mm)

The dimensions given for the pegs include the extra length and width required
for mounting and turning on the lathe.

CONSTRUCTION

PEGS

1 Cut the six square-sectioned blanks required for the pegs to length and prepare them for mounting between centres on the lathe (see the Note on page 47 and Fig 8.2).

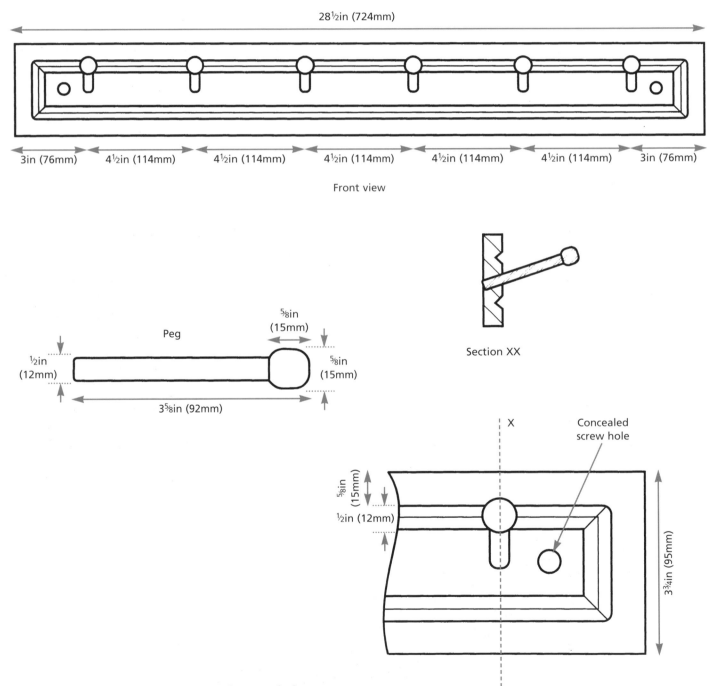

Fig 8.1 *Front view, section XX and peg with dimensions.*

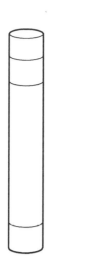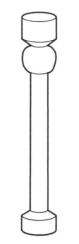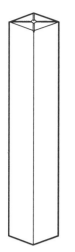

1 Prepare the square-sectioned piece for mounting on the lathe.

2 Turn it to a smooth cylinder with a diameter slightly larger than the widest section of the finished peg. Draw on the lines that show the boundaries of the different sections with a pencil.

3 Cut 'V' grooves at the section boundaries.

4 Round the top section to form a knob.

5 Make a ³⁄₈in (9mm) cylinder on the rest of the peg.

6 Finish with glasspaper and cut off the waste wood.

Fig 8.2 Steps for turning a peg.

2 Mount the first piece on the lathe, start at a relatively slow speed and use a large half-round gouge to turn a smooth cylinder with a diameter of ³⁄₄in (18mm). Use a rule and pencil to mark the position of the ends of the peg and also where the knob on the end is formed (see Fig 8.2). Increase the lathe speed and cut 'V' grooves at these points with a skew chisel (see Fig 8.2).

NOTE

PREPARING A BLANK FOR MOUNTING ON A LATHE

This operation must be done accurately or there will be excessive vibration when turning the wood. Locate the centres of the ends with diagonal lines and cut a cross on one end with a tenon saw, where the spur centre of the lathe will fit. Pierce a hole with a bradawl in the centre of the other end to accommodate the cup centre of the tailstock. Take the spur centre from the lathe and with a wooden mallet, tap it into the end of the wood where the cross was cut. Mount the wood on to the lathe and move the tailstock up to it so that the cup centre fits into the central hole previously made with the bradawl. Lubricate the cup centre with a couple of drops of oil and tighten the tailstock. The turned projects in this book use pine, which is not very tough and can split easily, particularly when turning fine detail, so use very sharp chisels and make shallow cuts.

Fig 8.3 Rack construction.

3 Use a small half-round gouge to form the knob (see Fig 8.2) and a skew chisel with a scraping cut to make the shaft of the pegs. The shaft is ⅜in (9mm) in diameter (see Fig 8.2) and must be cut accurately to fit into the holes that will be drilled in the back of the mug rack. Use callipers set at the correct diameter to check this. Finish off with two grades of glasspaper, remove the peg from the lathe and saw off the waste wood (see Fig 8.2).

4 When one peg has been completed, use it as a pattern for the rest. Use callipers to ensure that all the parts are the same diameter. Always use the same peg as the pattern to avoid compounding any errors.

BACK

1 Select a suitable piece of pine and mark out a rectangle to the required size, using a rule, try square and pencil, with the grain direction running along the length of the wood. Cut off any waste wood and use a jackplane to smooth the edges, paying particular attention to the end grain. Smooth the end grain with coarse and medium-grade glasspaper.

2 Cut the decorative 'V' groove around the face of the back with a router. Set up the router fence so that the outside edge of the 'V' sloped cutter will be ⅝in (15mm) from the edge of the back. Cut the groove and use a folded piece of glasspaper to clean it up if required.

3 Mark the positions of the holes for the pegs using a pair of dividers set at 4½in (114mm) and 'walk' across the face of the piece, starting 3in (76mm) in from one end. Also mark the positions of the holes for the screws that will be used to fix the rack to the wall. Use a gimlet to pierce holes to guide the drill bit.

4 As the pegs are sloped, I made a jig from some pieces of scrap wood to ensure that the angle of the drill was correct and constant when drilling the peg holes. This consists simply of two wedge-shaped pieces of wood with a slope of 3:1 that fit on either side of the drill stand, with a piece of plywood nailed across the top (see Figs 8.4 and 8.5). The mug

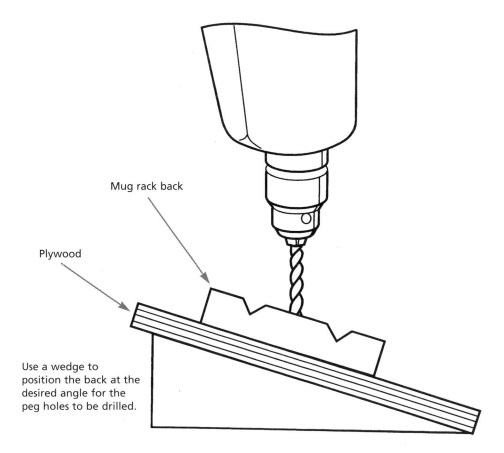

Mug rack back

Plywood

Use a wedge to position the back at the desired angle for the peg holes to be drilled.

Fig 8.4 Set-up for drilling the peg holes at an angle.

rack back is laid on this and the drill bit enters it at an angle. Use a smaller-diameter drill bit to make pilot holes before using the ³⁄₈in (9mm) bit to drill the holes themselves.

5 The rack is fixed to the wall with two number 8 screws that are concealed by sinking them into the mug rack back and covering the heads with small plugs of pine. Drill the two ³⁄₁₆in (4mm) screw holes vertically through the back with the drill held in the drill stand. Using a ¹⁄₂in (12mm) bit, drill two holes half-way through the back so that the screw heads will disappear into them. Make two ¹⁄₂in (12mm) diameter plugs, ¹⁄₄in (6mm) thick, to fit over the screw heads (see page 28). I used a couple of slices of the

waste wood from the end of the pegs after they had been turned, but failing this suitable pieces could be made using a plug cutter. Fix the plugs in the holes temporarily using only slight pressure, so that they will be varnished with the rest of the back. They can be pushed out from behind when the time comes to fix the rack to the wall.

ASSEMBLY AND FINISHING

1 Glue the pegs into the holes, and wipe off any surplus glue with a damp rag.

2 Because the kitchen environment can be damp and steamy, finish the rack with two coats of polyurethane varnish.

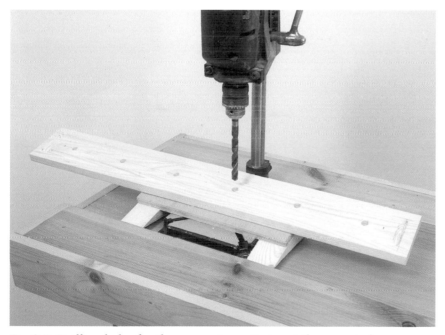

Fig 8.5 Drilling holes for the pegs using a jig to get the correct slope.

9 Egg Racks

DESIGN 1
DEGREE OF DIFFICULTY: EASY
TIME TO MAKE: 15 HOURS

DESIGN 2
DEGREE OF DIFFICULTY: MEDIUM
TIME TO MAKE: 20 HOURS

THESE two projects both serve the same purpose but the method of construction is different. Design 1 holds nine medium-sized eggs, is wall-mounted and can be made with the usual tool set. Design 2 is free-standing, holds 12 eggs and requires a lathe.

In both designs the holes for the eggs are 1½in (38mm) in diameter, which is about correct for medium-sized eggs. Large eggs will also sit in the holes but small ones might fall through. If you buy small eggs, simply make the holes slightly smaller.

CUTTING LIST

DESIGN 1

Back (1)	Pine	12¾ x 6 x ¾in (324 x 152 x 18mm)
Egg shelves (3)	Pine	6 x 3½ x ¾in (152 x 89 x 18mm)

ALSO REQUIRED:

Plastic screw caps (2)		

DESIGN 2

Top stand section (1)	Pine	3¾ x 1 x 1in (95 x 25 x 25mm)
Middle stand section (1)	Pine	3½ x 1 x 1in (89 x 25 x 25mm)
Lower stand section (1)	Pine	1½ x 1 x 1in (38 x 25 x 25mm)
Egg shelves (2)	Pine	6 x 6 x ¾in (152 x 152 x 18mm)
Base (1)	Pine	4¾ x 4¾ x 1¾in (121 x 121 x 43mm)

The dimensions given for the turned pieces make no allowance for waste.

DESIGN 1

This egg rack is wall-mounted and is finished with varnish and hinged plastic screw caps to match some of the other pieces made for the kitchen.

CONSTRUCTION

SHELVES

1 Mark out the three egg shelves on a piece of ¾in (18mm) pine, using Fig 9.1 as a guide to the angles required. Use a sliding bevel set from a protractor or a 60° set square to draw the lines that radiate from the centre (see Fig 9.2) and a compass to draw the overall semicircles for the edges of the shelves. The centres of the egg holes are found when the smaller semicircle is drawn so that it intersects the radial lines. At this point, pierce a hole with a gimlet to guide the drill bit.

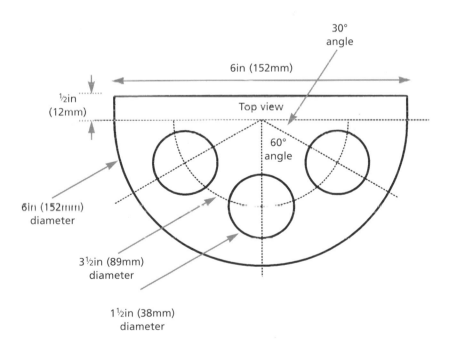

Fig 9.1 Top view of shelf with dimensions.

Fig 9.2 Drawing the radial lines that locate the egg holes.

Fig 9.3 Cutting the egg holes with a hole saw.

BACK

1 Draw out the shape of the back on a piece of ¾in (18mm) pine and mark the positions of the shelf housings and screw holes. Use one of the shelves to establish the correct width for the housing. Cut out the back, then smooth the straight edges with a plane and the curved edges with files and glasspaper.

2 All the egg holes are made before the shelves are cut out. When the positions of the holes have been determined, drill a ⅛in (3mm) pilot hole before using a 1½in (38mm) diameter hole saw to form the egg holes themselves (see Fig 9.3). Use the hole saw to cut from both sides of the wood so that a clean cut is made on both faces. (A hole saw works best if it is not forced to cut too quickly. Start slowly and allow it to rotate smoothly throughout the cut.)

3 Cut around the outside shape with a bandsaw as close as possible to the outside of the pencil line. Smooth the edges with a flat file to eradicate all the marks left by the saw cuts and then use glasspaper to eradicate the file marks.

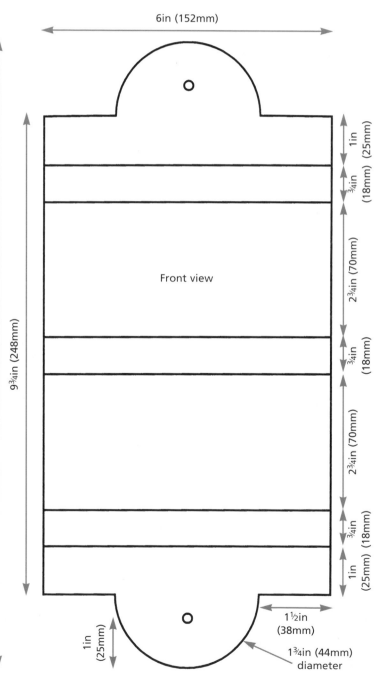

Fig 9.4 Front view with dimensions.

2 Mark the depth of the housings on the edges of the back with a marking gauge. Cut the sides of the housings with a tenon saw and remove the waste wood with a bevel-edged chisel. Try the shelves in the housings to test the accuracy of the fit. You should aim to get it so that the shelf will slot fully home with hand pressure only. Always err on the tight side – planing off a couple of shavings is a simple adjustment to make.

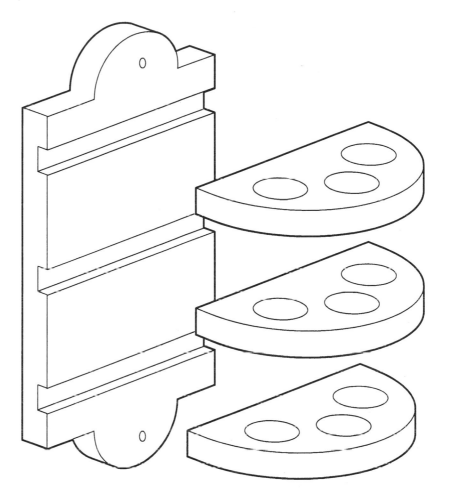

Fig 9.6 Construction.

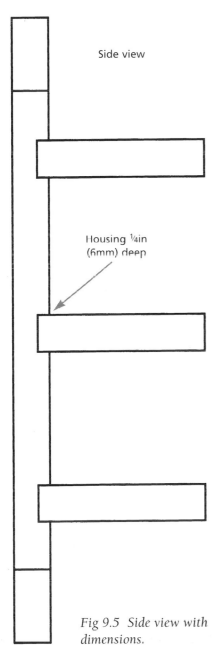

Side view

Housing ¼in (6mm) deep

Fig 9.5 Side view with dimensions.

ASSEMBLY AND FINISHING

1 Fix the shelves in place with glue and apply two or three coats of polyurethane varnish to the completed rack.

DESIGN 2

The central stand of this free-standing egg rack is turned as one complete piece. It is then sawn into three so that the pieces can be fitted into the holes in the centre of the shelves. The project uses sawn stock, which requires care in selection (see the Note, right).

NOTE

SELECTING SAWN STOCK

Take care when choosing pieces of sawn stock, as defects are not as easy to spot as when the wood has been planed. The faults to look for are loose knots, decayed knots, splits and resin pockets. Sort through the stock and select pieces with large knot-free areas or only small, light-coloured knots. Do not attempt to select away all the knots, as they are part of the character of the wood – simply choose pieces with fewer knots.

CONSTRUCTION

STAND AND BASE

1 Select a piece of pine without any knots, about 1¼in (32mm) square and 11in (279mm) long. This allows for some waste when mounting on the lathe and turning the square section into a cylinder. Prepare the wood for the lathe (see the Note on page 47), mount it between centres and turn it to a smooth cylinder with a diameter of 1in (25mm). Use callipers to ensure that the cylinder is the correct diameter.

2 Use a rule and pencil to indicate the position of the three narrow sections of the stand where it fits into the two shelves and the base. Cut these with a scraper to exactly ¾in (18mm) in diameter – the size to which the holes that accommodate them will be made (see Fig 9.9).

3 Mark the positions of the ends of the shallow concave curves on the straight parts of the stand and form the curves with a ½in (12mm) gouge (see Fig 9.10). Cut the ball on the top with a skew chisel: start by forming a deep 'V' cut at the top and base of the ball and then use the skew chisel with a cutting action to form the ball shape.

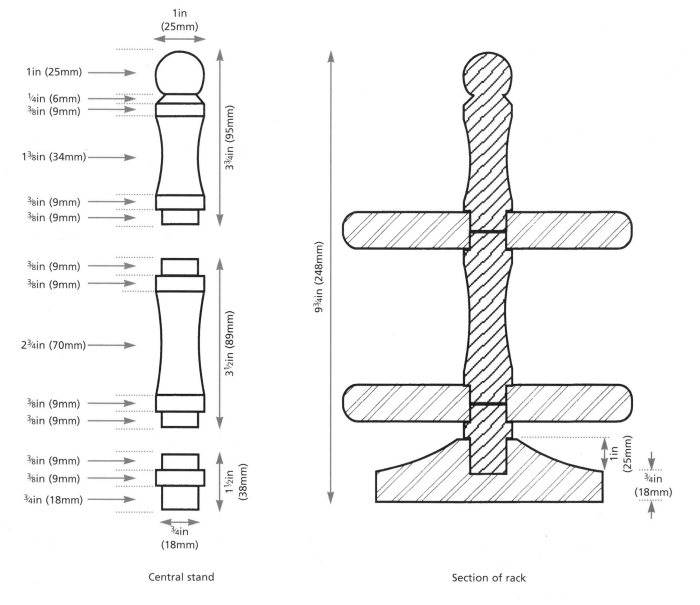

Central stand

Section of rack

Fig 9.7 Central stand and section of rack with dimensions.

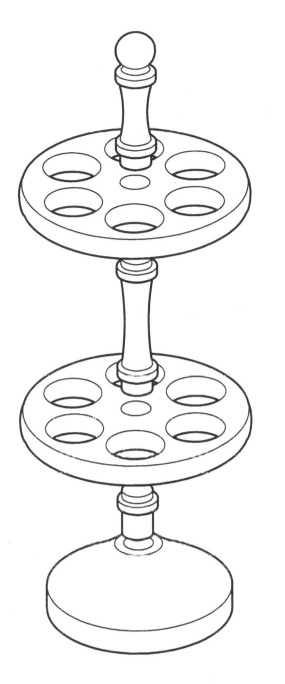

Fig 9.8 *Construction.*

Fig 9.9 *The central stand with some of the recesses that will eventually take the shelves.*

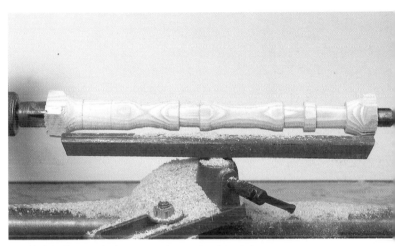

Fig 9.10 *Parts of the central stand with the concave shaping formed.*

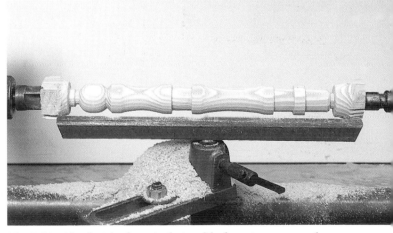

Fig 9.11 *The finished central stand before it is removed from the lathe.*

4 Push the tool rest out of the way, turn up the speed of the lathe and smooth the surface with medium-grade and fine glasspaper (see Fig 9.11). Put the tool rest back in place and use a parting tool to cut through the remaining wood at both ends of the stand so that it can be removed from the lathe. Use a tenon saw to cut the stand into three pieces.

5 Select a piece of suitably thick pine for the base and draw a 4¾in (121mm) diameter circle on it. Cut around the circle in the waste wood area and mount it on to the lathe face plate to smooth the edge and remove the saw marks. Turn the tool rest through approximately 90° and cut the concave shapes on the face of the base with a gouge. Smooth to a fine finish with glasspaper and remove from the lathe. Use a spade bit to drill a ¾in (18mm) hole in the centre of the base for the central stand.

SHELVES

1 Draw two 6in (152mm) diameter circles on a piece of ¾in (18mm) pine board. Cut these out using a bandsaw, mount them on the face plate of the lathe and use a gouge to round and smooth the edges. Use glasspaper to remove any tool marks.

2 Remove the discs from the lathe and use a compass to draw the inner circle that locates the distance from the centre of the shelf for the centres of the egg holes. With a protractor, draw the radial lines that project from the centre of the shelf and bisect the inner circle 60° apart, to locate the centres of the egg holes. Drill ⅛in (3mm) pilot holes at these points.

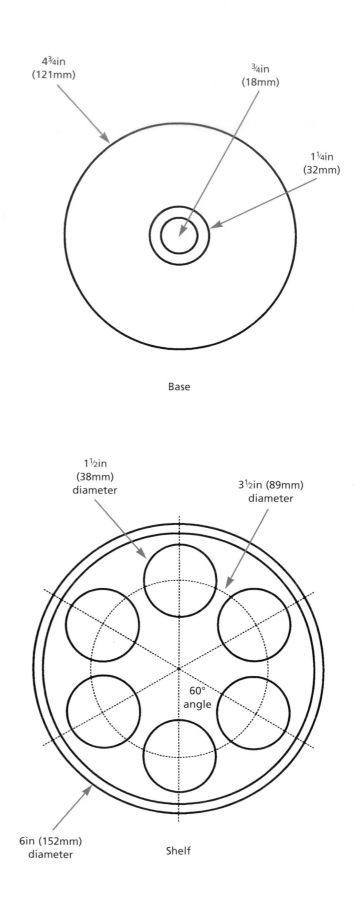

Base

Shelf

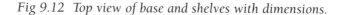

Fig 9.12 *Top view of base and shelves with dimensions.*

Fig 9.13 The completed egg shelves.

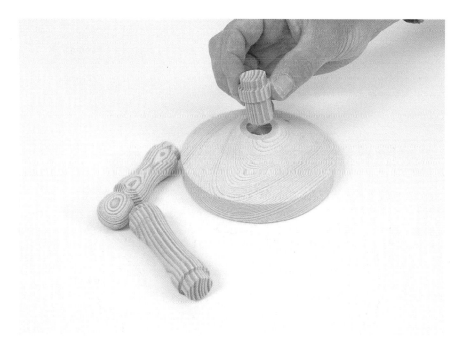

Fig 9.14 Fitting the lower part of the stand into the base.

With a 1½in (38mm) hole saw mounted in a power drill, cut out the egg holes. Use the drill in a vertical stand to keep the hole saw perpendicular to the surface and saw the holes from both sides of the shelves to avoid tearing the wood on the back surface (see Fig 9.13). A hole saw works best if it is not forced to cut too quickly. Start slowly and allow it to rotate smoothly throughout the cut.

ASSEMBLY AND FINISHING

1 Smear glue on the narrow areas of the pieces that make up the central stand. Place the short lower pieces into the base and fit it into the lower shelf (see Fig 9.14). Glue in the central section of the stand and then the top shelf. Finally fit in the top section of the stand.

2 Carefully remove any surplus glue before it dries and apply two coats of polyurethane varnish to give the rack a hard, durable finish

Kitchen Shelf Unit

DEGREE OF DIFFICULTY: MEDIUM
TIME TO MAKE: 20 HOURS

These kitchen shelves are made to look like the type of furniture that might have been seen in a Victorian farmhouse. The lower shelf is for plates and the top one for dishes and saucepans. Along the edges of the top and base there is a traditional moulded decoration, and the two sides are shaped with a smooth curve to add visual interest. Originally, such a unit would have been used for the best willow pattern plates and gleaming copper pots and pans.

The project is made from pre-jointed pine boards that are fixed at the corners with housing joints. Extensive use is made of a router for cutting the joints and decorative moulding. If you do not have a router, alternative ways of making these features are suggested in the instructions.

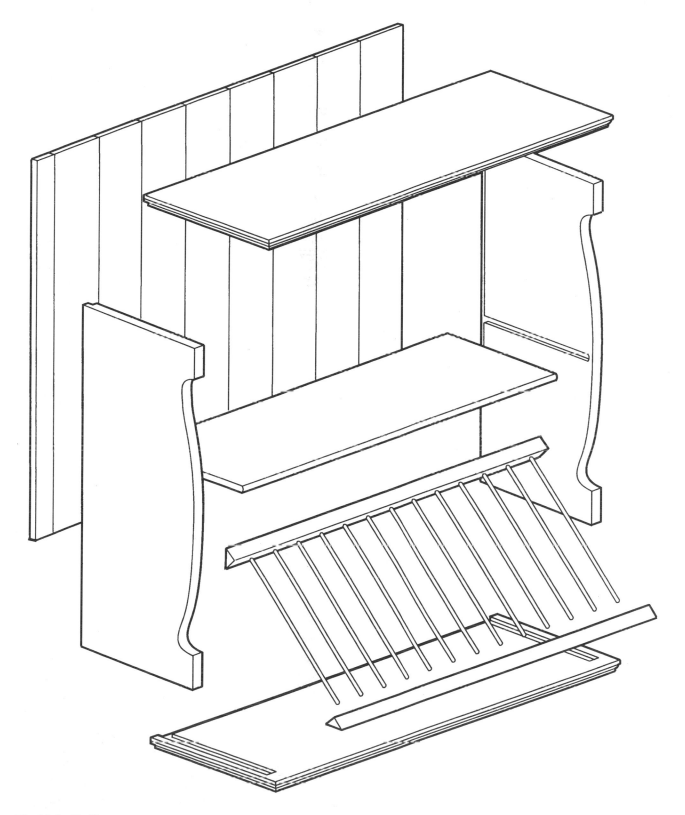

Fig 10.1 *Shelf unit construction.*

CUTTING LIST		
Sides (2)	Pre-jointed pine board	25⅞ x 10 x ¾in (657 x 254 x 18mm)
Top (1)	Pre-jointed pine board	31 x 11 x ¾in (787 x 279 x 18mm)
Base (1)	Pre-jointed pine board	31 x 11 x ¾in (787 x 279 x 18mm)
Shelf (1)	Pre-jointed pine board	28½ x 9⅛ x ¾in (723 x 232 x 18mm)
Back planks (9)	Pine cladding	26⅛ x 3¾ x ⅜in (663 x 94 x 9mm)
Plate rack ends (2, cut from 1 piece)	Pine	28 x 1⅛ x 1in (711 x 28 x 25mm)
Plate rack dividers (13)	Hardwood dowel	12⅛ x ⅜in diameter (308 x 9mm diameter)

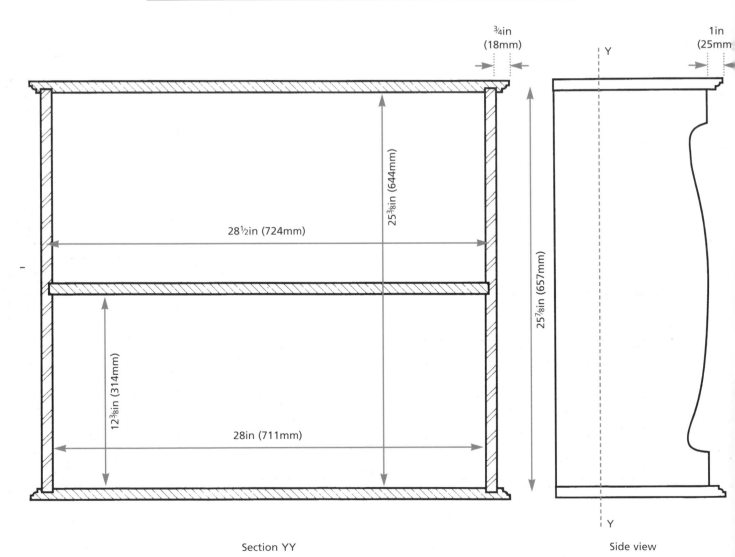

Fig 10.2 Side view and section YY.

CONSTRUCTION

CARCASS

1 You will need five pine boards large enough to make the sides, top, base and shelf. Purchase them as near as possible to the sizes required so that there will not be too much waste. Alternatively, purchase one large board and cut all the pieces from it – this will be more cost effective.

NOTE

MAKING A TEMPLATE

To make a template from the patterns given in this book, first mark up a grid of squares of the required size on a piece of card. Sketch in the pattern shape, cut it out and then draw around it to mark out the shape on the wood. If the shape is symmetrical, you need only make a template for one half: when you have drawn around it, turn it over and draw around it again to complete the shape.

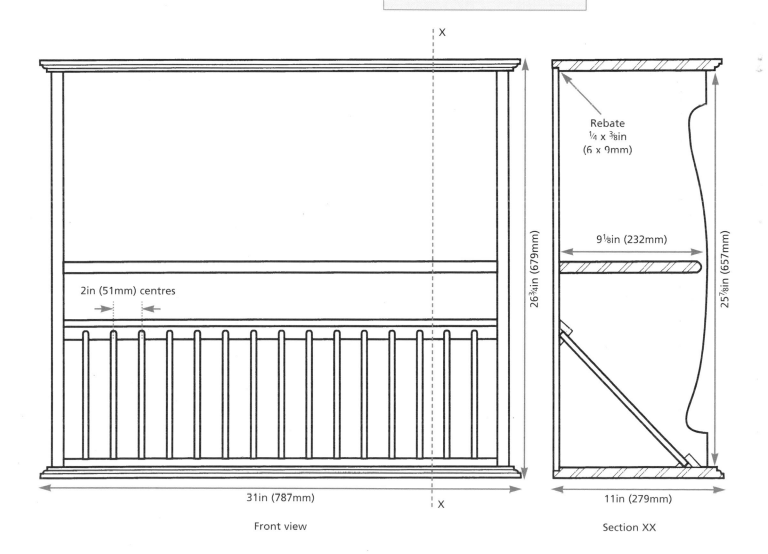

X

2in (51mm) centres

26³⁄₄in (679mm)

31in (787mm)

X

Front view

Rebate
¼ x ⅜in
(6 x 9mm)

9⅛in (232mm)

25⅞in (657mm)

11in (279mm)

Section XX

Fig 10.3 Front view and section XX.

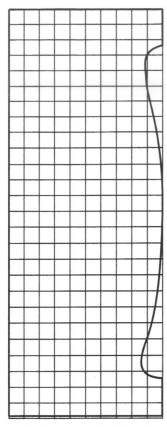

Each square = 1in (25mm)

Fig 10.4 Template for sides.

Fig 10.5 Eradicating the saw marks on a convex curve with a rasp.

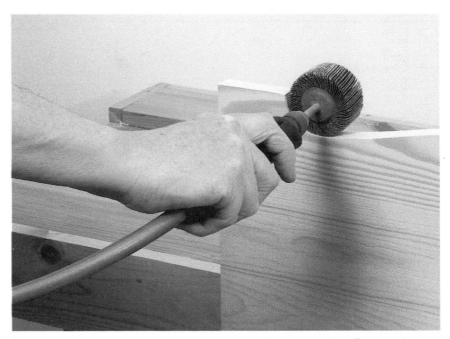

Fig 10.6 Smoothing the acute concave curved section with a flapwheel.

SIDES

1 Using a rule, T square and pencil, mark and cut out the two sides. Make a template for the side shape by squaring up the shape in Fig 10.4 on to card (see the Note on page 61) and then mark it out on to the wood.

Cut around the curves with a jigsaw and smooth the edges. For smoothing the long convex curves use a rasp (see Fig 10.5) followed by a file, and for the tight concave curves use a flap wheel attached to a drill (see Fig 10.6) or a half-round file – the latter requires a lot more effort. Use medium-grade and fine glasspaper to take out all the marks left by the files.

2 On the inside surfaces of the sides, use a pencil to mark the position for the housing joints for the central shelf to fit into. Cut over the pencil lines with a marking knife as this will give a good clean edge to the housings, particularly if you are cutting them by hand rather than with a router.

3 To cut the housing with a router, use a straight cutter set to a depth of $\frac{1}{4}$in (6mm). Because the housing is not near the edge, it is not possible to use the fence on the router as a guide. Instead, clamp a straight-edged piece of scrap wood to the workpiece so that the base plate can be guided along it (see Fig

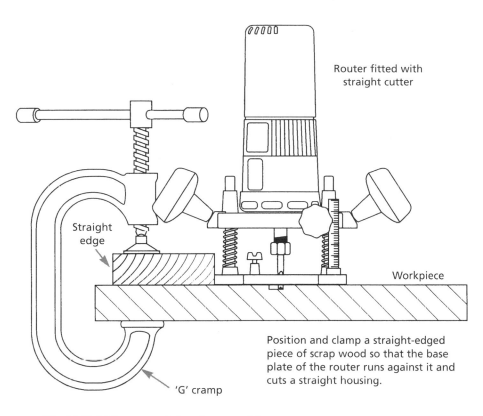

Router fitted with
straight cutter

Straight
edge

Workpiece

'G' cramp

Position and clamp a straight-edged
piece of scrap wood so that the base
plate of the router runs against it and
cuts a straight housing.

Fig 10.7 Using a straight edge to guide a router.

10.7). Use a half-round gouge to round the blind end of the housing to match the rounded front edge of the central shelf.

If you do not have a router, you can make the housings by hand with a tenon saw, bevel-edged chisel and half-round gouge. Use the chisel and gouge to carve out approximately 2in (51mm) of the blind end of the housing – this will give enough room to use a tenon saw to cut down the sides of the trench (see Fig 10.8). Use a bevel-edged chisel to clean out the waste wood between the saw cuts.

4 To complete the sides, cut a through rebate on the back inside edges to house the back of the unit. The rebate can be made using a router or a rebating plane.

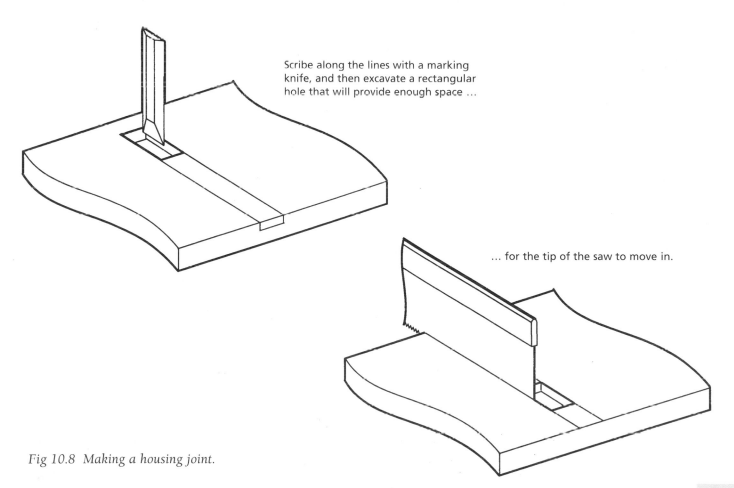

Scribe along the lines with a marking
knife, and then excavate a rectangular
hole that will provide enough space ...

... for the tip of the saw to move in.

Fig 10.8 Making a housing joint.

SHELF, TOP AND BASE

1 Mark out and cut the central shelf. Use a plane, file and glasspaper to round the front edge. Slot the shelf into the sides to ensure that it fits accurately.

2 The top and base are exactly the same size and shape and are made in the same way. Mark out a rectangle, ensure that the corners are square, cut it to size and plane the edges. Use a block plane for smoothing the end grain followed by glasspaper. It is important that the edges are flat and smooth because the beading cutter now used in the router, for making the decorative moulding, has a bearing on the end that rubs against the edge of the wood to guide it. If the edge is wavy, the decorative moulding will also be wavy.

An alternative way of making a decorative edge is to glue on ready-made pine moulding strips.

3 In the underside of the top and the top surface of the base, cut the housings for the sides. These are made in the same way as before except that the blind ends of the housings are square and not rounded. Assemble the top, base and sides without gluing to ensure that they fit together without too many gaps, and make any corrections required.

4 To house the back of the cabinet, the back inside edges of the top and base have rebates in them, which are stopped short of the ends so that they do not show when the cabinet is assembled. The easiest way to make these rebates is with a router fitted with a straight cutter. It is difficult to make them with a rebating plane.

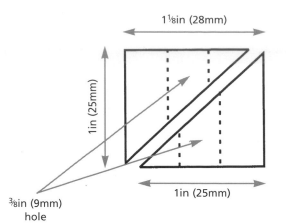

1⅛in (28mm)

1in (25mm)

Block size is 1 x 1⅛in (25 x 28mm) before sawing to allow for width of saw cut

1in (25mm)

⅜in (9mm) hole

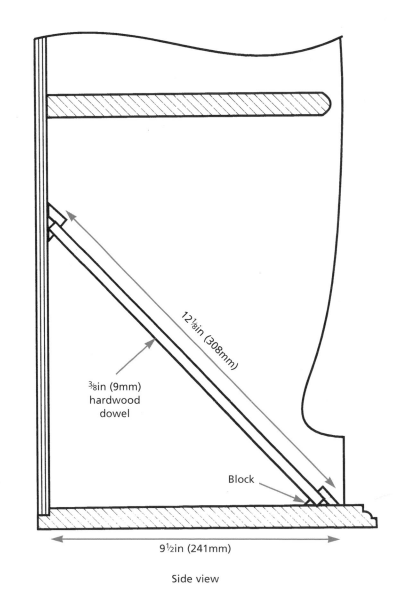

12⅛in (308mm)

⅜in (9mm) hardwood dowel

Block

9½in (241mm)

Side view

Fig 10.9 Details of triangular blocks for plate rack with dimensions.

5 Glue and assemble the sides, top and base and clamp with sash cramps. Ensure that the assembly is square by measuring across the diagonals and make any adjustments with a long sash cramp across the longest diagonal before the glue has time to set (see the Note on page 136). When everything is dry, glue and fit the central shelf.

BACK

The back is made from ³⁄₈in (9mm) tongue and groove cladding that fits into the rebates cut in the sides, top and base. The cutting list specifies nine lengths to make up the required width – however, only part of the last piece is required as the lengths do not fit in exactly. Make sure that the cladding planks are placed so that the face side will be seen from the front.

1 Cut the cladding into the required lengths and pin the first length into the rebate. Place several pins along the long edge into the sides and into the top and base, and a couple into the central shelf. Now slot the remaining planks into place and pin.

2 When you have almost finished, it will be obvious that a complete plank will not fit into the remaining gap. Measure the gap, cut a plank to the required width and pin it into place.

PLATE RACK

The plate rack is made from a number of lengths of ³⁄₈in (9mm) hardwood dowel that slot into holes drilled into two triangular-sectioned end pieces. These end pieces are made from a single rectangular-sectioned length of pine that is split down the middle across the diagonal of the section.

1 Cut and plane a rectangular-sectioned piece of pine to length. Use a rule and pencil to make a mark in the centre of the wide side every 2in (51mm) along the length of the piece. Use a bradawl to pierce a guide hole at each of these marks to guide the drill. It helps if the drill is used in a vertical drill stand. Fit a ³⁄₈in (9mm) bit into the drill and make holes through the piece every 2in (51mm). If you are not confident about drilling the holes accurately, drill a smaller-diameter pilot hole first.

2 With a power saw set to cut at 45°, slice the wood along its length. Cut the dowel into the correct lengths and glue them into the two triangular-sectioned pieces (see Fig 10.10). When the glue has dried, trim any dowel ends that stick right through the triangular blocks with a craft knife.

ASSEMBLY AND FINISHING

1 Before fixing the plate rack into the shelf, apply two coats of polyurethane varnish to both the plate rack and the inside of the carcass – this is easier than varnishing after the whole unit has been assembled.

2 Glue and pin the plate holder into the shelf and drill two holes in the back ready to fix the unit to the wall. Finally, apply two coats of polyurethane varnish to the rest of the carcass.

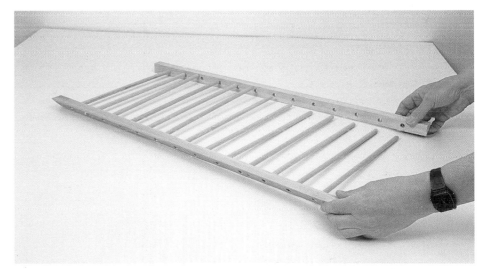

Fig 10.10 Connecting the two halves of the plate rack with dowels.

Wine Racks

DESIGN 1
DEGREE OF DIFFICULTY: EASY
TIME TO MAKE: 15 HOURS

DESIGN 2
DEGREE OF DIFFICULTY: MEDIUM
TIME TO MAKE: 25 HOURS

It is important to store wine properly, whether it is 'plonk' or an expensive vintage. If it is stored in an upright position the cork will dry out and shrink. This will lead to a deterioration in the quality of the wine because air will enter past the cork. The way to overcome this problem is to store the bottles on their sides, in a wine rack.

CUTTING LIST

DESIGN 1

Backs (2)	Pine	7¾ x 5¾ x ¾in (197 x 146 x 18mm)
Side to hold bottle necks (1)	Pine	37¼ x 5¾ x ¾in (946 x 146 x 18mm)
Side to hold bottle bases (1)	Pine	37¼ x 5¾ x ¾in (946 x 146 x 18mm)

ALSO REQUIRED:

Plastic screw caps (2)	

DESIGN 2

Sides (2)	Pine	18⅜ x 9 x ¾in (460 x 229 x 18mm)
Shelves with large holes (4)	Pine	30¼ x 2⅝ x ¾in (768 x 67 x 18mm)
Shelves with small holes (4)	Pine	30¼ x 1⅞ x ¾in (768 x 48 x 18mm)
Pegs (8)	Hardwood dowel	9 x ⅜in diameter (229 x 9mm diameter)

DESIGN 1

This rack uses the available space efficiently as it is designed to be fixed to a wall, which is ideal if your kitchen is short of floor space. It is unusual because the labels can be read at a glance without taking the bottles from the rack. It will accommodate bottles with sloping necks such as those used for hock, and also those with traditionally shaped shoulders.

The rack is sturdy and easy to use, but the dimensions of the holes are for standard bottles only and not for the larger sparkling wine bottles, although it could be altered to accommodate these. The rack shown is for eight bottles, but the design could be altered for a different number of bottles.

Pine is used throughout and there are no difficult joints. The sides are joined to the back with wood screws that are concealed below the surface with filler. The shape of the back has

a family resemblance to the wall-mounted egg rack on page 51.

CONSTRUCTION

1 Mark out and cut four rectangles from pine board for the two sides and two back pieces. Designate one of the sides to be the one that will have the larger holes to hold the bases of the wine bottles.

2 On this side mark the centres of the holes using a pair of dividers set to the required dimensions. Using a try square, draw a cross to indicate where to drill. Drill a series of pilot holes with a ⅛in (3mm) drill before using a 3⅜in (86mm) hole saw fitted to a drill in a drill stand to cut the holes themselves (see Fig 11.3). To make a clean cut, use the hole saw on both faces of the wood. (A hole saw works best if it is not forced to cut too quickly. Start slowly and allow it to rotate smoothly throughout the

cut.) Smooth the inside edges of the holes with a small-diameter drum sander.

3 Make a template for the end shapes by squaring up the shape in Fig 11.2 on to card. Mark the shape on to the ends of the first side piece and cut it out with a jigsaw. Smooth the long straight edges with a plane and the curves with a file and glasspaper.

Mark out and cut the side with the smaller holes in exactly the same way, but make the holes with a 2in (51mm) hole saw.

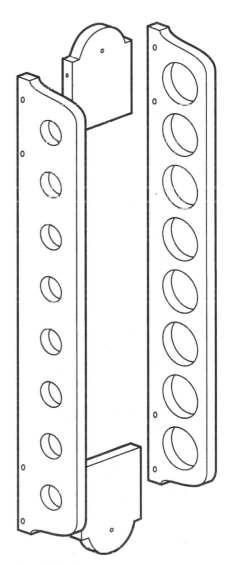

Fig 11.1 Construction.

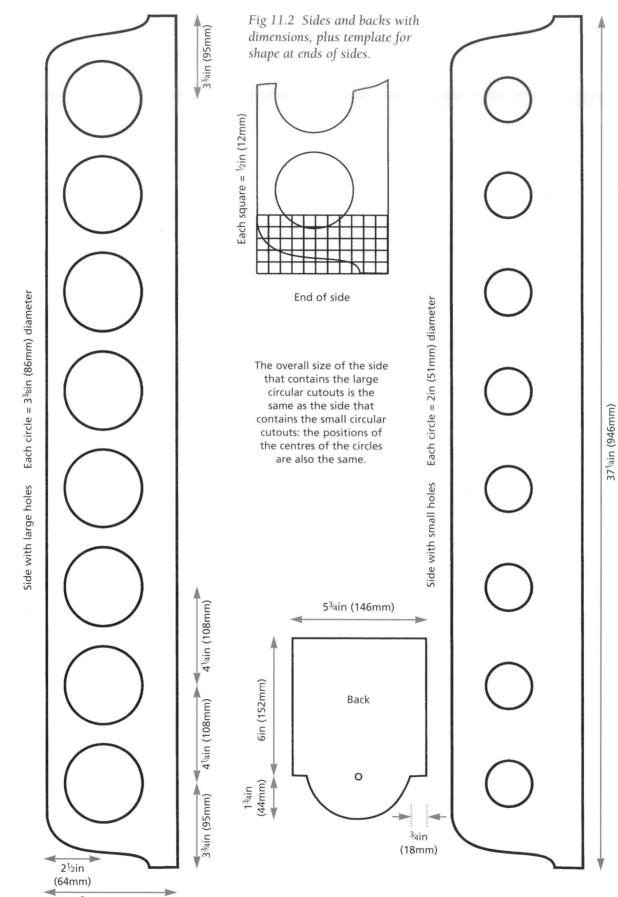

Fig 11.2 *Sides and backs with dimensions, plus template for shape at ends of sides.*

End of side

3¾in (95mm)

Each square = ½in (12mm)

The overall size of the side that contains the large circular cutouts is the same as the side that contains the small circular cutouts: the positions of the centres of the circles are also the same.

Side with large holes   Each circle = 3⅜in (86mm) diameter

Side with small holes   Each circle = 2in (51mm) diameter

37¼in (946mm)

4¼in (108mm)

4¼in (108mm)

3¾in (95mm)

2½in (64mm)

5¾in (146mm)

5¾in (146mm)

6in (152mm)

1¾in (44mm)

Back

¾in (18mm)

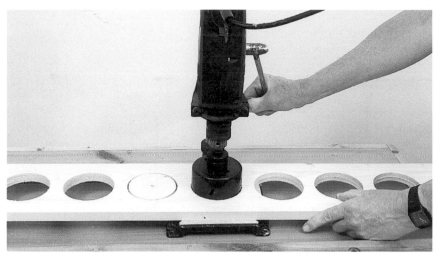

Fig 11.3 Using a large hole saw to make the holes that fit the bottle bases.

4 The two back pieces are the same size and shape. Mark the semicircular shape at one end of both of them, using a suitably sized paint can as a template. Cut out the shape with a jigsaw and smooth the edges. Drill holes for the screws that will fix the rack to the wall.

ASSEMBLY AND FINISHING

1 Drill and countersink holes for the screws in both sides so that they can be fixed to the backs. Glue and screw the parts together and wipe off any surplus glue with a damp rag. Use neutral-coloured wood filler to fill in over the screw heads, and when this is dry glasspaper the filler flush with the wood surface.

2 Finish the rack with blue glaze applied to a surface that has been distressed with a wire brush (see pages 33-4). Apply a coat of polyurethane varnish over the glaze.

3 Use two white plastic screw caps to conceal the heads of the screws that are used to fix the rack to the wall.

DESIGN 2

This floor-standing rack is an example of 'knock-down' furniture. It is designed to be taken apart if, for example, you are moving house. All the joints are through mortise and tenons, but instead of being held in place with glue they are fixed with a peg that fits through the projecting ends of the tenon (see Fig 11.4). The rack can be disassembled for storage in a couple of minutes by pulling out the pegs.

As in the wall-mounted wine rack, the bottles are stored horizontally. The rack has room for 24, but could easily be made larger or smaller. Pine is used throughout, but instead of a natural varnished finish a transparent glaze of colour is applied over everything except the dowels, which are left a neutral colour for contrast.

CONSTRUCTION

The wine shelves are two different sizes. The front shelves, which hold the necks of the bottles, have 2in (51mm) diameter semicircles cut in them and the rear shelves, which hold the lower ends of the bottles, have 3⅜in (86mm) diameter semicircles. The shelves are made in pairs so that the circles can be cut in them before the wood is sawn down the centre to form semicircles. There are four pairs of shelves, two with large holes and two with small holes.

1 Mark out a length of pine for one pair of shelves. Note that the shelves with small holes are narrower than those with large holes. Mark the tenons on the ends, the positions of the holes for the pegs, and the positions of the centres of the circles for the bottle cutouts. Drill ⅛in (3mm) pilot holes for the centres of the circles and the peg holes. When marking the positions of the pilot holes for the pegs, make sure they are positioned so that the pegs will pull the mortise

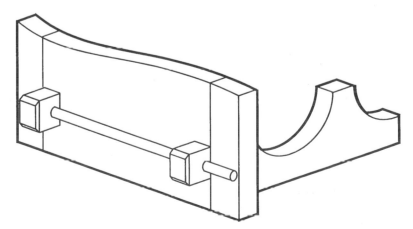

Fig 11.4 Dowelling pegs holding shelves in place.

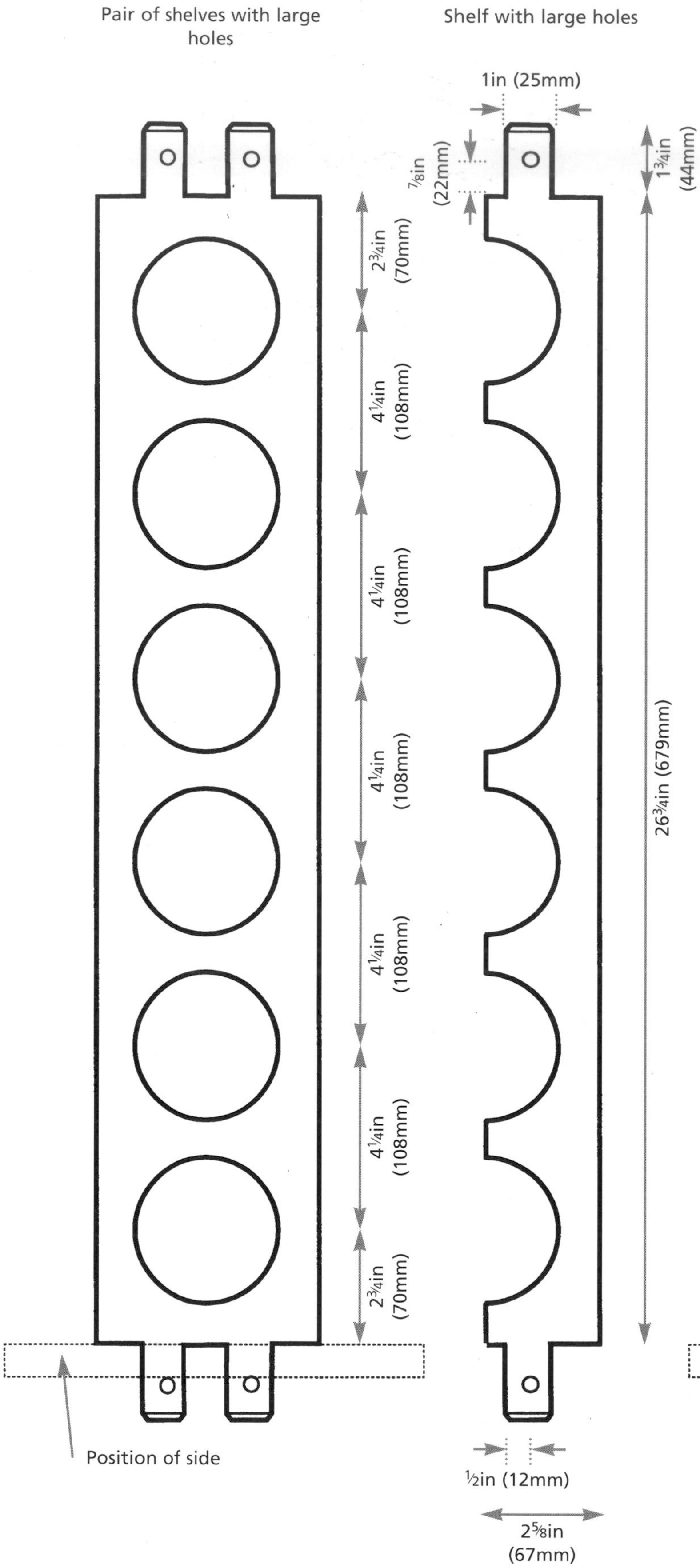

Pair of shelves with large holes

Shelf with large holes

Pair of shelves with small holes

Shelf with small holes

1in (25mm)

$\frac{7}{8}$in (22mm)

$1\frac{3}{4}$in (44mm)

$2\frac{3}{4}$in (70mm)

$4\frac{1}{4}$in (108mm)

$4\frac{1}{4}$in (108mm)

$4\frac{1}{4}$in (108mm)

$4\frac{1}{4}$in (108mm)

$4\frac{1}{4}$in (108mm)

$2\frac{3}{4}$in (70mm)

$26\frac{3}{4}$in (679mm)

Position of side

$\frac{1}{2}$in (12mm)

$2\frac{5}{8}$in (67mm)

1in (25mm)

$\frac{7}{8}$in (22mm)

$1\frac{3}{4}$in (44mm)

$2\frac{3}{4}$in (70mm)

$4\frac{1}{4}$in (108mm)

$4\frac{1}{4}$in (108mm)

$4\frac{1}{4}$in (108mm)

$4\frac{1}{4}$in (108mm)

$4\frac{1}{4}$in (108mm)

$2\frac{3}{4}$in (70mm)

$26\frac{3}{4}$in (679mm)

Position of side

$\frac{1}{2}$in (12mm)

$1\frac{7}{8}$in (48mm)

Fig 11.5 Shelf with large holes.

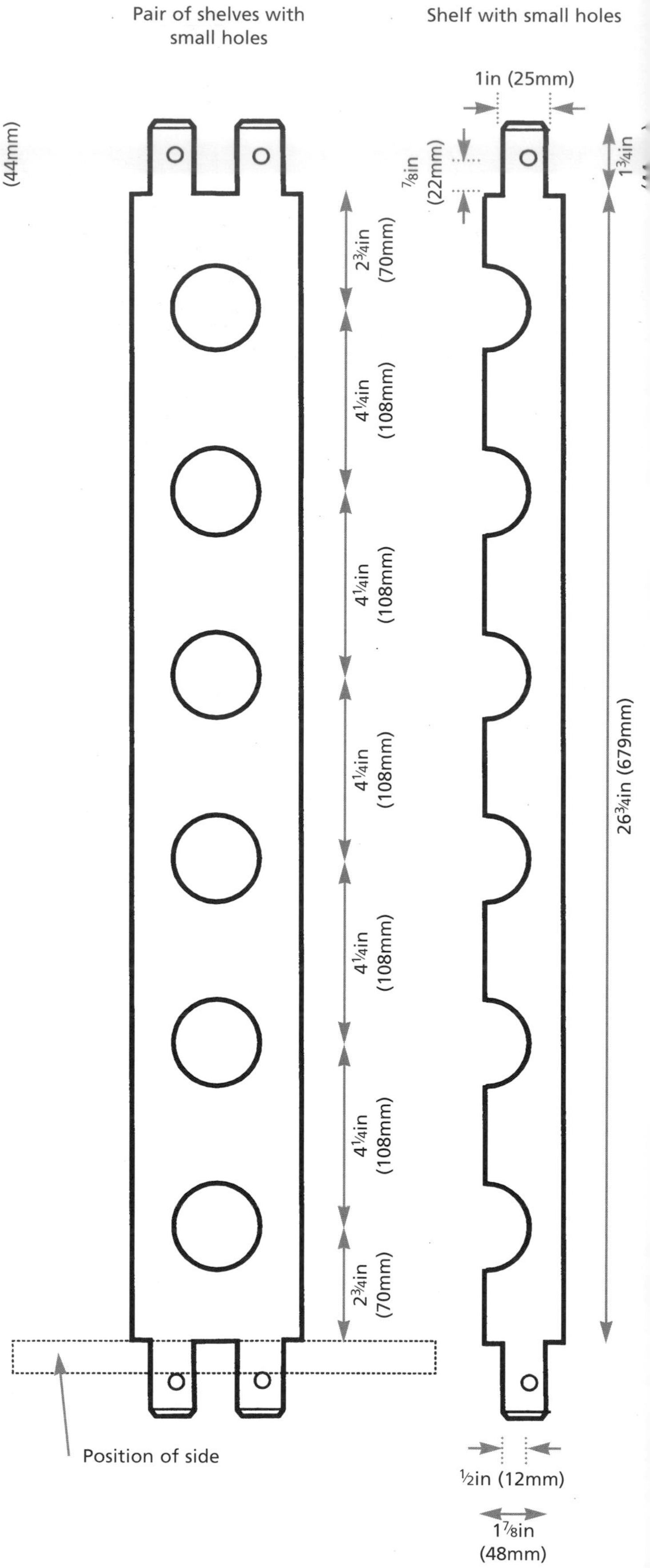

Fig 11.6 Shelf with small holes.

Fig 11.7 Construction.

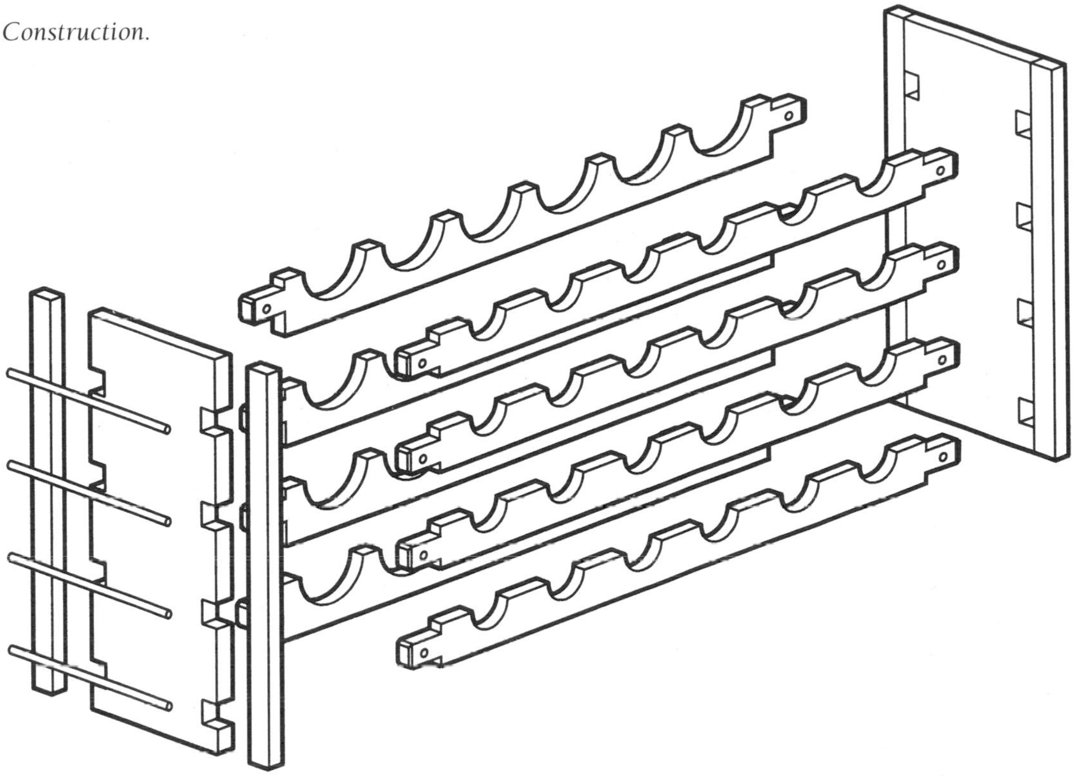

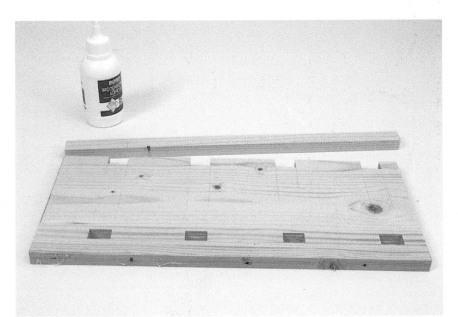

and tenon joints tightly together. Cut out the tenons on both ends of this first pair of shelves.

Use this first piece to mark the position of all the holes and the tenons on the rest of the pieces. To do this, lay it on top of the next pair of shelves, draw around the tenons at the ends and push a gimlet through the pilot holes to pierce the wood underneath (see Fig 11.8). Do this for all four pairs of shelves and drill pilot holes in all of them where the wood has been pierced.

2 Now drill all the ⅜in (9mm) holes for the pegs and use two different-sized hole saws to cut the holes for the bottles. To make a clean cut, use the hole saw on both faces of the wood. (A hole saw works best if it is not forced to cut too quickly. Start slowly and allow it to rotate smoothly throughout the cut.)

Next, saw the pairs of shelves down the centre and cut the tenons

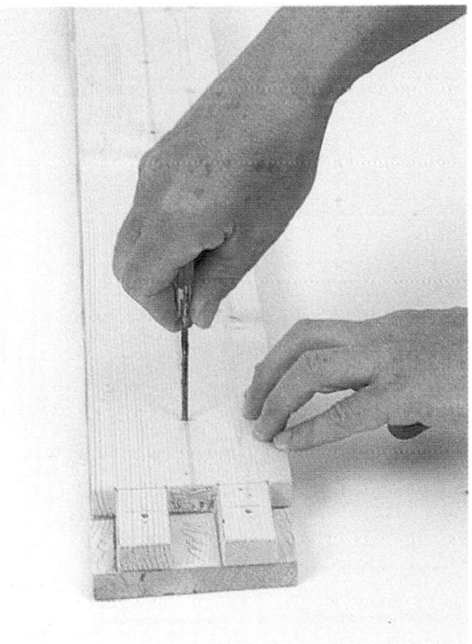

Fig 11.8 Using a shelf to mark the hole positions on another shelf.

Fig 11.9 Assembling one of the sides.

on the ends. Smooth the inside
edges of the circular cutouts with a
small-diameter drum sander. Using a
file, chamfer the ends of the tenons
to make it easier to assemble the
rack.

3 Cut two lengths of pine board
for the sides. It can be quite
difficult to cut accurate square
mortises in the centre of a piece of
board, so here the easy method is
used. The sides are made from three
pieces of wood. Form the mortises
by cutting the sides of the holes in
both edges of the central pieces with
a tenon saw and coping saw. After
that, glue and pin two pieces of pine
on to the outside edges to form the
complete side (see Fig 11.9). Punch
the pin heads below the surface and
make good the resulting holes with
pine-coloured filler.

4 Slot the tenons into the
mortises to ensure that they fit
accurately and make any
adjustments that are required. Look
closely to make sure that the peg
holes are just clear of the outside
face of the sides, so that the
dowelling pegs will hold the joint
firmly. If they are not, adjust the
shoulders of the tenons.

5 Cut the pegs to size from
lengths of ³⁄₈in (9mm)
hardwood dowel. Sharpen the ends
slightly with a pencil sharpener to
make it easier to locate the peg holes
and plane a small flat on the sides
for the same reason.

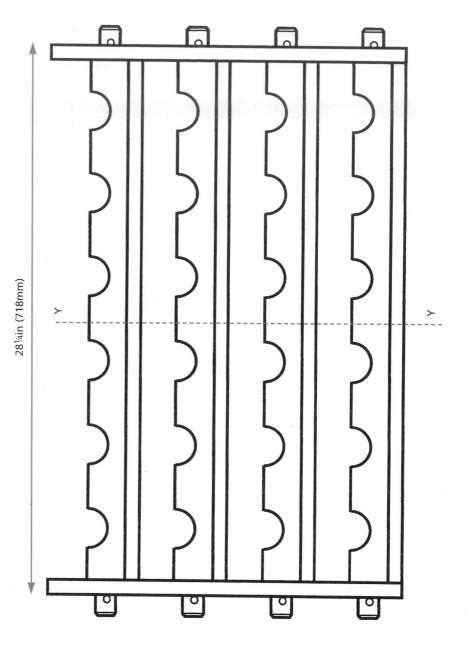

28¼in (718mm)

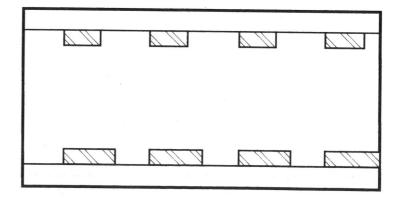

Section YY

Fig 11.10 Front view and section YY.

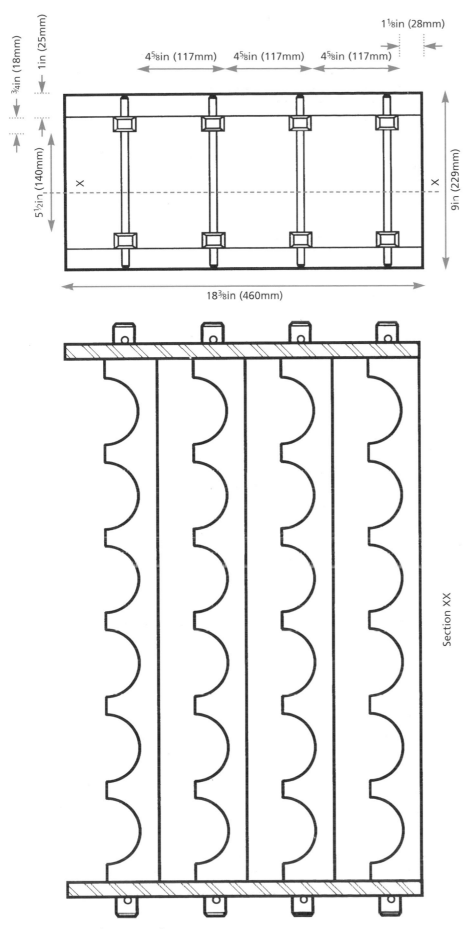

¾in (18mm)

1in (25mm)

5½in (140mm)

4⅝in (117mm)   4⅝in (117mm)   4⅝in (117mm)

1⅛in (28mm)

9in (229mm)

X   X

18⅜in (460mm)

Section XX

Fig 11.11 Side view and section XX.

ASSEMBLY AND FINISHING

1 Assemble the pieces by putting all the shelves into one of the sides and pushing in the pegs. Place this on the second side and push the pegs into position. If everything fits accurately, take the rack apart and finish it with blue glaze and polyurethane varnish in the same way as for the wall-mounted wine rack (see page 69). Reassemble to complete.

THE HALL

HALLS ARE OFTEN SMALL AND IN SOME INSTANCES NOT MUCH MORE THAN A PASSAGEWAY TO GIVE ACCESS TO THE OTHER ROOMS IN THE HOUSE. IN THESE CIRCUMSTANCES FLOOR SPACE IS AT A PREMIUM, BUT POTENTIAL STORAGE SPACE IS STILL AVAILABLE BY HANGING ANY CUPBOARDS OR SHELVES ON THE WALL.

IN A SMALL HALL IT MAKES SENSE, FOR EXAMPLE, TO HANG THE TELEPHONE ON THE WALL OR PLACE A FREE-STANDING TELEPHONE ON A SHELF. SIMILARLY, A SMALL SPACE WILL BECOME CLUTTERED IF THE OCCUPANTS OF THE HOUSE DROP THEIR SHOES ON THE FLOOR WHEN THEY CHANGE INTO SLIPPERS, SO SOLVE THE PROBLEM BY MAKING A HANDY WALL-MOUNTED SHOE CUPBOARD.

12

Shoe Cupboard

DEGREE OF DIFFICULTY: MEDIUM
TIME TO MAKE: 18 HOURS

FOR many years we kept our shoes on a shelf in the base of a wardrobe in the bedroom. However, because this was not always the most convenient place to store them, there were often a large number of shoes strewn around the hall. If this problem sounds familiar, this is the project for you.

The cupboard is not intended to meet all your shoe storage requirements, but simply to keep your most frequently used shoes both out of sight and to hand. It is designed to hang on the wall and the top is extended slightly so that it can be used as a shelf. If extra storage is required, it would be comparatively easy to expand the design to include two or three tiers, although in that case it might be best to make the cupboard floor standing.

The cupboard is hinged on the lower edge and the box that contains the shoes is fixed to the inside of the door (see Fig 12.1). To make the construction as simple as possible, I have used dowel joints for the main carcass and simply glued and pinned the plywood together to make the interior box. The dowel joints are made using a dowelling jig to drill the holes and hardwood dowel pegs that are purchased ready-made. The carcass is made from pre jointed pine boards so that there is no need to make up wide planks.

CUTTING LIST

Carcass sides (2)	Pre-jointed pine board	13¾ x 6½ x ¾in (349 x 165 x 18mm)
Carcass top (1)	Pre-jointed pine board	37 x 7 x ¾in (940 x 180 x 18mm)
Carcass base (1)	Pre-jointed pine board	34½ x 6½ x ¾in (876 x 165 x 18mm)
Carcass back (1)	Plywood	35 x 13½ x ¼in (889 x 343 x 6mm)
Door (1)	Pre-jointed pine board	34⁷⁄₁₆ x 12¹⁵⁄₁₆ x ¾in (875 x 328 x 18mm)
Shoe box base (1)	Plywood	33¼ x 5⅜ x ⅜in (845 x 137 x 9mm)
Shoe box sides (2)	Plywood	12 x 5⅜ x ⅜in (305 x 137 x 9mm)
Shoe box top (1)	Plywood	34 x 12 x ⅜in (864 x 305 x 9mm)
Shoe box back (1)	Plywood	33¼ x 5 x ⅜in (845 x 127 x 9mm)

ALSO REQUIRED:

Short length of brass chain
1½in (38mm) brass hinges (3)
1in (25mm) magnetic catch (1)
1½in (38mm) pine knob (1)
1in (25mm) screw eyes (2)

NOTE

USING PRE-JOINTED PINE BOARDS

Pine board is supplied covered in shrink-wrapped plastic, which not only keeps it clean but also retains the moisture in the board at the same level as when it was manufactured. When the board is unwrapped this allows the moisture content in the board to change, particularly if it is placed in a dry environment such as a centrally heated house, which can lead to problems such as bending and warping. To prevent this, unwrap the board just before it is made up into the project. Very often, the construction will hold the boards flat. Applying the varnish finish will also reduce any tendency to warp because the varnish helps to stabilize the moisture content. If, after unwrapping the boards, construction of the project is delayed, the boards should be stored flat with some weights placed on top of them to prevent any warping.

Before work is started on the pine boards, make sure that your bench is free from any small wood chips and other pieces of detritus, because if the boards are laid face down on them their surface will become indented and marred.

CONSTRUCTION

1 Choose a suitable piece of pre-jointed pine board for the top and use a pencil, try square and ruler to mark out a rectangle to the correct size. When choosing the board, bear in mind that the top and front are the pieces that will be most noticeable, so try to choose a board without any large, ugly defects such as resin pockets or loose knots (see the Notes on page 53 and right).

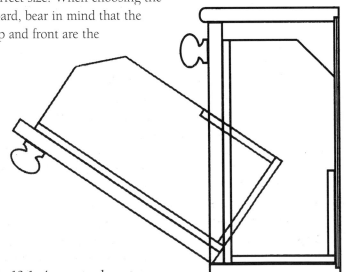

Fig 12.1 Access to shoe storage.

The door and shoe box assembly is hinged at the front so that it can drop forward. The amount it can open is limited by a short length of chain.

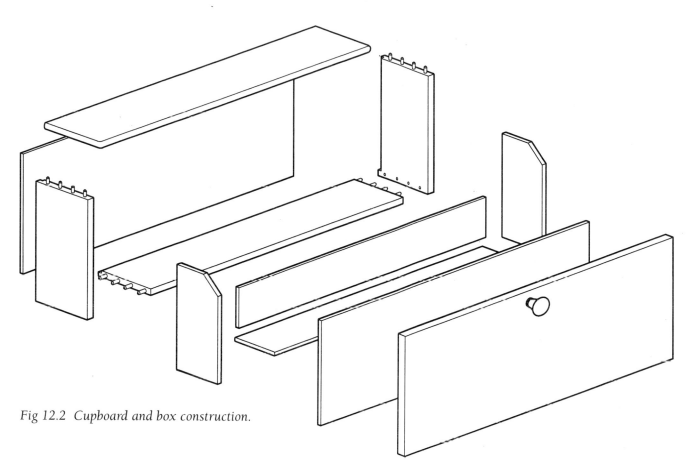

Fig 12.2 Cupboard and box construction.

Cut out the shape with a suitable saw and smooth all the sides with a plane. The front and side edges of the top are rounded. This can be achieved in a number of ways – I use a plane and glasspaper. Mount the board in the vice and plane a chamfer at 45° degrees along both corners of the edges, then plane off the corners left by doing so, until a nearly rounded shape is achieved. Use glasspaper to remove any final corners (see Fig 19.5 on page 115). It is slightly more difficult to do this on the end grain but good results can be achieved with a block plane.

On the underside of the back edge, use a router to cut a stopped rebate, measuring ¼ x ¼in (6 x 6mm), that will eventually be used to house the plywood back.

2 Mark out and cut the base and two sides in a similar way to the top, but this time do not round

any of the edges. Use a router to cut the rebates on the back edges to house the back. Note that the rebate on the sides is stopped at the base, but the rebate in the base is a through rebate.

On each piece, indicate the front edge with a pencil mark, and also mark with pairs of letters (AA, BB, etc.) the pieces that will match up at the corners. This will avoid any confusion when making the dowel joints and gluing the carcass together.

Drill the dowel holes using a dowelling jig, which takes time to set up but produces accurate results. Put a depth stop on the drill bit so that the dowel holes are not too deep (see the Note on page 82). This is important when drilling the holes in the top, as it would be quite easy to drill right through the ¾in (18mm) thickness.

3 Assemble the carcass dry, with just a few dowel pegs fitted and lightly clamped with sash cramps, to check that the joints fit. Make any adjustments required and then glue up the joints and clamp them – this is a two-person job. Before the glue dries, check the carcass for squareness and make any necessary adjustments (see the Note on page 136).

DOOR

1 On a wide board, mark out the rectangle for the door, cut it to size and plane the edges. Test it in the carcass to ensure that it fits. There should be a clearance of about ¹⁄₃₂in (0.75mm) all round between the door and the sides of the carcass. The door is fixed to the base with three 1½in (38mm) brass hinges. (Three are required because when the box is filled with shoes all the weight will be on the hinges.)

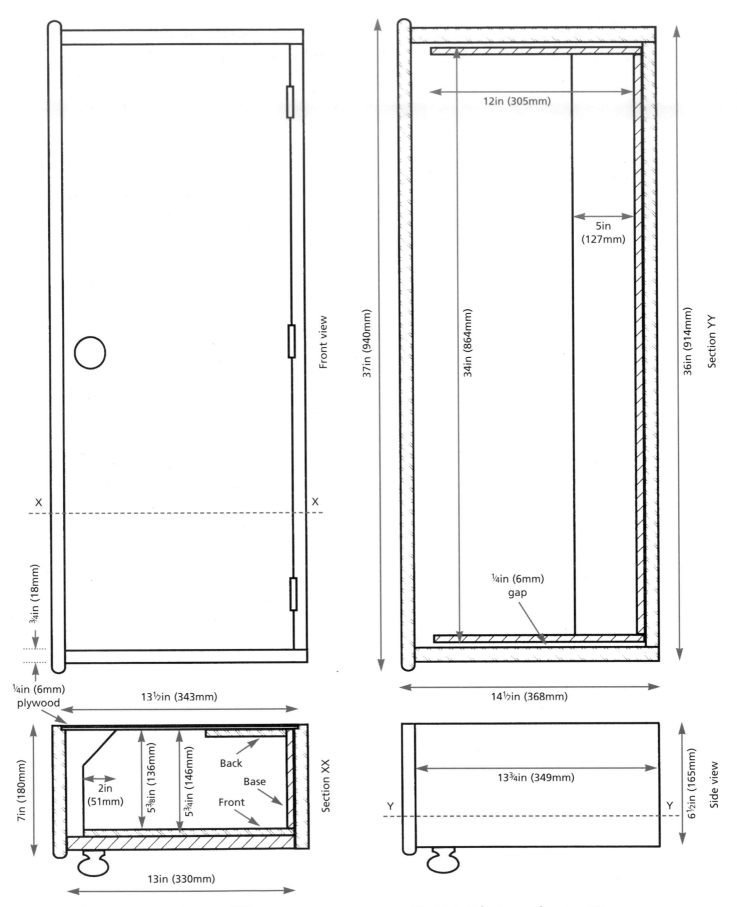

Front view

37in (940mm)

¾in (18mm)

¼in (6mm)
plywood

13½in (343mm)

7in (180mm)

2in
(51mm)

5⅜in (136mm)

5¾in (146mm)

Back

Base

Front

Section XX

13in (330mm)

12in (305mm)

5in
(127mm)

34in (864mm)

36in (914mm)

Section YY

¼in (6mm)
gap

14½in (368mm)

13¾in (349mm)

6½in (165mm)

Side view

Fig 12.3 Front view and section XX.

Fig 12.4 Side view and section YY.

NOTE

FITTING RECESSED HINGES

Place a hinge on the door, with the hinge knuckle protruding from it. Draw around the hinge with a pencil. With a marking gauge, scribe a line on the door front where the hinge is to be placed, corresponding to half the thickness of the hinge knuckles.

Using a try square, steel rule and marking knife, cut around the pencil lines, then use a saw to cut down the recess at the ends. Remove the waste wood with a bevel-edged chisel and place the hinge into the recess. Mark the position of the screw holes with a bradawl and then drill them with a bit that has a slightly smaller diameter than the hinge screws. Follow this procedure for all the hinges on the door and on the carcass.

Fit the hinges with a single screw in each flap and test to see if the door swings and fits in a satisfactory way. If not, adjust the hinge recesses: they may require deepening, or packing with a piece of card. If the door is refitted several times, the heads of brass screws may become damaged. To overcome this, use steel screws initially and then substitute brass screws when all the necessary adjustments have been made.

2 Mark the position for the hinges on the door, about 1½in (38mm) from the sides and in the centre. The hinge flaps are recessed into the door and carcass, so that they fit flush with the surface of the wood (see the Note, left).

3 Remove the door from the carcass, leaving the hinges in place on the door: when the box is made, it fits over the hinges. Fix a knob on the door using glue and a screw.

BACK

Select a piece of ¼in (6mm) plywood that is large enough for the back with a little to spare. Place this on the workbench and position the carcass on top of it. With a pencil, trace around the inside back edge of the carcass on to the plywood to get the exact size required. Cut out the shape and fix it to the back of the carcass with 1in (25mm) panel pins. These are slanted so that they fix into the sides (see Fig 12.5).

SHOE BOX

The entire inner shoe box is made from ⅜in (9mm) plywood. All the edges and corners are fixed together with glue and ⅞in (20mm) oval brads. To ensure that putting them in is straightforward, always drill small pilot holes in the top piece to be fixed, to avoid splitting the wood and to keep the nails upright. When the nails have been hammered home, punch the heads below the surface and fill in the holes with suitably coloured filler (see Fig 12.6). On the long edges, put in one nail approximately every 4in (102mm).

1 Using a T square, rule and pencil, lay out all the pieces on a single sheet of plywood in the most economical position (i.e. without wasting too much wood). Check all the diagonals to ensure that the corners are square, and then cut out the pieces with a suitable saw. Use a plane and glasspaper to smooth the edges.

2 Using nails and glue, join the base to the two sides, followed by the back and the front.

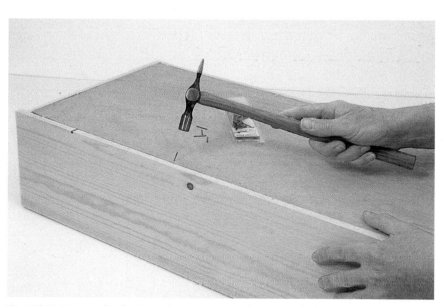

Fig 12.5 Fixing the back to the carcass with pins and glue.

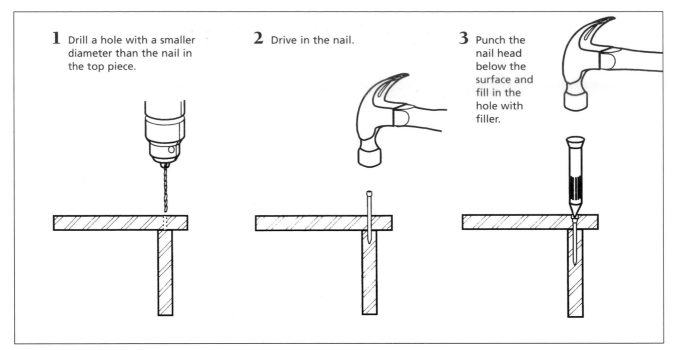

1 Drill a hole with a smaller diameter than the nail in the top piece.

2 Drive in the nail.

3 Punch the nail head below the surface and fill in the hole with filler.

Fig 12.6 Shoe box nailing technique.

ASSEMBLY AND FINISHING

1 Drill screw holes in the front of the box and countersink them, then join the box to the door using several screws and glue (see Fig 12.7). Fill over the screw heads with filler, and when it is dry smooth it flush with the surface using glasspaper. Now fit the entire front on to the carcass using the hinge holes made earlier.

2 Drill two holes in the back of the cupboard that will be used to hang the cupboard on the wall. Fit a magnetic catch to prevent the front dropping open, and two screw eyes that will be used for connecting a length of chain to prevent the front opening too far.

3 Apply two coats of emulsion (acrylic) varnish to all the pine parts but ignore the plywood. Fit the chain to complete (see Fig 12.8).

Fig 12.7 Screwing the shoe box to the back of the door.

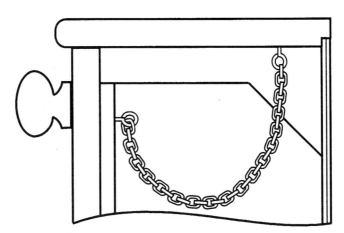

The screw eyes are placed approximately 2in (51mm) from one end.

Fig 12.8 Position of chain.

13 Telephone Shelf

DEGREE OF DIFFICULTY: MEDIUM
TIME TO MAKE: 15 HOURS

TRADITIONAL styling is combined with the beauty of pine in this handy telephone shelf. The top is designed to have a large enough surface for a telephone and answering machine, with a shelf underneath that will hold several telephone directories. The shallow drawer is to hold a pad and pen for those urgent messages.

A traditional-style telephone shelf may seem a little anachronistic, but it is intended to complement the coat rack on page 86 and so would have looked odd if the styling was not the same. Of course, it is possible to buy Georgian-style television cabinets, so there is a precedent!

CUTTING LIST

CARCASS

Top (1)	Pine	16½ x 9 x ¾in (419 x 229 x 18mm)
Sides (2)	Pine	15 x 8½ x ¾in (381 x 216 x 18mm)
Lower shelf (1)	Pine	12 x 8½ x ¾in (305 x 216 x 18mm)
Drawer runners (2)	Hardwood	7 x ⅜ x ⅜in (179 x 9 x 9mm)

ALSO REQUIRED:

2in (51mm) plastic corner blocks (2)

DRAWER

Front (1)	Pine	11¹⁵⁄₁₆ x 3 x ¾in (303 x 76 x 18mm)
Sides (2)	Plywood	7¼ x 2⅜ x ½in (184 x 60 x 12mm)
Back (1)	Plywood	9⁷⁄₁₆ x 2⅜ x ½in (240 x 60 x 12mm)
Base (1)	Plywood	10⁷⁄₁₆ x 7¼ x ¼in (265 x 184 x 6mm)

ALSO REQUIRED:

Plastic screw caps (2)

CONSTRUCTION

CARCASS

1 On a piece of pine board, draw the two rectangles for the sides, cut them out and smooth the edges. Make a template for the classical design at the base of the sides by squaring up the shape from Fig 13.3 on to card (see the Note on page 61) and then mark it out on the wood. Use an appropriate saw to cut around the curves (I use a bandsaw, but others such as a jigsaw would

also do the job). To smooth the concave curves, use a drum sander or flap wheel followed by fine glasspaper. For the concave curves, use files followed by medium-grade and then fine glasspaper.

> ### NOTE
>
> #### USING A DEPTH STOP
>
> When drilling holes that must not pass right through the woods – for example, when making concealed dowel joints – stick a piece of tape around the drill bit to act as a guide for the depth of the hole.

2 Cut out the top, round the edges with a plane and smooth with two grades of glasspaper. Cut the lower shelf to size.

3 Drill the holes for the dowel joints in the top of the sides and the telephone shelf using a dowelling jig. Use a depth stop on the drill bit (see the Note below). This is particularly important when making the holes in the top, as it would be easy to drill right through the wood. Assemble the parts without using glue to check the fit and make any adjustments required. Apply glue to the joints and clamp the parts together. Before the glue has set, check that the carcass is square and adjust the position of the cramps if necessary (see the Note on page 136).

4 Cut two lengths of hardwood for the drawer runners, and when the glue on the carcass has set fix them to the inside with glue and pins. It helps to place the pins accurately if small pilot

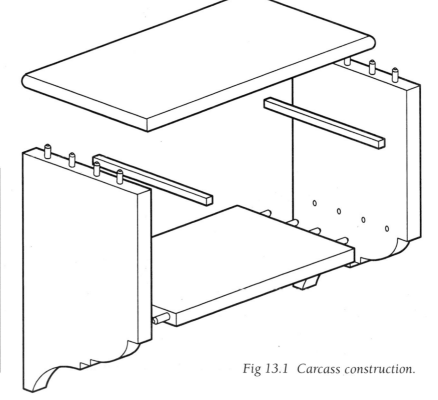

Fig 13.1 Carcass construction.

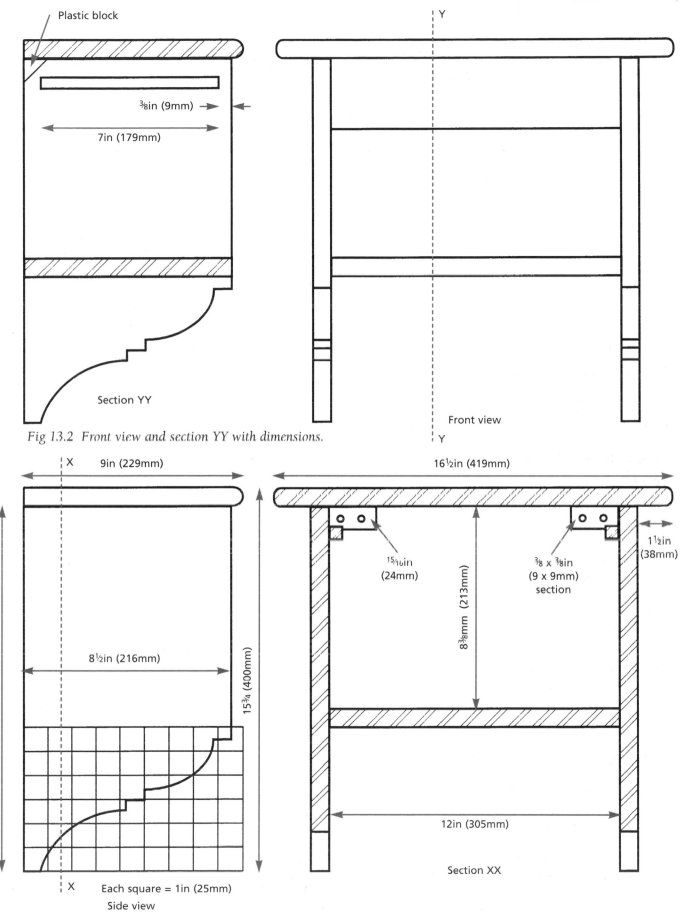

Plastic block

⅜in (9mm)

7in (179mm)

Section YY

Y

Front view

Y

Fig 13.2 Front view and section YY with dimensions.

X 9in (229mm)

16½in (419mm)

15in (381mm)

8½in (216mm)

15¾ (400mm)

¹⁵⁄₁₆in (24mm)

⅜ x ⅜in (9 x 9mm) section

1½in (38mm)

8⅜mm (213mm)

12in (305mm)

Section XX

Each square = 1in (25mm)

X

Side view

Fig 13.3 Side view and template, and section XX with dimensions.

holes are drilled through the rail before fixing. The front ends of the rails act as a backstop for the back of the drawer front. Punch the pin heads below the surface of the wood so that they will not interfere with the smooth running of the drawer. To enable the shelf to be fitted to the wall, screw two plastic corner blocks to the underside of the top at the back edge.

DRAWER

The shallow drawer is made from plywood with a pine front. Grooves are cut in the sides so that the drawer can be hung on the two rails fitted to the inside of the carcass.

1 Saw the two sides and the back from a sheet of ½in (12mm) plywood. Make the two shallow grooves in the sides using a router fitted with a ⅜in (9mm) straight cutter. Cut the front from a suitable piece of pine and use a tenon saw to mark the rebates on the end that will eventually house the plywood sides. Along the lower back edge of the drawer front cut the rebate for the plywood base, again using a router. If you do not have a router, all the rebates can be made with a plough plane.

2 Fix the back to the sides with a glued butt joint strengthened with 1in (25mm) oval brads. Although this is a simple joint it will be strong enough, particularly when the plywood drawer base has been fitted. Use the same technique to fix the sides to the drawer front. Make sure that the assembly is square, and when the glue is dry punch all the nail heads below the surface of the wood.

3 To mark out the size of the base accurately, lay the assembled drawer on a sheet of ¼in (6mm) plywood and draw around the outside edges with a pencil (see Fig 13.5). Saw the base to size and fix it into place with glue and ¾in (18mm) panel pins. There is no need to fit a handle to the drawer, as the bottom edge of the front protrudes beyond the plywood base to provide a finger grip for this purpose.

ASSEMBLY AND FINISHING

1 Apply two coats of antique pine brushing wax, followed by beeswax furniture polish. Slot the drawer into place to complete.

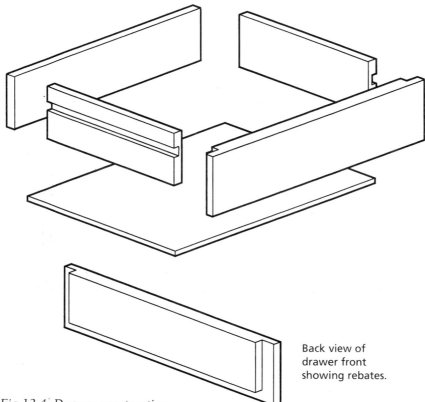

Back view of drawer front showing rebates.

Fig 13.4 Drawer construction.

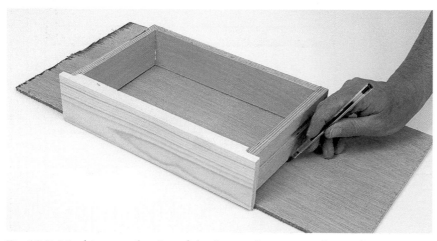

Fig 13.5 Marking out the size of the drawer base on to plywood.

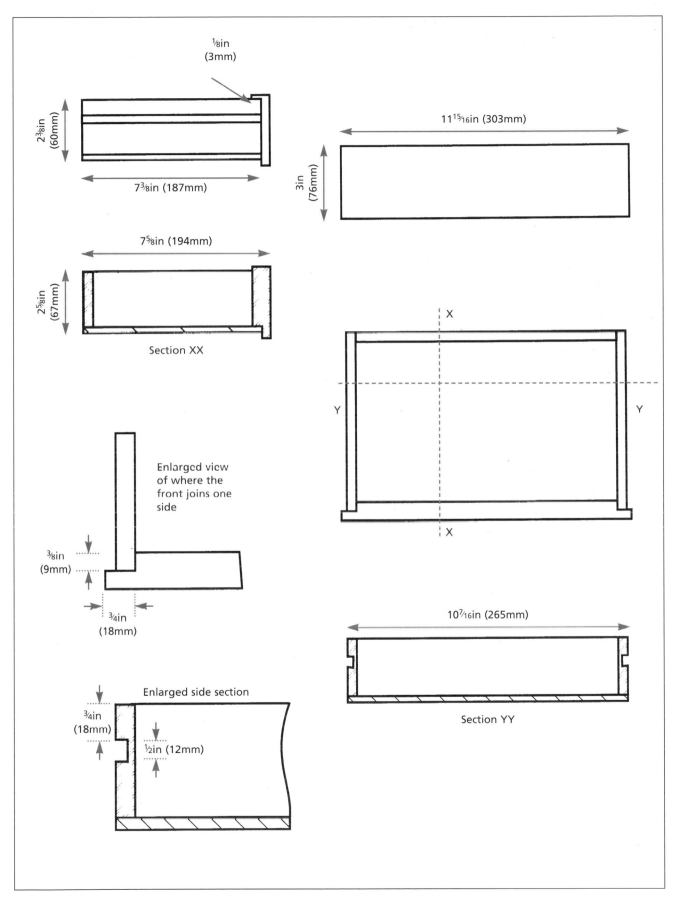

⅛in
(3mm)

2⅜in
(60mm)

7⅜in (187mm)

11¹⁵⁄₁₆in (303mm)

3in
(76mm)

7⅝in (194mm)

2⅝in
(67mm)

Section XX

X

Y   Y

X

Enlarged view
of where the
front joins one
side

⅜in
(9mm)

¾in
(18mm)

10⁷⁄₁₆in (265mm)

Enlarged side section

¾in
(18mm)

½in (12mm)

Section YY

Fig 13.6 Side, top and front views of drawer with dimensions, plus sections XX and YY.

14

Coat Rack

DEGREE OF DIFFICULTY: MEDIUM
TIME TO MAKE: 12 HOURS

A<small>T</small> the most basic level, a coat rack could consist simply of a few nails banged into the wall, but even here you would need to consider how many nails would be required and how high above the floor they should be. The first decision to be taken for the coat rack shown here was whether it should be free-standing or wall-mounted. Although there are advantages to both, I decided to fix it to a wall, as a free-standing hanger takes up extra floor space in a small hall.

The number of pegs was calculated by multiplying the number of people in the house by two (as each person has two top coats) and then adding one for luck. The coats can be doubled up temporarily when visitors arrive. The pegs are shaped so that the coats hang near the end away from the wall, with a knob on the end that is not so large that the loop in a coat will not go over it, but large enough for the coat not to slip off accidentally. A shelf is included to hold small items such as gloves or a dog lead, and the traditional styling complements that of the telephone shelf on page 81.

CUTTING LIST

Back (1)	Pine	25¾ x 6¾ x ¾in (645 x 171 x 18mm)
Sides (2)	Pine	6¾ x 4⅝ x ¾in (171 x 117 x 18mm)
Top (1)	Pine	28¼ x 5¼ x ¾in (718 x 133 x 18mm)
Pegs (5)	Pine	6½ x 1 x 1in (165 x 25 x 25mm)

ALSO REQUIRED:

Brass mirror plates (2)

The dimensions given for the pegs include the extra length and width required for mounting and turning on the lathe.

CONSTRUCTION

1 Mark out rectangles of the required size for the back, top and two sides. Ensure that they are square, cut them out and smooth the edges with a plane.

2 Make a template for the concave curve in the front edge of the sides by squaring up the shape in Fig 14.2 on to card (see the Note on page 61) and then marking

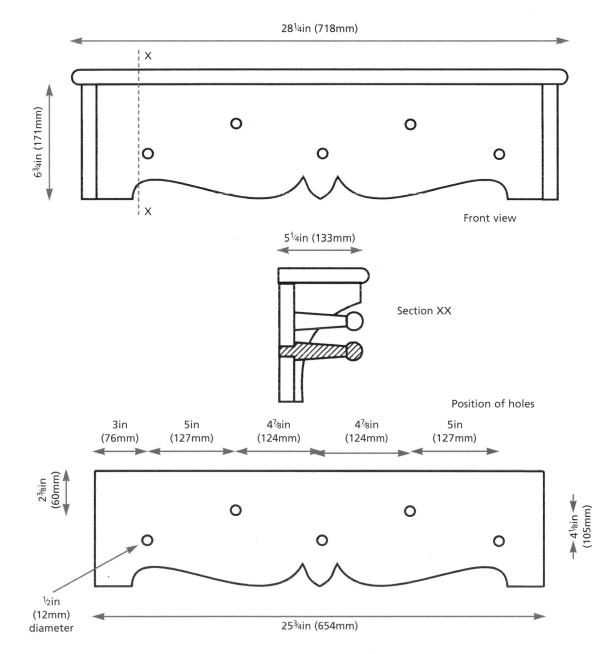

Fig 14.1 Front view, section XX and position of holes with dimensions.

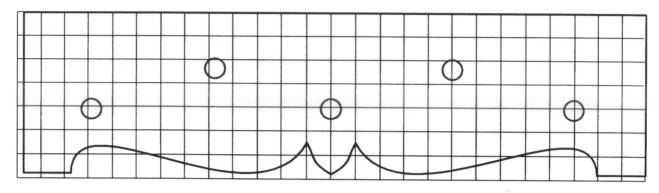

Back   Each square = 1in (25mm)

Fig 14.2 Templates for back and sides.

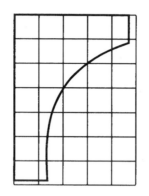

Side   Each square = 1in (25mm)

it out on one of the side pieces. Cut out the curve: I used a bandsaw, but as the radius of the curve was too tight for the blade that was fitted I made some extra 'relieving' cuts to help it to cut around the curve (see Fig 14.3). Smooth the resulting curved shape, preferably with a drum sander, which gives a quick result but does create a lot of dust. Use the first side to mark out the curved shape for the second side and cut it out as before.

3 Round the front and side edges on the top with a plane, followed by medium-grade and fine glasspaper. Make a template as before for the shape on the bottom edge of the back and mark it out on to the wood. Use a bandsaw or jigsaw to cut around the curves, then smooth the edges with a half-round file and flap wheel. Mark the positions of the holes for the pegs

and drill a ⅛in (3mm) pilot hole before using a ½in (12mm) bit for the final size.

4 Concealed dowel joints are used to connect the sides to the back and top. The top edge of the back is fixed to the top with glue.

Using a dowelling jig, drill all the holes for the dowels and glue the pegs into both ends of the back and the top edges of the sides. (For the coat rack shown, ¼in (6mm) ready-made dowel pegs were used.) Allow these to dry before applying glue to the rest of the joints.

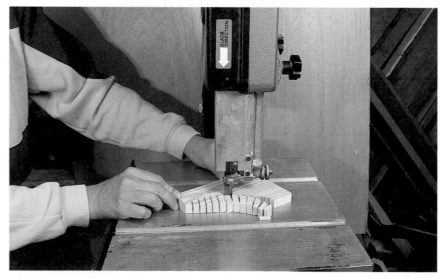

Fig 14.3 Cutting the curved shape on the side with a bandsaw.

Assemble the sides with the back and then place the top in position. Clamp together with sash cramps until dry.

5 The coat rack will be fixed to the wall with mirror plates – attach these now.

TURNING THE PEGS

1 Prepare all five pieces of wood from which the pegs will be cut, for mounting on the lathe (see the Note on page 47, and Fig 14.5).

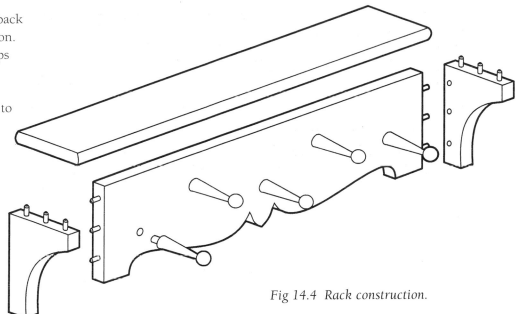

Fig 14.4 Rack construction.

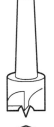
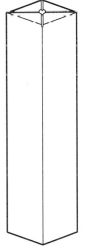

1 Prepare the square-sectioned pieces for mounting on the lathe.

2 Turn the square section to a cylinder and mark on the position of the 'V' grooves with a pencil.

3 Cut the 'V' grooves with a skew chisel.

4 Turn the ball on the end of the peg with a half-round gouge.

5 Cut the taper, with a half-round gouge.

6 Use a scraper chisel to form the part that fits into the back of the coat rack.

7 Glasspaper the peg and cut off the waste wood from the ends.

Fig 14.5 Turning a peg.

2 Mount the wood between the lathe centres, switch to a slow speed and turn the square section to a cylinder with a 1in (25mm) half-round gouge.

3 Use a ruler and pencil to mark the position of the 'V' grooves and shoulder and then cut them using the point of a skew chisel (see Fig 14.5).

4 Speed up the lathe and use a ½in (12mm) half-round gouge to form the ball on the end of the pegs and to cut the taper (see Fig 14.5). Make constant checks with callipers to ensure that all the diameters are correct.

The diameter of the part that fits into the back must be accurate to fit into the ½in (12mm) holes. Use a skew chisel with a scraping action for this part (see Figs 14.5 and 14.7), as it is easier to be accurate with this method, although it is slower than using a cutting action.

5 Speed up the lathe once again and, using a strip of emery paper wrapped around the peg, hold it at both ends to give a final smooth surface. Remove the peg from the lathe and cut off the waste wood (see Fig 14.5).

6 When the first peg has been made, use it as a guide for cutting the remaining pegs, taking measurements with callipers to ensure that all the round sections are the same in diameter.

ASSEMBLY AND FINISHING

1 Fix the pegs into the back of the rack with glue.

2 Apply two coats of antique pine brushing wax, followed by beeswax furniture polish.

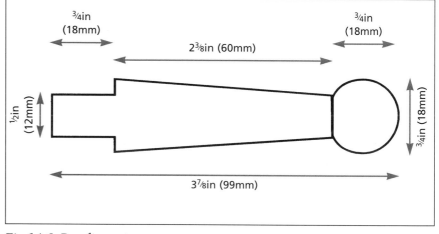

Fig 14.6 Peg dimensions.

Fig 14.7 Using a skew chisel with a scraping action to turn the ends of the peg accurately.

15

Mirror with Shelf

DEGREE OF DIFFICULTY: MEDIUM
TIME TO MAKE: 15 HOURS

A MIRROR in the hall is an essential part of any furnishing scheme – this is where you take a quick glance to ensure that everything is in place before you set out to face the world. This design incorporates a small shelf to hold a hairbrush or lipstick, so that if necessary a quick 'repair job' can be undertaken.

The unit is made from pine with box comb joints at the corners, so named because they are often seen on the corners of small boxes. These joints are easily made using either hand or power tools and, glued together with a modern adhesive, are very strong. The mirror is ¼in (6mm) thick and in the interests of economy is not bevelled, although the design would accommodate a bevel-edged mirror without problems. It is designed for placing in a small hall, perhaps in a town house or flat

CUTTING LIST		
Sides (2)	Pine	15 x 5½ x ¾in (381 x 140 x 18mm)
Top (1)	Pine	19 x 1½ x ¾in (483 x 38 x 18mm)
Base (1)	Pine	19 x 5½ x ¾in (483 x 140 x 18mm)
Back (1)	Plywood	18 x 14 x ¼in (457 x 356 x 6mm)
ALSO REQUIRED:		
17⅞ x 13⅞ x ¼in (454 x 353 x 6mm) mirror (1)		
Brass picture turns (8)		
Brass mirror plates (2)		

CONSTRUCTION

1 Select some pine boards large enough to accommodate the pieces and, using a rule and pencil, mark out the rectangles for the sides, top and base. Make a template for the side curves by squaring up the shape from Fig 15.2 on to card (see the Note on page 61) and mark them out on the wood. Cut along the straight edges with a suitable saw and then plane them square and flat. Cut the curves with a jigsaw and smooth them with a drum sander.

2 On the ends of the base, top and sides where box comb joints are to be formed, use a marking gauge to scribe a line corresponding to the thickness of the plank. Decide how many pins are required and use a pair of dividers to mark the pin width and the spaces between them. Draw the lines that mark the width of the pins parallel to the side of the plank. Indicate the areas of waste wood by cross-hatching with a pencil. Cut the sides of the pins with a tenon saw, ensuring that the kerf is in the waste wood area. Remove the waste wood between the pins with a coping saw (see Fig 15.3). Do not cut right up to the line at the base of the pins: stop just short and remove the last small pieces by chopping with a bevel-edged chisel, held perpendicular to the surface and on the line at the base of the pins (see Fig 15.4).

3 Slot the joints together without glue to test the fit and make any adjustments that may be required. If the joints are too tight, remove a few shavings from the sides of the offending pins with a chisel. If they are too loose, pack them out with small pieces cut, preferably, from a sheet of light-coloured veneer, or from thin buff-coloured card. Cut the pieces the same length and width as the pins and glue them to the sides of the pins that need correcting. Do not be tempted to fit the joints together too often, as this will loosen them. When the joints fit together accurately, still do not glue them, as the rebates to hold the mirror are yet to be cut.

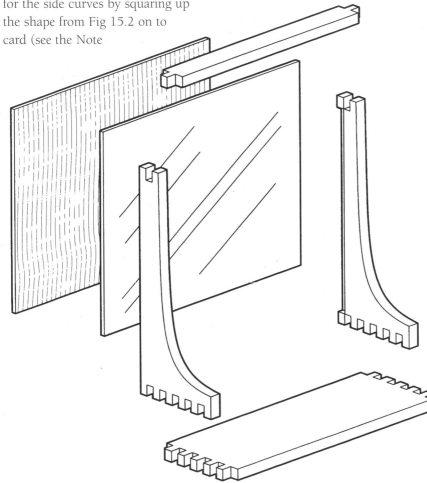

Fig 15.1 Mirror and shelf construction.

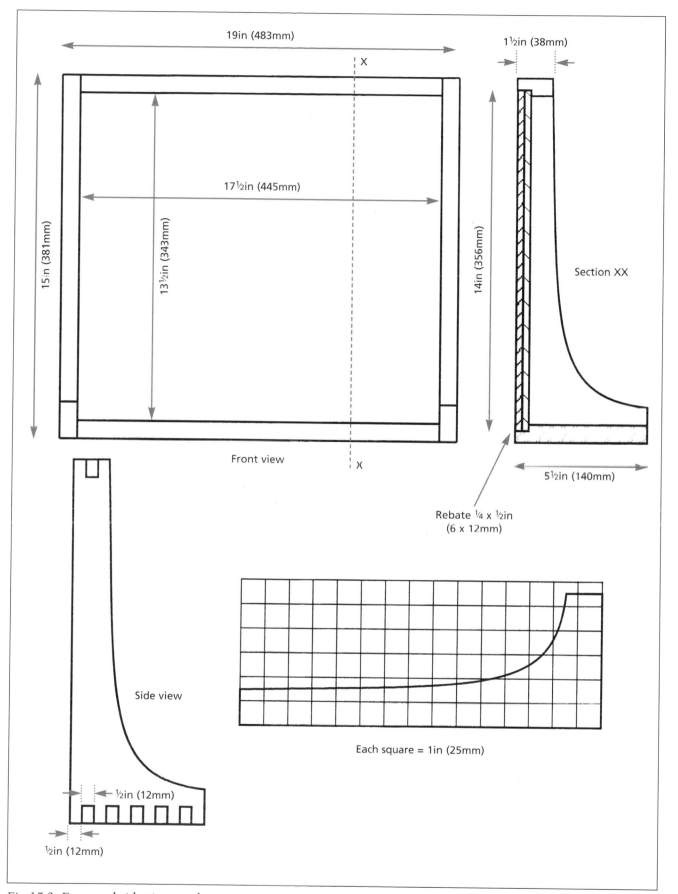

19in (483mm)

1½in (38mm)

X

17½in (445mm)

15in (381mm)

13½in (343mm)

14in (356mm)

Section XX

Front view

X

Rebate ¼ x ½in
(6 x 12mm)

5½in (140mm)

Side view

½in (12mm)

½in (12mm)

Each square = 1in (25mm)

Fig 15.2 Front and side views and section XX with dimensions, plus template for side curve.

4 Mark the positions of the stopped rebates that will house the plywood back and the mirror on the two sides, and the through rebates on the top and base. Cut these with a router, using a ¼in (6mm) straight cutter.

ASSEMBLY AND FINISHING

1 Apply plenty of glue and assemble the structure. Use sash cramps to pull the joints completely closed and leave them in place while the glue sets. Before it does, check that the structure is square and make any adjustments that are necessary (see the Note on page 136).

2 When the glue has set, clean up the corners of the rebates where the sides butt up to the top and base with a small bevel-edged chisel. Use a block plane to level the ends of the pins on the outside faces of the joints flush with the surrounding wood and smooth all the surfaces with a random orbital sander. Start with a medium-grade pad and use a fine pad to finish.

3 Apply three coats of emulsion (acrylic) varnish and when it is dry, measure, mark and cut out the plywood back. Fit the brass picture turns (see Fig 15.5) and mirror plates to the frame and fix the mirror (purchased cut to size) and back in place.

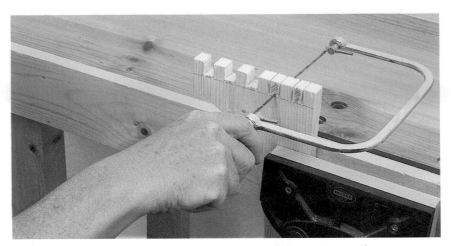

Fig 15.3 *Using a coping saw to remove most of the waste wood between the pins.*

Fig 15.4 *Cutting the gap between the pins back to the line.*

Fig 15.5 *Fitting the picture turns.*

The Living Room

To achieve a stylish, uncluttered look in your home, good storage is important. It is either that, or do without most of the things that people find essential for comfortable living. Pictures in magazines and books show interiors that are models of clean and uncluttered, functional living space. The reality behind any such room is that the interior designer will have spent as much time specifying its hidden assets as its public face. Good storage is the secret of a clean and tidy living environment.

Any old storage is not good enough — it does not help to hide things in the cupboard under the stairs in an unplanned fashion. Firstly, they can get forgotten and remain there taking up valuable space for years; secondly, even if you remember where things are, they are usually so difficult to retrieve behind all the other clutter that it is often too much trouble to find and use them.

To save space efficiently, storage should be planned so that certain pieces of furniture are designed specifically for a single purpose. This way, items such as CDs and magazines cannot get lost and forgotten, but will always be to hand.

16 Nest of Tables

DEGREE OF DIFFICULTY: MEDIUM
TIME TO MAKE: 25 HOURS

NESTING tables are a classic way to provide adaptability and functionality without taking up valuable floor space when not in use. They can be placed in their stacked position beside an armchair to take a reading lamp, and still be available immediately if friends arrive, to be scattered around for cups of coffee. Whenever you require several occasional tables but only have space for one, this solution is worth considering.

There is a drawback, however: it takes almost three times as long to make this nest of tables as it does to make a single example. Bearing this in mind, I have opted for a simple design and jointing technique in order to minimize the construction time. Pine is used throughout and, again in the interests of simplicity, all the joints are made with hardwood dowels. However, it is worth taking some extra time to finish the tables with a pseudo-liming technique to enhance the design.

The instructions below are for making the smallest of the tables, although they are all made in exactly the same way. You can save construction time if the three tables are 'mass produced' by cutting all the legs and then all the rails, before making all the joints. In this way, tools such as the dowelling jig are only set up once for use on all three tables.

The tables have only three sides – the fourth side is missing to allow the smaller tables to slide under the larger ones. The front legs are made from two separate pieces joined at the corners where two sides meet and the back legs are single pieces of wood.

CUTTING LIST

SMALL TABLE

	Top (1)	Pre-jointed pine board	14 x 13½ x ¾in (356 x 343 x 18mm)
A	Wide leg parts (4)	Pine	13¼ x 1½ x ¾in (336 x 38 x 18mm)
B	Narrow leg parts (2)	Pine	13¼ x ¾ x ¾in (336 x 18 x 18mm)
C	Lower side rails (2)	Pine	10¾ x 1¼ x ¾in (273 x 31 x 18mm)
D	Lower front rail (1)	Pine	10 x 1¼ x ¾in (254 x 31 x 18mm)
E	Upper side rails (2)	Pine	10¾ x 1¾ x ¾in (273 x 44 x 18mm)
F	Upper front rail (1)	Pine	10 x 1¾ x ¾in (254 x 44 x 18mm)

MEDIUM TABLE

	Top (1)	Pre-jointed pine board	16 x 15¼ x ¾in (406 x 387 x 18mm)
G	Wide leg parts (4)	Pine	14¼ x 1¾in x ¾in (362 x 44 x 18mm)
H	Narrow leg parts (2)	Pine	14¼ x 1 x ¾in (362 x 25 x 18mm)
I	Lower side rails (2)	Pine	11½ x 1¼ x ¾in (292 x 31 x 18mm)
J	Lower front rail (1)	Pine	12 x 1¼ x ¾in (305 x 31 x 18mm)
K	Upper side rails (2)	Pine	11½ x 1¾ x ¾in (292 x 44 x 18mm)
L	Upper front rail (1)	Pine	12 x 1¾ x ¾in (305 x 44 x 18mm)

LARGE TABLE

	Top (1)	Pre-jointed pine board	18½ x 16½ x ¾in (470 x 419 x 18mm)
M	Wide leg parts (4)	Pine	15¼ x 2 x ¾in (387 x 51 x 18mm)
N	Narrow leg parts (2)	Pine	15¼ x 1¼ x ¾in (387 x 31 x 18mm)
O	Lower side rails (2)	Pine	12¼ x 1¼ x ¾in (311 x 31 x 18mm)
P	Lower front rail (1)	Pine	14 x 1¼ x ¾in (356 x 31 x 18mm)
Q	Upper side rails (2)	Pine	12¼ x 1¾ x ¾in (311 x 44 x 18mm)
R	Upper front rail (1)	Pine	14 x 1¾ x ¾in (356 x 44 x 18mm)

CONSTRUCTION
FRONT AND SIDES

1 Mark and cut all the legs (parts A and B) to size and plane the edges, including the slope on the base of the legs. It is important that the long edges are planed exactly square, as this determines how flat and true the sides will be when the legs are assembled with the rails. Cut the rails (parts C, D, E and F) to size and for the same reason, make sure the ends are as square as possible.

2 Match up the rails and legs in the groups that make up the sides (see Fig 16.3) and mark to identify all the pieces and where they connect, so that when they are glued and assembled there will be no mistakes. Use a dowelling jig to drill the holes for the dowel joints and assemble the three sides without glue to check that they fit accurately. Make any adjustments that may be required before gluing each side together and clamping.

When dry, plane the faces of the joints so that all the parts are flush and level with each other. Finish them with a random disc sander fitted with medium-grade and fine glasspaper pads.

3 As the tables are to be finished with a pseudo-limed effect (see page 35) wire brush the sides – it is easier to do this now rather than after the table has been assembled.

4 Reset the dowelling jig and make the dowel joints to join the three sides together. As before, test the joints for fit and make any adjustments that may be necessary before gluing them together. It is important to wipe off any excess glue with a damp cloth before it has time to dry, otherwise it might fill the pores that have been opened up with the wire brush and spoil the paint effect that is applied later. If this does happen, it can be corrected by wire brushing the affected areas.

TOP

1 Select pieces of pre-jointed pine board without any large, ugly knots (see the Notes on pages 53 and 76) and mark out the rectangle for the top. Ensure that this is exactly square and the correct size before cutting it out and planing the edges.

Note that the grain direction runs from one side of the table to the other and not from front to back. This is because the tables will tend to warp across the grain, so when the main direction is from side to side the upper rails of the two sides (parts E), joined firmly to the back of the top, will prevent it from bending. If the grain ran from front to back there would be only a single rail to fulfil this function, which would not be as effective.

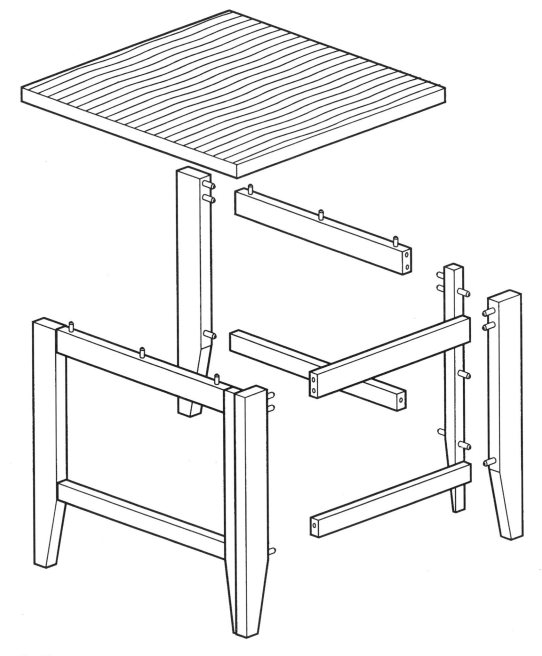

Fig 16.1 Small table: construction.

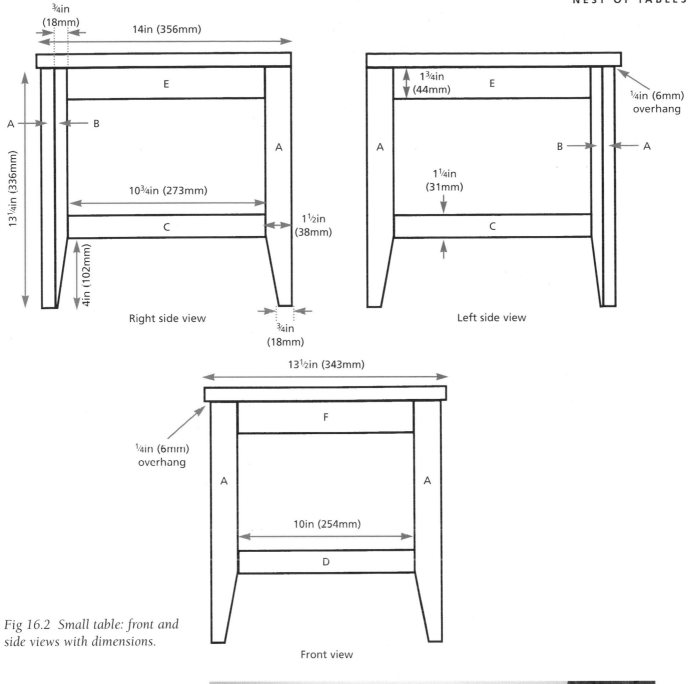

¾in (18mm)

14in (356mm)

E

A ← → ← B

13¼in (336mm)

10¾in (273mm)

C

1½in (38mm)

4in (102mm)

Right side view

¾in (18mm)

1¾in (44mm)

E

¼in (6mm) overhang

A

B → ← A

1¼in (31mm)

C

Left side view

Fig 16.2 Small table: front and side views with dimensions.

13½in (343mm)

¼in (6mm) overhang

F

A

A

10in (254mm)

D

Front view

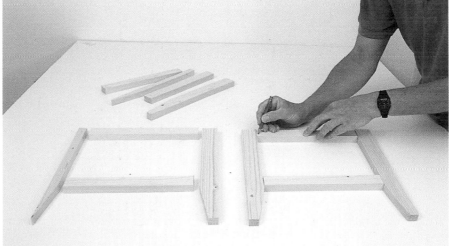

Fig 16.3 Matching the rails to the legs and marking them for identification.

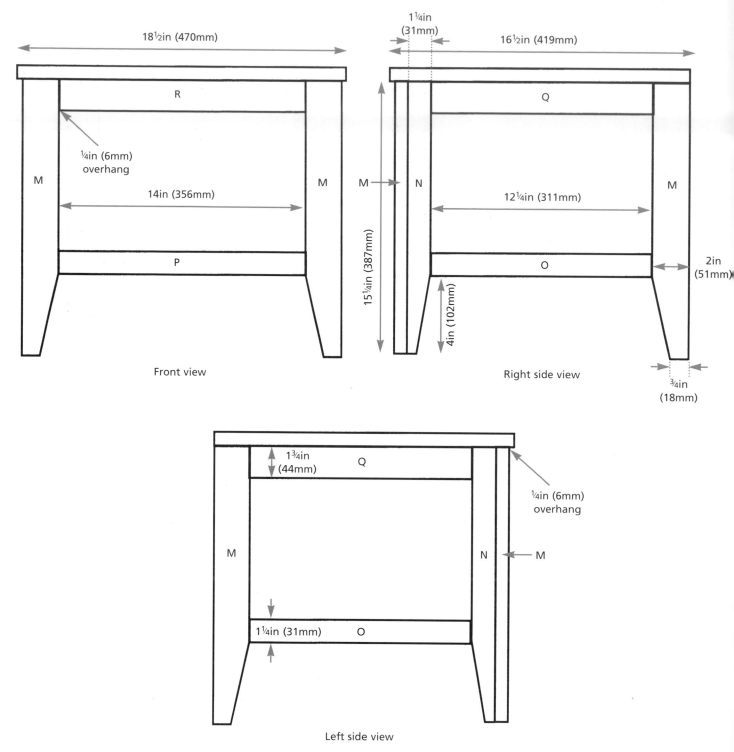

Fig 16.4 Large table: front and side views and dimensions.

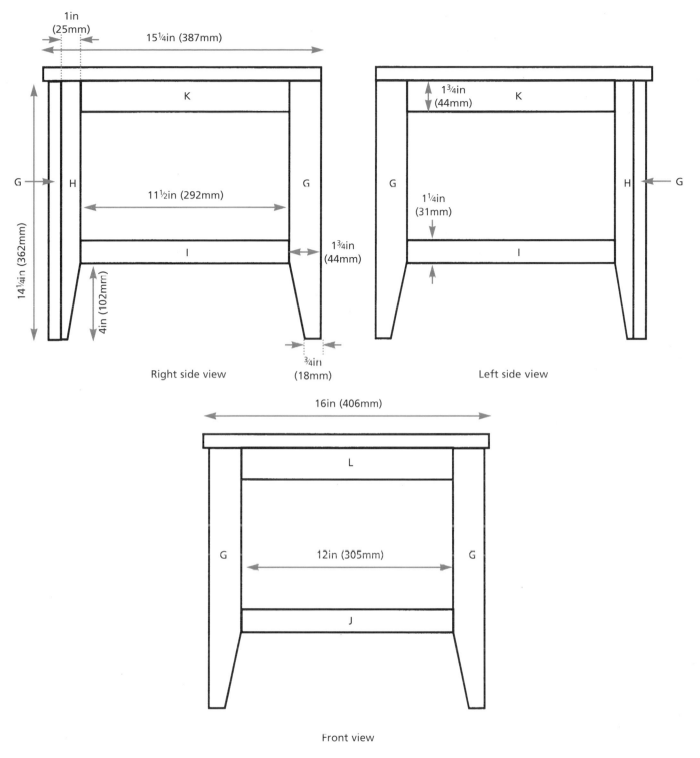

1in
(25mm)

15¼in (387mm)

K

G   H   G

11½in (292mm)

I   1¾in
(44mm)

14¼in (362mm)

4in (102mm)

¾in
(18mm)

Right side view

1¾in
(44mm)

K

G   H   G

1¼in
(31mm)

I

Left side view

16in (406mm)

L

G   G

12in (305mm)

J

Front view

Fig 16.5 Medium table: front and side views with dimensions.

ASSEMBLY AND FINISHING

1 Use the wire brush to provide the required surface on the tabletop.

2 On the back of the top and upper rails (parts E), make the dowel joints to fix the top in position. Test for fit before joining them permanently with glue.

3 Follow the instructions for pseudo-liming on page 35 to give the table an interesting pale finish.

   Make and finish the medium and large tables in the same way.

17 CD Rack

DEGREE OF DIFFICULTY: MEDIUM
TIME TO MAKE: 12 HOURS

Compact discs are used to store digitally recorded music and have largely taken the place of vinyl discs and magnetic tapes. They are also used for storing computer software. This CD rack design will accommodate either, so it is suitable for both the music and computer enthusiast. The rack will hold 12 discs, but this could be increased if required by cutting more parts. It is made from oak and pine, and the design makes a feature of the colour contrast between the different types of wood. For aesthetic reasons, try to select your wood so that there are no knots on the edges when the pieces are stacked together.

To make the rack, a number of small pieces are stacked into two columns with gaps of $^7/_{16}$in (11mm) in between – this just accommodates a CD, which has a thickness of $^3/_8$in (10mm). The discs are held in place by two of their corners slotting into the two columns. The thickness of the pieces of pine that dictate the depth of the disc slots is crucial – fortunately, the wood I obtained was sold as $^1/_2$in (12mm) thick but turned out to be $^7/_{16}$in (11mm), which was just right. This is a fairly common fault (or advantage), so take a rule with you when purchasing and be selective.

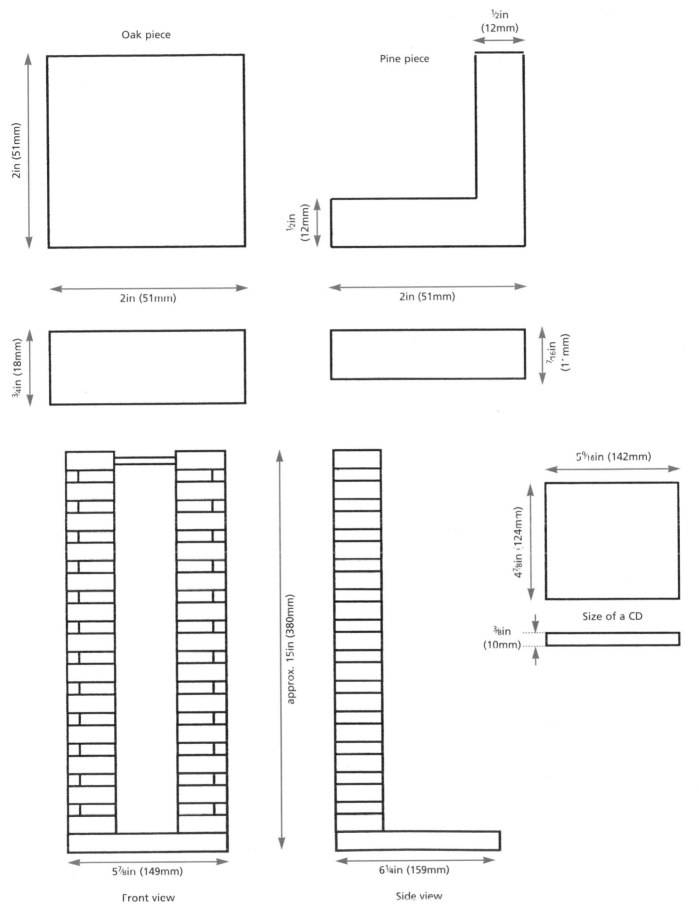

Oak piece

Pine piece

2in (51mm)

½in (12mm)

½in (12mm)

2in (51mm)

2in (51mm)

¾in (18mm)

7⁄16in (11mm)

approx. 15in (380mm)

5⁷⁄8in (149mm)

Front view

6¼in (159mm)

Side view

5⁹⁄16in (142mm)

4⁷⁄8in (124mm)

Size of a CD

⅜in (10mm)

Fig 17.1 *Rack components, front and side views with dimensions.*

CUTTING LIST		
Thick pieces (26)	Oak	2 x 2 x ¾in (51 x 51 x 18mm)
Thin 'L' shaped pieces (24)	Pine	2 x 2 x ⁷/₁₆in (51 x 51 x 11mm)
Base (1)	Pine	6¼ x 6 x ¾in (159 x 152 x 18mm)
Spacer (1)	Hardwood dowel	2¾ x ⅜in diameter (70 x 9mm diameter)

CONSTRUCTION

1 Along the length of a piece of oak 2in (51mm) wide and ¾in (18mm) deep, rule a line every 2in (51mm) plus an allowance for the width of the saw kerf. Saw the wood into 2in (51mm) square blocks and remove any splinters left by the saw cuts with glasspaper. In a similar way, mark a strip of ⁷/₁₆in (11mm) thick pine into 2in (51mm) lengths, but also draw lines that define the 'L' shapes required and indicate the waste wood areas with crosshatching (see Fig 17.2). Cut these out also.

2 Arrange the pieces in the order in which they will be glued up, ensuring that they are all the same way up and have the end grain facing in the same direction (see Fig 17.4).

Gluing these pieces together so that they form straight columns can be difficult, because when pressure is applied on the ends with a sash cramp the pieces in the centre slide out of alignment. The solution is to make an 'L' shaped splint to hold the pieces rigid while they are clamped (see Fig 17.5). Apply glue to the pieces and line them up in the splint, with newspaper placed along its inside edges so that the pieces are not inadvertently stuck to it. Hold the pieces firmly in place with 'G' cramps and then use a sash cramp to apply pressure on the ends.

Once the two columns have been glued firmly together, clean the glue and old pieces of newspaper off the faces with a plane, drum sander and glasspaper on a block.

3 Mark out and cut the base from a piece of pine. Drill and countersink two holes for the screws in the base.

ASSEMBLY AND FINISHING

If the base is not exactly flat, or the columns are not straight when they are fixed to it, the columns may not be the same distance apart at the base as they are at the top. To avoid this problem, a piece of hardwood dowel is inserted between the two oak blocks at the top of the column.

1 Glue and fit the hardwood dowel into ⅜in (9mm) holes, ½in (12mm) deep, which should be drilled in the blocks when the columns are glued and screwed to the base. Before the glue is dry, check that a CD will fit into the slots at both ends of the columns and adjust the distance between the columns if required. Wipe off any surplus glue.

If the design is modified to accommodate more CDs, you will need to insert extra spacers between the columns: twice as tall would require one extra spacer.

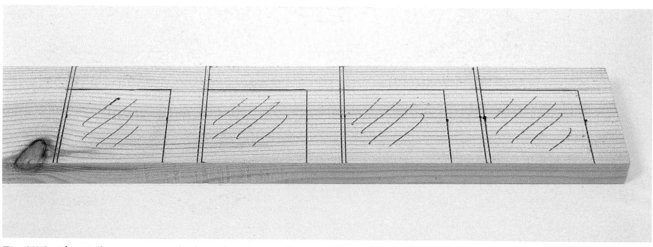

Fig 17.2 The 'L' shapes are marked on the pine sections and cross-hatched to indicate the waste wood.

2 Finish the rack with emulsion (acrylic) varnish to enhance the grain. Do not attempt to varnish inside the slots – simply apply it to the outsides.

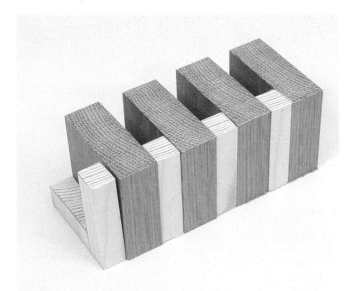

Fig 17.4 *The pieces are assembled so that the end grain is always on the same side.*

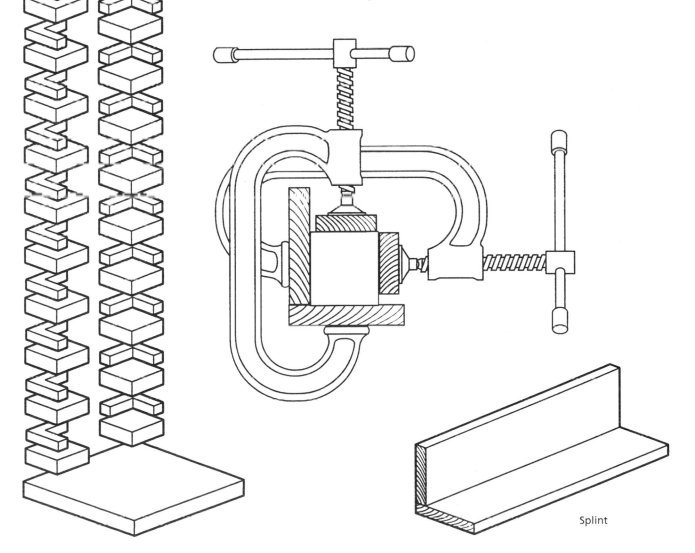

Fig 17.3 *Rack construction.*

Fig 17.5 *Clamping the pieces with a splint.*

Splint

Magazine Rack

DEGREE OF DIFFICULTY: EASY
TIME TO MAKE: 10 HOURS

THIS rack was designed to remove the problem of newspapers and magazines left lying around on furniture and floors. It is intended to stand on the floor, conveniently to hand by a favourite chair, with enough capacity for around a month's worth of periodicals.

The rack is made from a combination of pine boards and plywood, and uses some sawn stock (see the Note on page 53). The construction is uncomplicated, with simple housing joints for the partitions and joints that are screwed and glued to hold the two sides together. Most of the wood is finished with clear varnish, while the plywood partitions are further enhanced by colouring with mahogany wood stain before varnishing.

CUTTING LIST

Narrow side (1)	Pre-jointed pine board	14½ x 9½ x ¾in (368 x 241 x 18mm)
Wide side (1)	Pre-jointed pine board	14½ x 10¼ x ¾in (368 x 260 x 18mm)
Bases (2)	Pine	7 x 3½ x 1½in (178 x 89 x 38mm)
Partitions (5)	Plywood	9¾ x 9¾ x ¼in (248 x 248 x 6mm)

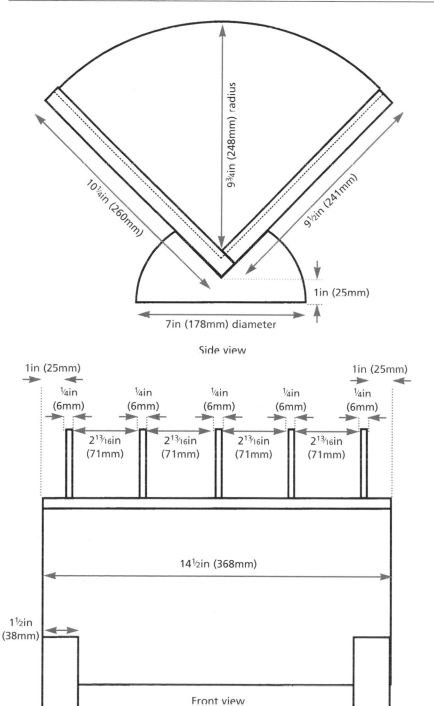

Fig 18.1 Front and side views with dimensions.

CONSTRUCTION

SIDES

1 On a piece of pre-jointed pine board, mark out the two sides using a try square, rule, straight-edge and pencil. Cut along these lines with a panel saw and plane the edges square and smooth so that any high spots are removed. On one of the sides, mark the position of the slots that hold the partitions, then butt both sides edge to edge and duplicate these marks on the second side.

2 Cut the slots with a ¼in (6mm) straight cutter to a depth of ¼in (6mm), making a couple of passes with the router. Note that the slots stop about ½in (12mm) short of one of the edges on the wider of the two sides: this is where the narrow side is butted and screwed to it. The router must be set up so that it is guided by a piece of wood clamped to the workpiece (see Fig 10.7 on page 63), as the fence cannot be set wide enough to do the job.

3 Drill and countersink holes in the wide side and fix the two sides together with glue and screws. To ensure that the slots all line up, place a few pieces of scrap ¼in (6mm) plywood in them when the holes are being drilled and the screws put in place, but make sure they are not glued in permanently. Before the glue is dry, wipe off any surplus and use a try square to test that the two pieces are at right angles to each other (see Fig 18.3). If they are not, adjust them with a sash cramp laid across the two edges further away from the joint.

4 Fill over the screw heads with neutral-coloured filler, putting enough in the holes to ensure that

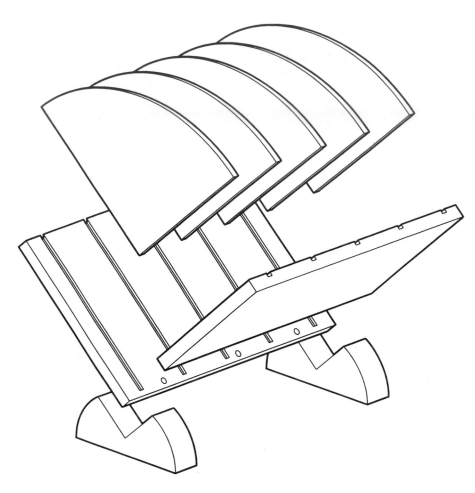

Fig 18.2 Rack construction.

Apply two coats of emulsion (acrylic) varnish to the sides and bases. Paint the partitions with deep red mahogany stain and then apply a protective coat of emulsion (acrylic) varnish. Do not allow any varnish to run into the partition housings, as this might make them harder to fit.

2 When the finish is absolutely dry, apply glue sparingly to the partitions and fit them in place. Any glue that is left on the surface can be wiped off with a damp cloth before it dries.

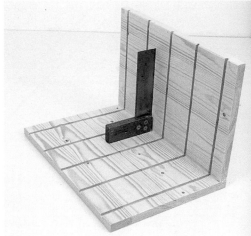

Fig 18.3 Checking that the sides are orthogonal.

the filler stands proud of the surface of the wood. When the filler is dry, smooth with glasspaper until it is flush with the surface.

PARTITIONS AND BASES

1 Mark out the quadrant of a circle of the correct radius on a suitable piece of ¼in (6mm) plywood using a trammel arm (see Fig 20.6 on page 122). This consists of a length of wood with a pen or pencil pushed through a hole in one end and a nail pushed through the other to act as a pivot. Cut out the partition with a jigsaw and smooth the edges with glasspaper. Test the partition for accuracy of fit (see Fig 18.4), make any necessary adjustments and then use it as a template to mark out the remaining partitions. Cut these out in the same way.

2 On a piece of 1½in (38mm) pine, mark the bases by drawing two semicircles with a radius of 3½in (89mm). Use a set square to draw the right angles that indicate where to cut the recesses to take the sides of the rack. Cut around the outline with a jigsaw and smooth the curved edges with a drum sander. Stick the two bases to the sides with glue only.

ASSEMBLY AND FINISHING

1 Apply the varnish and stain before the partitions are assembled with the sides – otherwise it may be difficult to reach down between the partitions and apply the stain smoothly and accurately.

Fig 18.4 Fitting a partition into the sides.

THE BATHROOM

BATHROOMS MAY BE HOT AND STEAMY PLACES BUT IN MOST HOUSES THEY ARE A STORAGE DESERT. USUALLY THERE IS A SINGLE BATHROOM CABINET WHERE THINGS ARE HIDDEN AWAY AND LITTLE ELSE BESIDES. FOUR YEARS AFTER WE MOVED INTO OUR HOUSE WE STILL STORED BATH SALTS, SHOWER GEL, SHAMPOO AND ALL THE REST OF THE ODDS AND ENDS THAT WOULD NOT FIT IN THE CABINET ON THE WINDOWSILL. ALTHOUGH THE BOTTLES LOOKED VERY ATTRACTIVE WITH THE SUNLIGHT SHINING THROUGH THEM, THEY WERE NOT EASILY ACCESSIBLE FROM THE BATH. NOW ALL THIS HAS CHANGED. IF YOU HAVE SIMILAR PROBLEMS THE SOLUTION — AS WELL AS THE SHAMPOO — IS AT HAND.

19

Bathroom Corner Cabinet

DEGREE OF DIFFICULTY: ADVANCED
TIME TO MAKE: 25 HOURS

THIS cabinet is designed to appeal to someone who has a traditionally furnished and fitted bathroom. Its features will complement Victorian-style baths and washbasins with brass taps and moulded porcelain.

Whenever widths greater than 6in (152mm) are called for, pre-jointed pine boards can be used. The complete cabinet can be made from three standard-sized boards measuring 35 x 12 x ¾in (889 x 305 x 18mm), with a few small pieces left over. Most of the parts are joined together with hardwood dowels and any metal fittings are made of brass.

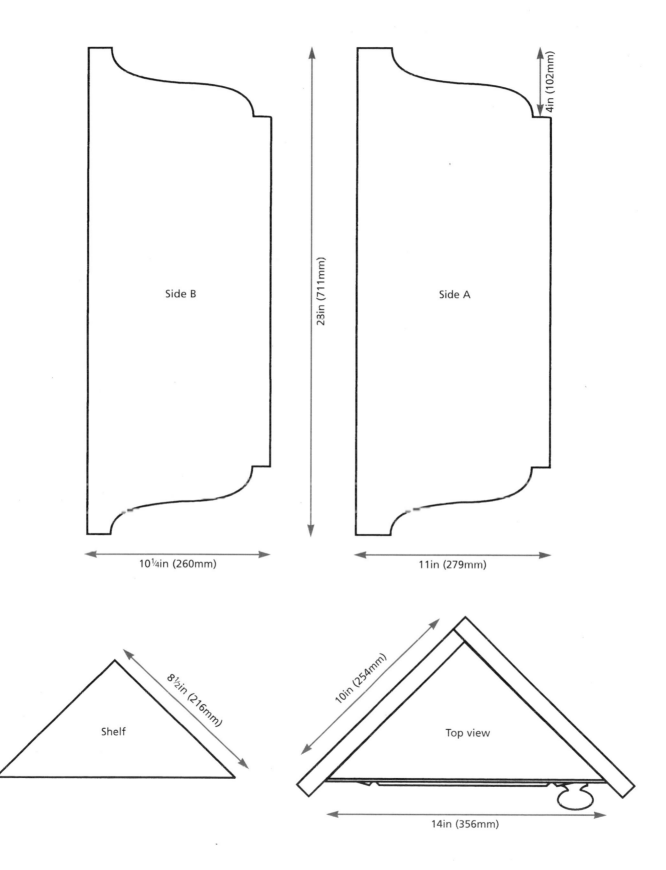

Fig 19.1 Sides, top and shelf with dimensions.

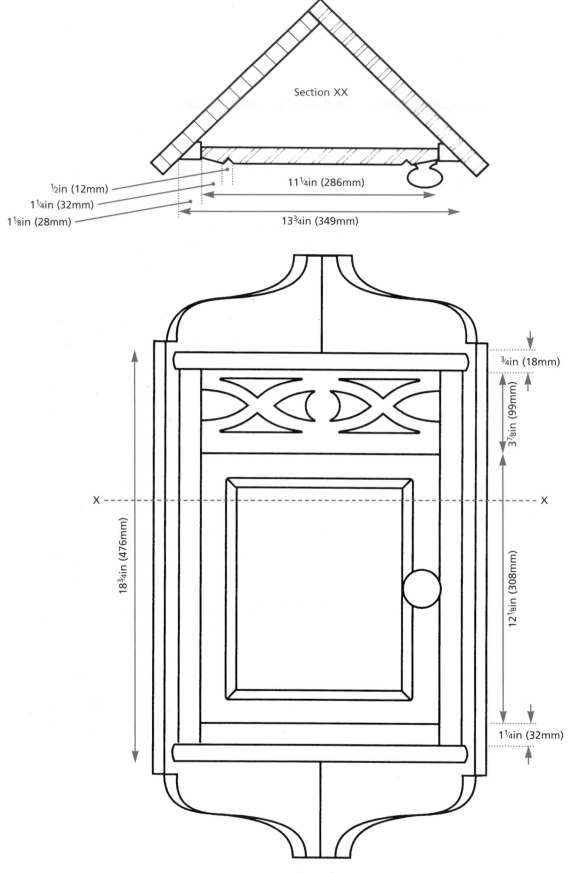

Section XX

½in (12mm)

1¼in (32mm)

1⅛in (28mm)

11¼in (286mm)

13¾in (349mm)

¾in (18mm)

3⅞in (99mm)

X — — — — — — — — — — — — — — X

18¾in (476mm)

12⅛in (308mm)

1¼in (32mm)

Front view

Fig 19.2 *Front view and section with dimensions.*

Side A

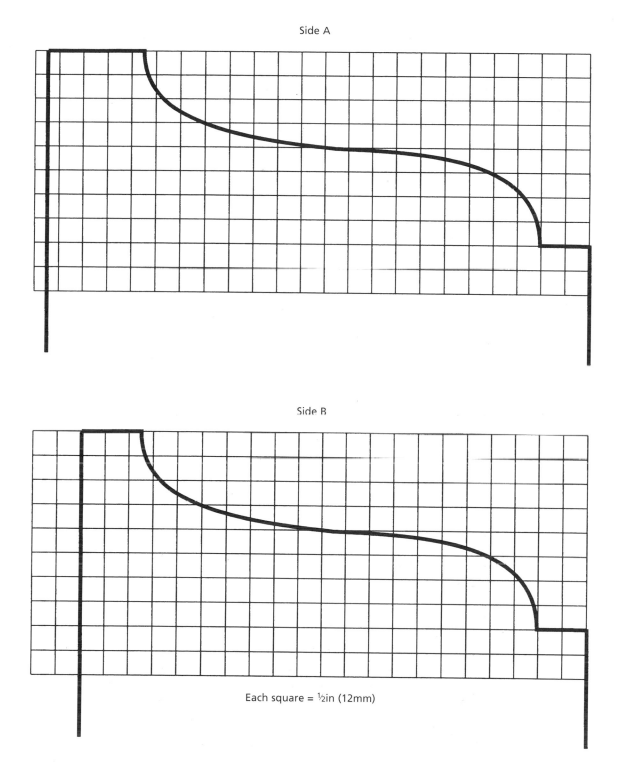

Side B

Each square = ½in (12mm)

Fig 19.3 Templates for top and base of sides.

CUTTING LIST		
Side A (1)	Pre-jointed pine board	28 x 11 x ¾in (711 x 279 x 18mm)
Side B (1)	Pre-jointed pine board	28 x 10¼ x ¾in (711 x 260 x 18mm)
Top and base (cut from 1 piece)	Pre-jointed pine board	10 x 10 x ¾in (254 x 254 x 18mm)
Shelf (1)	Pre-jointed pine board	8½ x 8½ x ¾in (216 x 216 x 18mm)
Front with fret (1)	Pine	11¼ x 3⅞ x ¾in (286 x 99 x 18mm)
Front base rail (1)	Pine	11¼ x 1¼ x ¾in (286 x 32 x 18mm)
Front sides (2)	Pine	17¼ x 1⅛ x ¾in (438 x 28 x 18mm)
Door (1)	Pre-jointed pine board	12⅛ x 11¼ x ¾in (308 x 286 x 18mm)

ALSO REQUIRED:

Lengths of ¼in (6mm) hardwood and ramin dowel
1½in (38mm) brass hinges (2)
1in (25mm) magnetic catch (1)
1½in (38mm) pine knob (1)

CONSTRUCTION

CARCASS

1 Using a rule, set square and pencil, mark out the edges of the sides on two pieces of pre-jointed pine board. Mark out the scroll shapes at the top and base of both sides using templates made by squaring up the shapes in Fig 19.3 on to card (see The Note on page 61). Note that side A is slightly narrower than side B. Cut out the overall shapes with a bandsaw and use a jigsaw to cut around the scrolls. (A jigsaw could be used to cut the long straight edges, but because it can easily wander off line it is best to use a bandsaw fitted with a wide blade, or alternatively a panel saw.)

Fig 19.4 Sides, top, base and shelf construction.

2 Plane the long straight edges flat and use a rasp, followed by a half-round file, followed by glasspaper to smooth the edges of the scrolls. Use the flat side of the file for smoothing the convex shapes and the half-round side for the concave curves.

3 The two sides are joined together using pegs made from ¼in (6mm) hardwood dowelling. On the wider side (side A), drill four ¼in (6mm) holes spread evenly along the length of the back edge. Hold the two sides together in their final position and drill into the edge of side B, through the holes in side A. It is quite difficult to hold the pieces in place while all the holes are drilled, so take time to place the

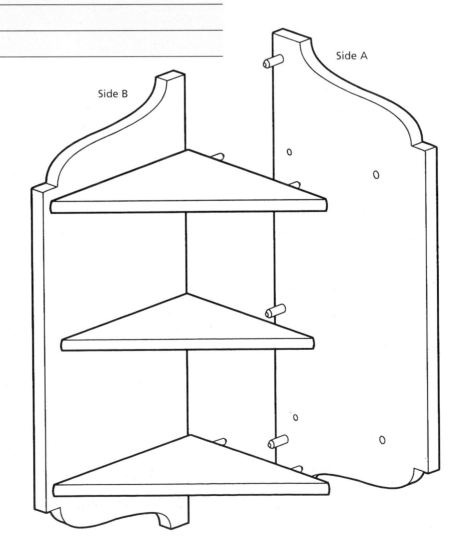

Side B

Side A

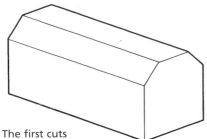

The first cuts
chamfer the corners.

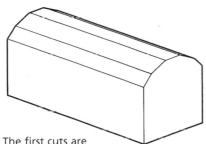

The first cuts are
smoothed off to leave
the edge as shown. Smooth off any
remaining corners with glasspaper.

Fig 19.5 Rounding an edge using a
plane and glasspaper.

first one accurately and insert the
dowel into position. This will help
to hold the pieces together while the
other holes are drilled.

When all the holes have been
made, take the two pieces apart and
apply glue to the dowels and the
edges, before fitting them together
again and hammering the dowels
into the holes. Use a couple of sash
cramps to hold the pieces while the
glue dries, but before it sets wipe off
any surplus with a damp rag. When
the glue has dried, plane the tops of
the dowels flush with the back
surface of side A.

4 Mark out the two triangular
pieces that form the top and
base on a piece of board measuring
10 x 10in (254 x 254mm). Ensure
that the board is exactly square
before drawing a diagonal line
between two of the corners and
sawing along it. Round the long
edges of both parts using a plane
and glasspaper (see Fig 19.5).

5 Draw lines on the sides to
indicate the positions of the top
and base. Fix these in place using
dowel pegs in the same way as for
joining the two sides together. After
gluing, I found it difficult to clamp
the assembly using conventional
cramps, so I used a string tourniquet
(see Fig 19.6). To do this, wrap a
length of nylon cord loosely around
the assembly a couple of times and

knot the ends together. Insert a
short length of scrap wood into the
loop, twist it round and secure. This
will have the effect of squeezing the
joints together. Protect the edges of
the cabinet with a layer or two of
corrugated cardboard or something
similar to ensure that the cord does
not mark the wood. When dry, clean
up the dowel ends with a plane.

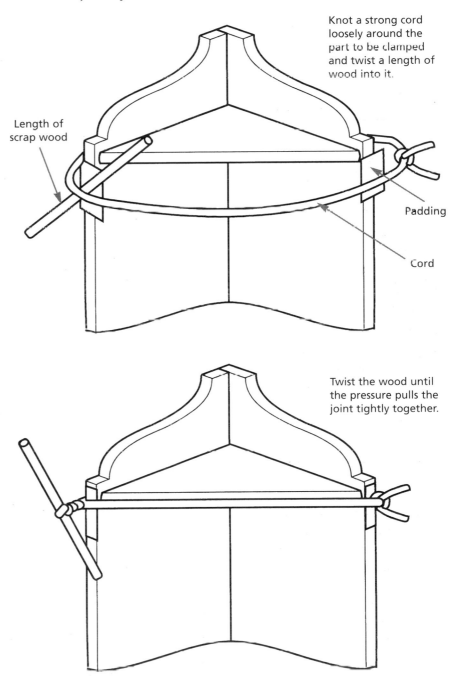

Knot a strong cord
loosely around the
part to be clamped
and twist a length of
wood into it.

Length of
scrap wood

Padding

Cord

Twist the wood until
the pressure pulls the
joint tightly together.

Fig 19.6 Using a tourniquet for clamping.

FRONT AND SHELF

The front of the cabinet is made up from four pieces of pine that are fixed at the corners with concealed dowel joints made with a jig.

1 To make the top piece of the front, start with a piece of knot-free pine that is slightly larger than the final size. The fret is the most difficult part to make, so it is important to make sure it is cut

correctly before forming the edges and putting in the dowels.

Draw the pattern for the fret on a piece of thin paper (e.g. photocopier paper) using Fig 19.8 as a guide (see the Note on page 61). Transfer the drawing to the surface of the wood using carbon paper. Place the ink

side of the carbon paper on to the surface of the wood, lay the thin paper pattern on top of this and hold the two layers of paper in place with sticky tape. Use a ballpoint pen to trace around the pattern, which will be transferred on to the wood surface. The resulting firm black line can now be used as a guide for cutting out the shapes.

A powered fret saw is the simplest and quickest tool to use for this process, but if you do not have one a coping saw is an adequate substitute (see Fig 19.9). Both

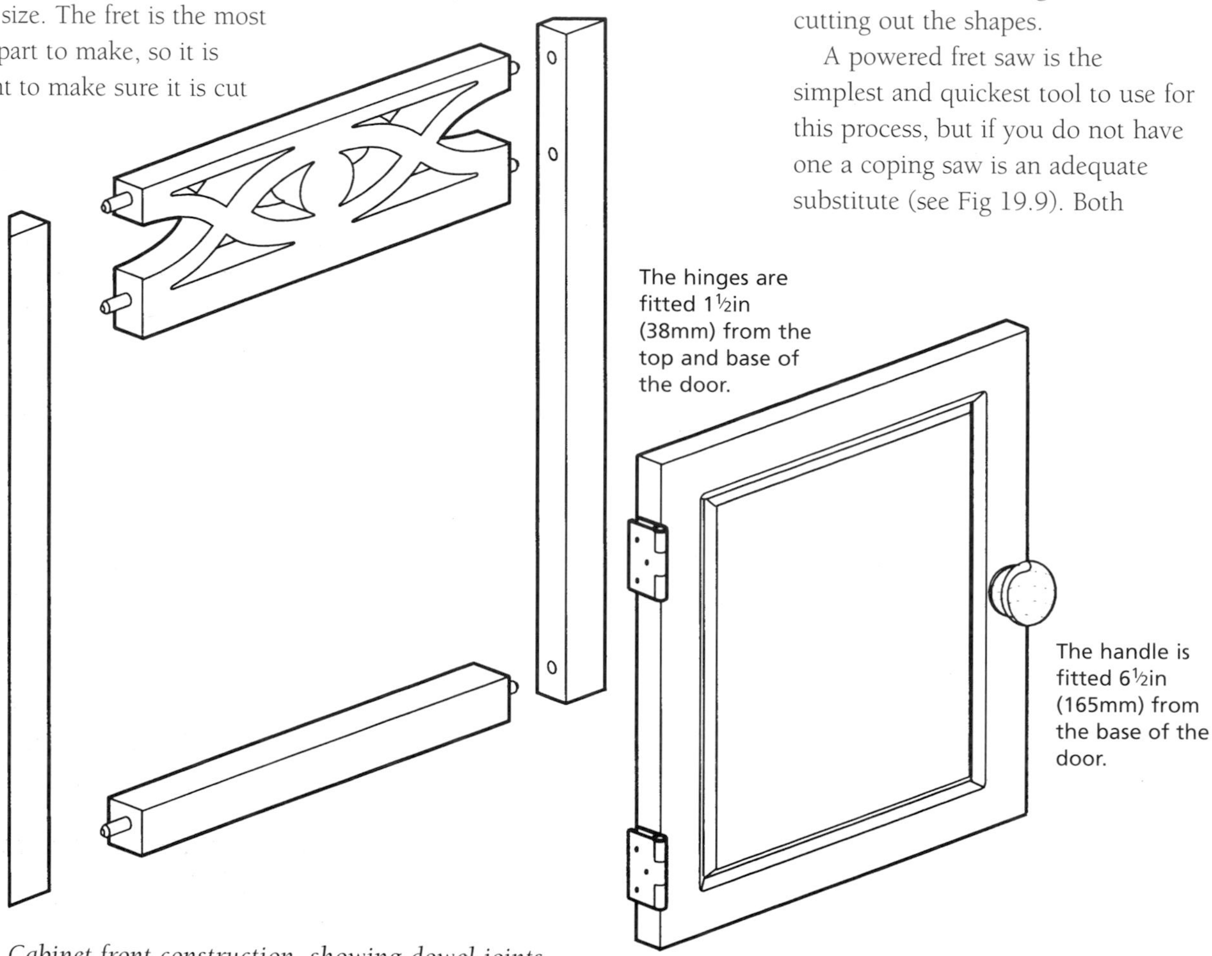

The hinges are fitted 1½in (38mm) from the top and base of the door.

The handle is fitted 6½in (165mm) from the base of the door.

Fig 19.7 Cabinet front construction, showing dowel joints.

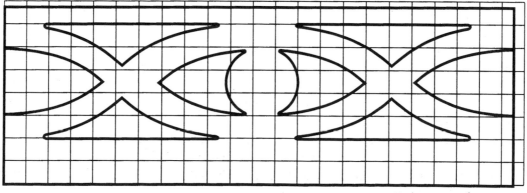

Each square = ½in (12mm)

Fig 19.8 Pattern for fret.

Fig 19.9 Cutting the enclosed shapes of the fret with a coping saw.

methods require a hole to be drilled inside each of the shapes to start the saw. When the shapes have been sawn out, use files and glasspaper to smooth the edges.

Finally, cut the piece of wood with the fret in it to the correct size and smooth the edges with a plane. Use a block plane for the end grain and guard against breaking the edges.

2 Cut and smooth the base rail for the front and ensure that it is exactly the same length as the fret.

3 To make the sides, use a power saw to cut a 45° bevel along the edge of a straight-grained piece of pine that is long enough to use for both sides. Smooth the bevel with a plane and then cut the piece to the correct width. Mark the required length for the sides and cut with a tenon saw.

4 The four pieces that form the cabinet front are joined at the corners with concealed dowels. Make the dowel pegs from a length of ¼in (6mm) ramin dowelling. To align them accurately, it is best to use a dowelling jig. When the dowel joints have been completed, assemble them without using glue and put the front into the carcass to test how accurately it fits into the recess. If any adjustments are required, make them now.

5 Glue is applied to the joints and the front glued into the carcass in one operation. Take the pieces apart, apply glue to the joints, reassemble the pieces and apply more glue all around the outside edges of the front. Push the front firmly into the recess in the carcass, so that the joints are forced together by the action of wedging the front between the sides. Wipe off any surplus glue with a damp rag and allow to dry.

6 Mark the position of the centre shelf on the inside of the sides, half-way between the top and the base. Cut it out from a piece of pre-jointed pine board, round the front and fit it into place with glue. Drill two holes in the sides that will be used to house the screws which fix the carcass to the wall.

DOOR

1 Mark out the rectangle for the door on some pre-jointed pine board and smooth the edges with a plane and glasspaper. Put this into the front to check that it fits – there should be a small gap all round. If the door fits into the front more accurately in one orientation than the other, mark it in some way so that when fitted permanently it is in the best position.

2 Use a router fitted with a 'V' grooving cutter (see Fig 3.13 on page 16) to form the decorative groove on the face of the door. The groove is the same distance from all four sides. When this is done, use a plane to make the decorative chamfer between the groove and the edges.

3 Slant the base of a small pine knob to an angle that corresponds to the angle of the chamfer on the face of the door, where the knob will be positioned. Drill a hole 6½in (165mm) from the base of the door and fix the knob in place with a screw and glue.

ASSEMBLY AND FINISHING

1 The door is hung using two 1½in (38mm) brass hinges. Mark the position for the hinges on the door, about 1½in (38mm) from the top and base. The hinge flaps are recessed into the door and door frame, so that they fit flush with the surface of the wood (see the Note on page 79). Fit the magnetic catch.

2 Fill any holes or gaps with neutral-coloured wood filler. Glasspaper the entire surface and apply two coats of polyurethane varnish.

20

Shower Caddy

DEGREE OF DIFFICULTY: ADVANCED
TIME TO MAKE: 20 HOURS

You know the feeling: you are in the shower, have an eye full of soap and are vainly trying to locate the shampoo before you remember that it is on the bathroom windowsill, on the other side of the room. Do you: (a) leave washing your hair until tomorrow; (b) trail wet footprints over the floor to get the shampoo; or (c) shout for someone else to fetch it for you? Fortunately, you will not have to take such awkward decisions if you make this shower caddy. It is constructed from pine and water-resistant plywood, and is finished with an application of waterproofing solution followed by polyurethane varnish – so it can hang in a corner on the wall close to the shower and hold all the soaps and lotions you might require.

CUTTING LIST		
Side A (1)	Pine	24½ x 7¼ x ¾in (622 x 184 x 18mm)
Side B (1)	Pine	24½ x 8 x ¾in (622 x 203 x 18mm)
Shelf fronts (3)	Pine	10⅜ x 2⅝ x ¾in (263 x 67 x 18mm)
Shelves (3)	Plywood	7 x 7 x ½in (179 x 179 x 12mm)

ALSO REQUIRED:

Plastic screw caps (2)

The dimensions given for the shelf front make no allowance for waste or the extra wood required
for the centre of the quadrant if the circles are cut out with a router,
as described in the text instructions.

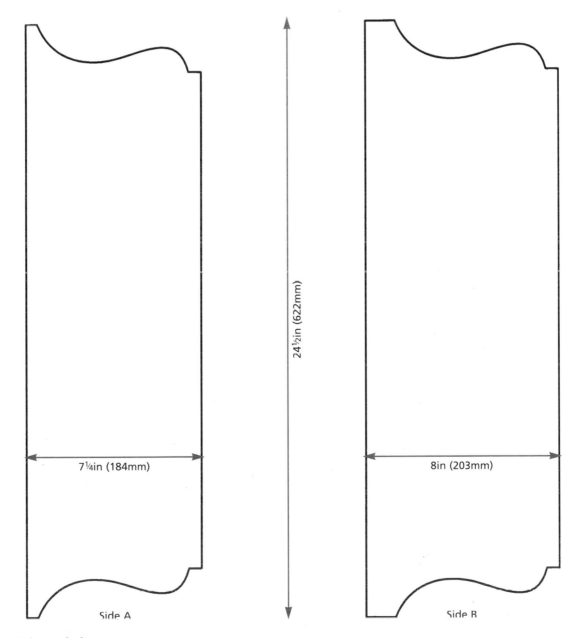

24½in (622mm)

7¼in (184mm)

8in (203mm)

Side A

Side B

Fig 20.1 Sides with dimensions.

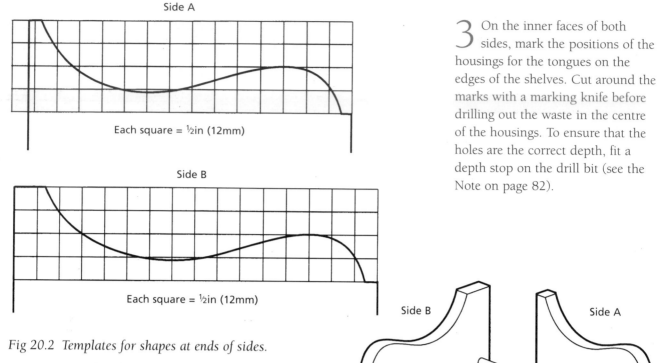

Side A

Each square = ½in (12mm)

Side B

Each square = ½in (12mm)

Fig 20.2 Templates for shapes at ends of sides.

CONSTRUCTION

SIDES

1 Draw two rectangles on a suitable piece of pine board for the sides. Note that side B is wider than side A because of the overlap in the corner. Make templates for the classical serpentine shapes on the ends of the sides by squaring up the shapes in Fig 20.2 on to card (see the Note on page 61) and then mark them out on to the wood.

Cut around the curves with a bandsaw or jigsaw and remove the saw marks with a file, followed by glasspaper to achieve a smooth finish. Finish the straight edges with a plane.

2 The two sides are joined in the corner with through dowels: steel screws might rust in the steamy bathroom environment, although brass screws would be acceptable. Using a dowelling jig to ensure that the dowels are placed accurately, drill the holes. Assemble the two sides to test for fit but do not glue them together at this stage.

3 On the inner faces of both sides, mark the positions of the housings for the tongues on the edges of the shelves. Cut around the marks with a marking knife before drilling out the waste in the centre of the housings. To ensure that the holes are the correct depth, fit a depth stop on the drill bit (see the Note on page 82).

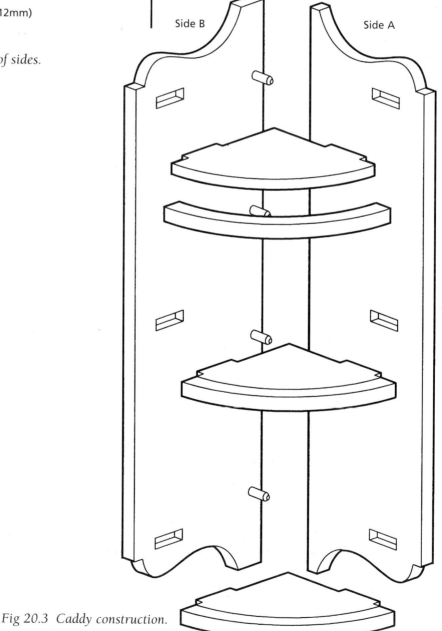

Side B   Side A

Fig 20.3 Caddy construction.

4 Use a bevel-edged chisel to remove the rest of the waste and clean out the corners of the housings. This is accomplished by holding the chisel vertically between the lines that mark the boundary of the housing and rapping the top with a mallet to chop out the waste wood. The method works best if the chisel is the same width as the housing (see Fig 20.4). Alternatively, the waste can be removed with a router instead of a drill, which leaves a lot less extra waste to remove.

Fig 20.4 Cleaning the waste wood from the housings with a bevel-edged chisel.

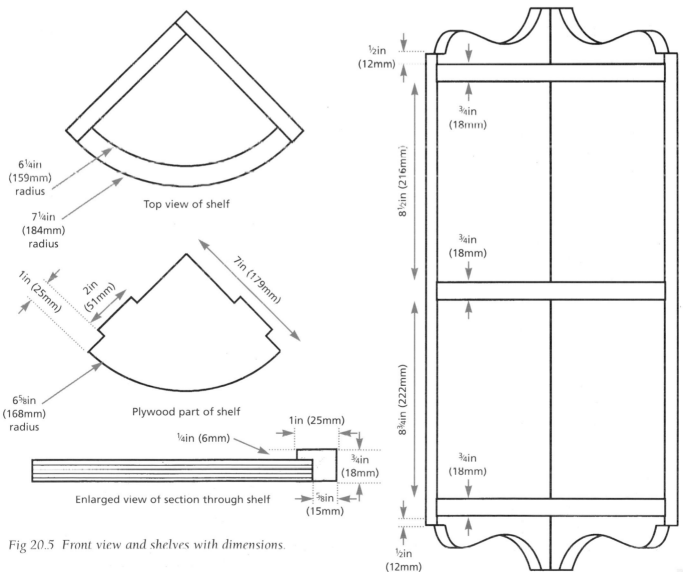

6¼in (159mm) radius

7¼in (184mm) radius

Top view of shelf

1in (25mm)

2in (51mm)

7in (179mm)

6⅝in (168mm) radius

Plywood part of shelf

1in (25mm)

¼in (6mm)

¾in (18mm)

⅝in (15mm)

Enlarged view of section through shelf

Fig 20.5 Front view and shelves with dimensions.

½in (12mm)

¾in (18mm)

8½in (216mm)

¾in (18mm)

8¾in (222mm)

¾in (18mm)

½in (12mm)

Front view

SHELVES

The three shelves are made from ½in (12mm) plywood with a front edging strip made from pine. To speed up the process, all three shelves can be made together in a mini production run, but for clarity the instructions below describe how one is made.

1 On a piece of plywood, mark out the shape of the shelf using a rule, try square and compass. If you do not have a large compass, you can improvise by making a trammel arm with which to draw the curve. This consists of a length of wood with a pen or pencil pushed through a hole in one end and a nail pushed through the other to act as a pivot (see Fig 20.6).

2 To cut the semicircular edge, use a router fitted with a circle cutting attachment and a straight bit. Use a panel saw to cut the straight edges, and a tenon saw to cut around the tongues that protrude from the sides, to fit into the shelf sides.

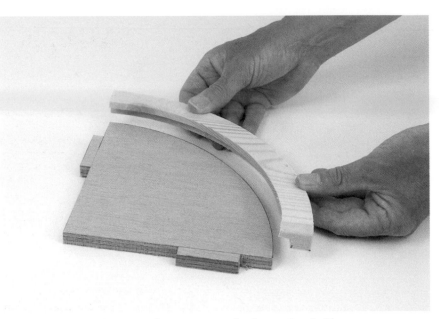

Fig 20.7 Fitting the pine edging strip to the front of a shelf.

3 Make the pine edging strip in the same way, but form a rebate in the inside edge using the router with a ⅜in (9mm) straight cutter, to house the plywood part of the shelf. Check to ensure that the edging fits before gluing it firmly in place (see Fig 20.7). When it is dry, trim the ends of the edging strip to line up with the edges of the plywood.

ASSEMBLY AND FINISHING

1 Assemble the two sides and the shelves without glue. To do this, slot the shelves into the narrowest side, then push on the other side before putting in the through dowels. If they all fit, glue them together and clamp until the glue is set. If they do not fit, make any adjustments that are required until they do.

2 Apply a coat of waterproofing solution and follow up with two applications of polyurethane varnish.

3 Drill two holes in the sides near the top for the screws that will hold the caddy on the wall. To conceal the screw heads, use hinged plastic screw caps.

Fig 20.6 An improvised trammel arm used to mark the quadrant shapes.

21

Towel Rail

DEGREE OF DIFFICULTY: ADVANCED
TIME TO MAKE: 25 HOURS

THE appearance and functionality of this towel rail will enhance a traditional-style bathroom that is furnished with pine accessories. It is made to hold a couple of large fluffy towels or several smaller hand towels. As it is free-standing it can be placed in front of a radiator or next to the bath or shower, so that it is to hand when required.

The parts of the stand are fixed together using mortise and tenon joints, which are in keeping with a traditional theme. With attention to detail they are easily made and form a strong structure. Making the legs requires access to a lathe. They are turned between centres and do not demand a very high skill level to achieve an acceptable result, so are ideal for the woodworker who is not very experienced on a lathe.

Pine is used throughout, but as some of the pieces (e.g. the legs) are a non-standard size, they will need to be planed to the size required from pieces of sawn timber (see the Note on page 53).

CUTTING LIST		
Stand bases (2)	Pine	12 x 3 x ¾in (305 x 76 x 18mm)
Turned legs (2)	Pine	27 x 2 x 2in (686 x 51 x 51mm)
Stand tops (2)	Pine	9 x 2½ x ¾in (229 x 64 x 18mm)
Towel rails (2)	Hardwood dowel	26½ x ¾in diameter (673 x 18mm diameter)
Lower rail (1)	Pine	24½ x 2¼ x ¾in (622 x 137 x 9mm)

The dimensions given for all turned parts includes an allowance for waste.

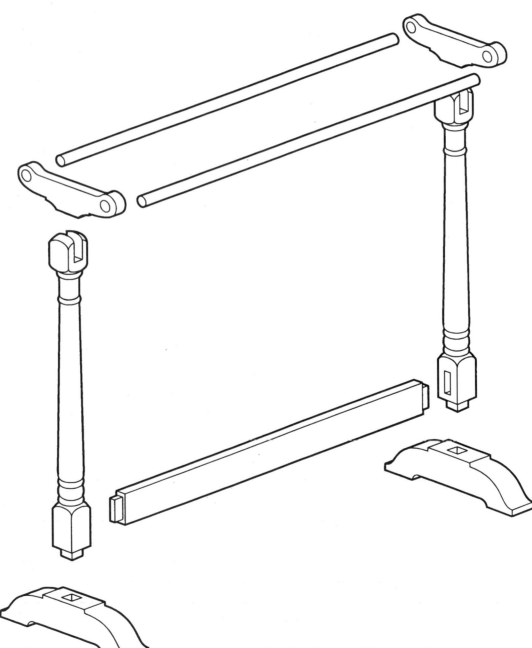

Fig 21.1 Towel rail construction.

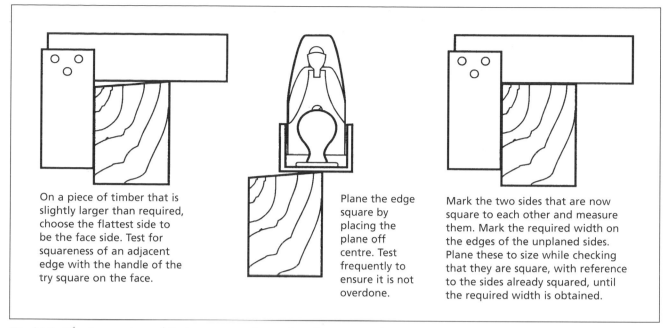

On a piece of timber that is slightly larger than required, choose the flattest side to be the face side. Test for squareness of an adjacent edge with the handle of the try square on the face.

Plane the edge square by placing the plane off centre. Test frequently to ensure it is not overdone.

Mark the two sides that are now square to each other and measure them. Mark the required width on the edges of the unplaned sides. Plane these to size while checking that they are square, with reference to the sides already squared, until the required width is obtained.

Fig 21.2 *Planing a piece of timber square, flat and to the correct size.*

CONSTRUCTION

STAND TOPS AND BASES

1 The two bases for the stands are made from pieces of pine with a section size of $1^3/4$ x 3in (44 x 76mm). If you are starting with a piece of oversized timber, follow the instructions in Fig 21.2 to plane it square and to the correct size.

2 Make a template for the base shape by squaring up the shape in Fig 21.3 on to card (see the Note on page 61) and then mark it out on to the pieces of wood you have just planed. Cut out the shape with a bandsaw and smooth the edges. A variety of tools can be used for this – I use a rotary rasp followed by a flap wheel, both of which are fitted

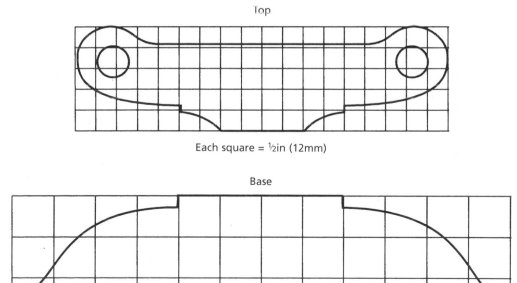

Top

Each square = ½in (12mm)

Base

Each square = 1in (25mm)

Fig 21.3 *Template for stand top and base.*

on a flexible drive shaft connected to a power drill. The rotary rasp can take off large amounts of wood very quickly and mistakes can easily be made; however, it is easier to control if the drill is run at a slow speed. Use glasspaper to achieve the final smooth finish required before varnishing.

3 The two top pieces are cut from pieces of ¾in (18mm) pine board. Mark out, cut and smooth the shapes in the same way as for the base pieces, but use a file to smooth the concave shapes at the ends. Round all the edges slightly with glasspaper.

4 Drill ¾in (18mm) holes in the pieces to accommodate the hardwood dowel towel rails. Use a spade bit, but to make the job easier drill a small pilot hole first. This will prevent the wood splintering on the back face if the holes are drilled from both faces – i.e. drill half-way through from one side, turn the piece over and finish off the hole.

LEGS

1 The legs are turned from pieces of straight-grained pine with a 2in (51mm) square section. The pieces should be 27¼in (692mm) long: this is a couple of inches longer than the final length, to allow for setting up on the lathe. Ensure that the section is square.

Prepare the wood for mounting between centres on the lathe (see the Note on page 47).

2 The first step is to cut the shoulders at either end, where the square section at the top and base meets the round section. Mark the position of the shoulders using a rule and pencil, select a slow speed on the lathe and use the point of a skew chisel to form the shoulder (see Fig 21.6).

3 The next stage is to turn the area between the two shoulders, to make a smooth cylinder to the maximum size allowed by the section size of the wood (see Fig 21.7). Do this using a 1in (25mm)

half-round gouge. When the cylinder has been made, mark the positions of all the beads and cut a groove either side of each bead with a skew chisel in the same way as for the shoulder (see Fig 21.8). Round the tops of the beads with a ½in (12mm) half-round gouge, used in a rolling motion around the tops. It

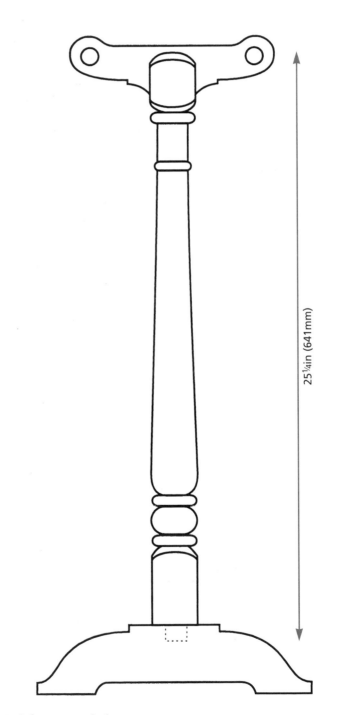

25¼in (641mm)

Fig 21.4 Side view with dimensions.

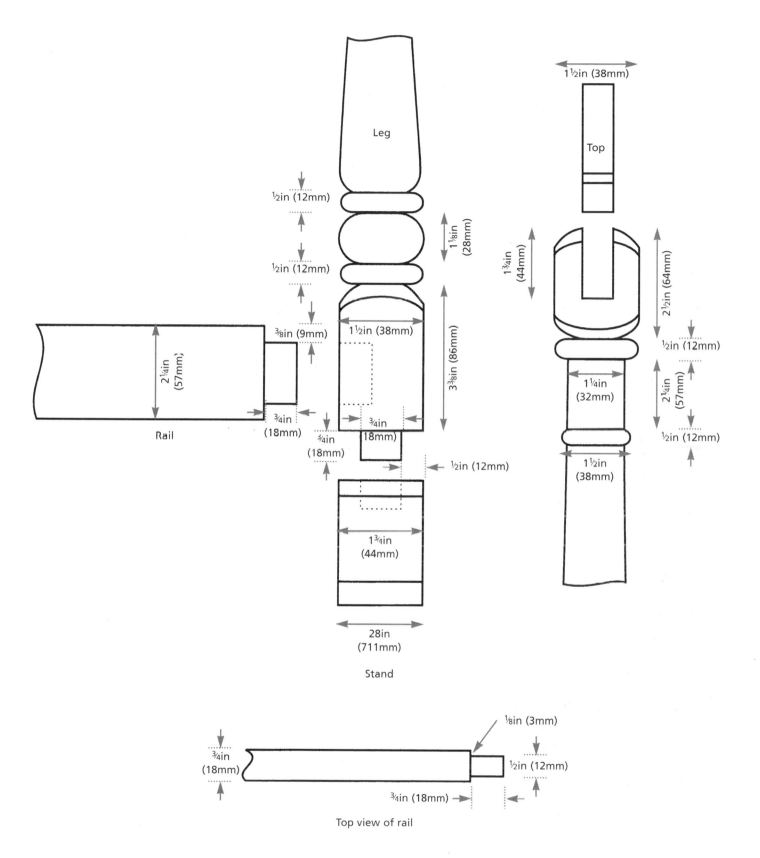

Fig 21.5 *Enlarged details of legs with dimensions.*

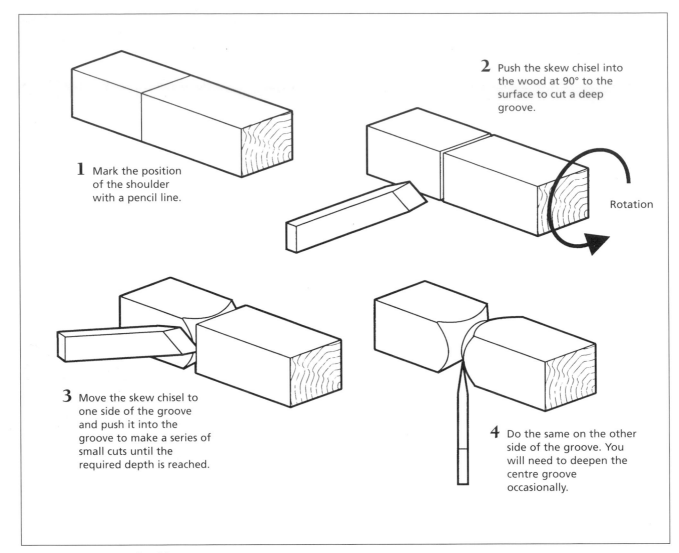

1 Mark the position of the shoulder with a pencil line.

2 Push the skew chisel into the wood at 90° to the surface to cut a deep groove.

Rotation

3 Move the skew chisel to one side of the groove and push it into the groove to make a series of small cuts until the required depth is reached.

4 Do the same on the other side of the groove. You will need to deepen the centre groove occasionally.

Fig 21.6 Turning a shoulder.

Fig 21.7 Turning the leg to a cylinder between the shoulders.

may be necessary to deepen the 'V' groove as the bead is being formed.

The two beads at the top of the legs have a short area of cylinder turned between them, which is the same thickness as the top of the tapered column immediately below them. Get the diameter of this correct and use it to gauge the width from the top of the tapered column. Cut the tapered column with a ½in (12mm) half-round gouge, and use a straight-edge laid along the column to check that there are no irregularities on the surface. When this has been done, cut a deep groove at the very top of the leg with a small gouge.

Use coarse and then medium-grade glasspaper to get the final finish. Increase the speed of the lathe for this and use the glasspaper on a cork block for the straight areas and a folded piece of glasspaper for smoothing the details. Once this has been completed, cut through the wood at the top of the leg to release it from the lathe.

4 Mount the second piece of wood for the other leg on to the lathe and use the first leg to mark out the positions of the various features (see Fig 21.9). Use callipers to take measurements from the first leg to get the dimensions of the beads on the second leg the same.

JOINTS AND RAILS

1 When both legs are finished, mark out the tenon on the bottom end of each leg with a mortise gauge. Saw down the cheeks of the tenon and across the shoulders with a tenon saw.

2 On the tops of the legs, mark out the slots that will eventually hold the tops of the stand. Cut down the sides of each slot with a tenon saw and remove the waste by cutting across the bottom of the slot with a coping saw. Fit the tops into the slots to test that the joints fit accurately, then put the legs to one side.

3 Mark the mortise that will hold the turned legs on the top edge of each stand base. Use the mortise gauge to mark out the parallel sides of the mortise and a try square and marking knife for the other sides. Drill out as much of the waste wood from the centre of the mortise as possible, using a depth stop on the drill to prevent making it too deep (see the Note on page 82). Use a

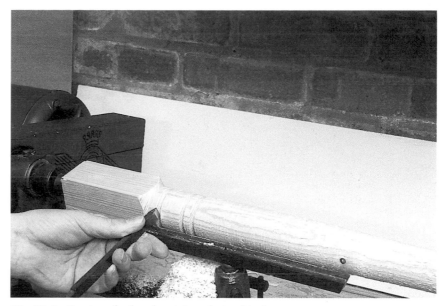

Fig 21.8 *Cutting the beads with a skew chisel.*

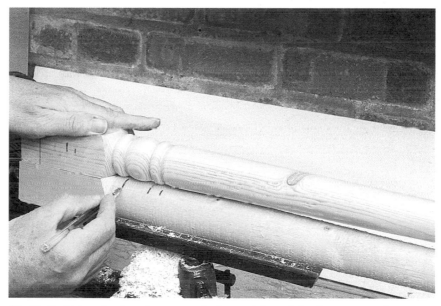

Fig 21.9 *Using the first leg to mark the position of the features on the second.*

bevel-edged chisel to chop out the rest of the waste wood. When the joint is complete, test it for fit and make any adjustments that are required.

4 Mark out and cut the lower cross rail and make tenons on both ends in the same way as before. Cut mortises to house the tenon on the base of the legs. Check the fit for accuracy.

5 Glue and assemble the two supports and hold them together with sash cramps (see Fig 21.11). Wipe off any surplus glue with a damp rag before it dries.

6 While you are waiting for the glue to dry, cut two lengths of ³⁄₄in (18mm) hardwood dowel for the towel rails. Use glasspaper to smooth the ends and round the edges of the ends slightly.

26½in (673mm)

23in (584mm)

Fig 21.10 Front view with dimensions.

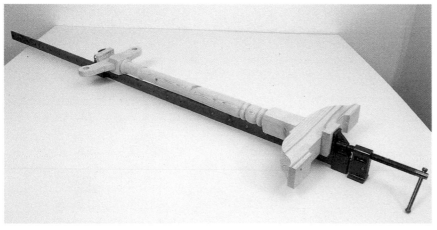

Fig 21.11 Clamping one of the legs.

ASSEMBLY AND FINISHING

1 When the glue is dry, assemble the complete towel rail. Glue the dowels into the tops of the stand leaving ½in (12mm) protruding. Glue and fit the lower rail into the base and clamp it until dry.

2 As the towel rail will be used in a hot, steamy bathroom, apply two coats of polyurethane varnish to finish.

22

Bathroom Cabinet with Mirror Doors

DEGREE OF DIFFICULTY: MEDIUM
TIME TO MAKE: 20 HOURS

Although simple to make, this bathroom cabinet must be constructed with some precision so that the doors slide smoothly. I purchased the glass mirror doors with recessed handles from a specialist shop. They measure 12⅛in (308mm) long x 9½in (241mm) wide, which is important because the rest of the cabinet dimensions depend on them. So, first obtain your mirror doors, and if they are the same size as mine the rest of the dimensions will work. If not, purchase larger mirrors and cut them to size, or alter the dimensions of the cabinet to suit. If you cannot find mirror doors with recessed handles, it would be possible to use plain mirrors and attach some small wooden blocks with superglue for the handles.

Pine is used for all parts except the back of the cabinet, which is made from plywood. The cabinet is made to hang on the wall and store small items of toiletry, and as it is not heavy you can use whichever lightweight fixing technique from Chapter 4 suits your particular wall type.

CUTTING LIST		
Top (1)	Pine	20½ x 6 x ¾in (521 x 152 x 18mm)
Base (1)	Pine	18 x 5½ x ¾in (457 x 140 x 18mm)
Sides (2)	Pine	12½ x 5½ x ¾in (318 x 140 x 18mm)
Shelf (1)	Pine	18½ x 3½ x ⅜in (470 x 89 x 9mm)
Back (1)	Plywood	18½ x 12¼ x ¼in (470 x 311 x 6mm)

ALSO REQUIRED:

12⅛ x 9½ x ⅛in (308 x 251 x 3mm) mirror doors (2)

CONSTRUCTION

CARCASS AND MIRRORS

1 Use a try square, ruler and pencil to mark out the rectangles for the top, base and sides on pieces of pine board, ensuring that the corners are square. Cut them out, making sure that the saw kerf is on the waste wood side of the marked lines. Plane the edges flat and square with a jackplane, before rounding the sides and front edge. Mark each piece clearly with pencil to identify which part it is (side, top etc.), and also which face is the inside and which the outside. Choose the face with the best appearance for the outside.

2 All the corners are connected by dowel joints made with a dowelling jig. Four hardwood pegs are used for each corner. Follow the technique described on page 26 for making concealed dowel joints, then join the sides together without glue to check that they all fit correctly. If not, take them apart and make any adjustments that are required.

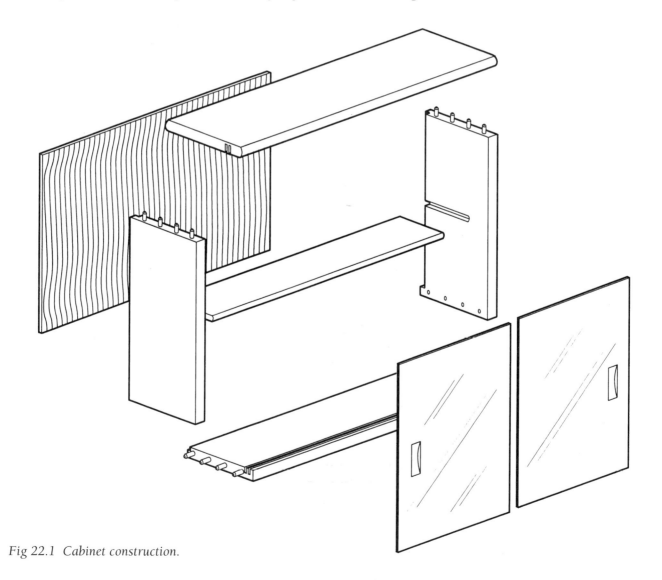

Fig 22.1 Cabinet construction.

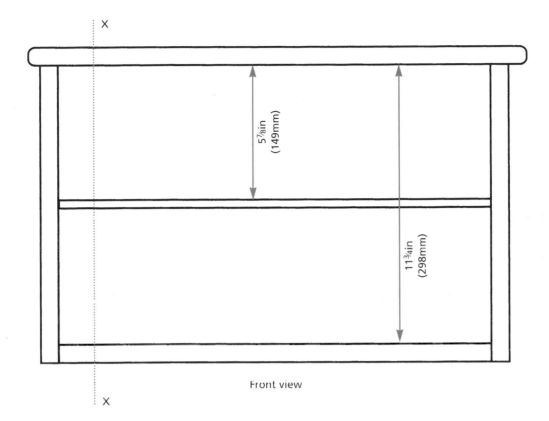

Front view

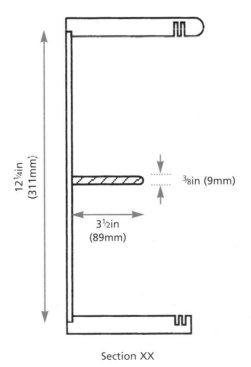

Section XX

Fig 22.2 Front view and section XX with dimensions.

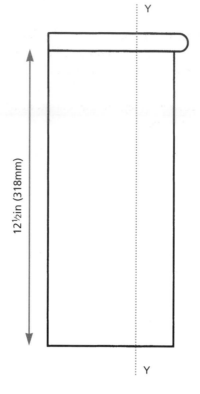

Side view

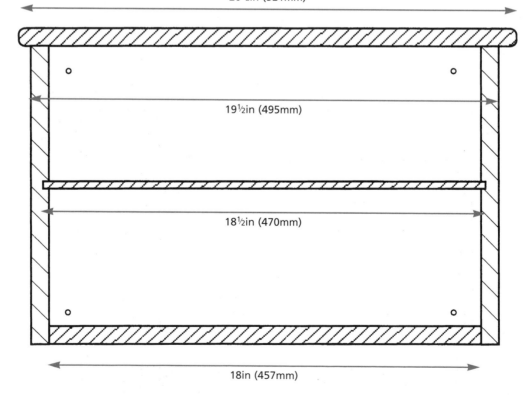

Section YY

Fig 22.3 *Side view and section YY with dimensions.*

3 On the inside back edge of the base, cut the ¼ x ¼in (6 x 6mm) rebate that will eventually house the plywood back, using a router with a ¼in (6mm) straight cutter. Repeat the operation on the two sides and the top. All the rebates are made on the back inside edges. On the two sides the rebates are stopped short of the bottom end, and in the top the rebates are stopped short of both ends. The base has a through rebate.

4 The mirrored sliding doors used here are ⅛in (3mm) thick, and so that they slide smoothly the grooves are made slightly oversize – ³⁄₁₆in (4mm) – using the appropriate-sized straight cutter. Cut two grooves along the front inside edge of both base and top; on the base they are from end to end but on the top they stop short so that they cannot be seen when the cabinet is assembled.

When the grooves have been cut, try one of the mirrors in them to ensure that it slides easily. The depth of the grooves is important because the mirrors are placed inside the grooves after the carcass has been assembled. They are pushed up into the top groove and then lowered into the base groove – if the top groove is not deep enough for this to happen the mirrors will not fit.

5 On the inside face of the two sides, mark out and cut with a router the stopped housings for the shelf, to a depth of ¼in (6mm). The front edge of this shelf is rounded, so the corresponding part of the housing must also have a half-round shape. This is done after the housing has been cut, by paring with vertical cuts using a ⅜in (9mm) half-round gouge.

6 Put the top in the vice and round the front edge and the two sides with a plane, followed by coarse and then medium-grade glasspaper. Use a block plane for the end grain.

7 Glue the dowels into the top and base, remove any surplus glue with a damp rag and leave to dry for about an hour. Assemble the carcass dry and check that the mirrors can be inserted and removed, because once these joints have been glued it will be difficult to correct any mistakes.

When you are satisfied with the fit of the mirrors, take the pieces apart, apply plenty of glue to each joint so that it squeezes out and clamp the carcass together with sash cramps. Check that it is square (see the Note on page 136), then use a damp cloth to remove any surplus glue, particularly in the mirror grooves, and leave to dry.

SHELF AND BACK

1 To make the shelf, cut the correct length from a piece of ⅜in (9mm) pine. I used cladding, as this is readily available in the correct thickness.

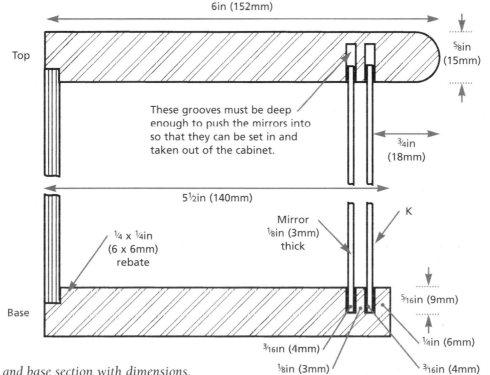

6in (152mm)

Top

⅝in (15mm)

These grooves must be deep enough to push the mirrors into so that they can be set in and taken out of the cabinet.

¾in (18mm)

5½in (140mm)

Mirror ⅛in (3mm) thick

K

¼ x ¼in (6 x 6mm) rebate

⁵⁄₁₆in (9mm)

Base

¹⁄₄in (6mm)

³⁄₁₆in (4mm)

⅛in (3mm)

³⁄₁₆in (4mm)

Fig 22.4 Top and base section with dimensions.

NOTE

IS IT SQUARE?

To test rectangular items for squareness, measure the distances between the two pairs of diagonally opposite corners. If the measurements are the same, the corners are square. If not, you will need to make adjustments until they are.

For this project, once I had glued the carcass and removed the sash cramps I tried the mirrors in the grooves. Although they went in without difficulty, when they were pushed up against the sides there was a small gap of about ¹⁄₁₆in (1.5mm) at the top of one end and at the bottom of the other. This indicated that the carcass was not exactly square. Fortunately, although PVA glue is apparently set after about an hour, it remains plastic for about 24 hours. I exploited this property by putting a sash cramp across the longer diagonal and tightening it until the carcass was exactly square (i.e. the diagonals were equal – see Fig 22.5) and the doors fitted without any gaps. Leaving the cramp in place, I fitted the shelf and back to help hold the carcass in the correct position. I left the cramp in place for a couple of days, and when it was removed the problem had been corrected.

The general procedure is the same for all rectangular items: test for squareness by measuring the diagonals, and then make any necessary corrections before the glue sets by adjusting a sash cramp across the diagonal.

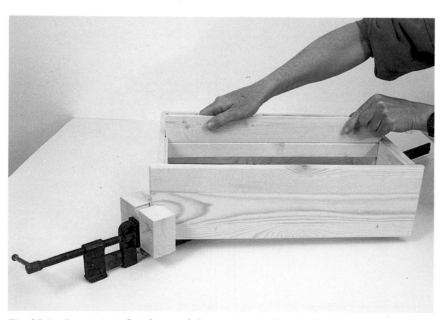

Fig 22.5 Correcting the shape of the carcass with a sash cramp.

2 Round the front edge using the same method as for the top, apply glue to the housings cut in the sides of the carcass and push the shelf into place from the back.

3 Mark out the rectangle for the back on a piece of ¹⁄₄in (6mm) plywood, cut it out and glasspaper the edges.

ASSEMBLY AND FINISHING

1 Place the back in position to check that it fits and draw a line across the width that corresponds to the position of the centre of the shelf. This is to facilitate stapling through the back into the shelf to secure it and prevent the shelf bending in the middle when objects are placed on it. If the fit is satisfactory, apply glue to the rebate around the edge of the carcass and across the back of the shelf. Fit the back and staple it. If you do not have a stapler, panel pins are equally acceptable.

2 Clean up and smooth the entire carcass with glasspaper. Drill four holes in the back of the cabinet for the screws that will hold it to the wall.

3 As the cabinet will be used in a hot, steamy atmosphere, to finish apply three coats of polyurethane varnish. Take care not to allow runs of varnish to get into the mirror grooves. The best way to avoid this is to ensure that there is very little varnish on the brush when you are painting over the area where the grooves are. If any varnish does get into the grooves, wipe it out immediately with a piece of rag wrapped around a small screwdriver or scrap of wood.

Bath Rack

DEGREE OF DIFFICULTY: MEDIUM
TIME TO MAKE: 15 HOURS

THIS design came about when I wanted to make all my bathroom furnishings from wood, so that they matched. The problem is, however, that a bath rack is suspended inches from a tub of hot, steamy water – an environment where a waterproof material such as plastic or a water-resistant hardwood is called for. As the rest of the bathroom was finished in pine, matching the bath rack seemed out of the question.

By coincidence, at about this time I came across a waterproofing solution used by builders on bricks and exterior wood. This is a clear solution that is applied by brush and penetrates below the surface of the wood to form a waterproof barrier. It is colourless, and if left for a short time any other wood finish such as paint or varnish can be painted over the top. This made my pine bath rack feasible.

137

CUTTING LIST		
Sides (2)	Pine	27¾ x 3¼ x ¾in (705 x 82 x 18mm)
Ends (2)	Pine	6⅜ x 1¾ x ¾in (162 x 44 x 18mm)
End rails (2)	Hardwood dowel	5⅞ x ⅜in diameter (149 x 9mm diameter)
Remaining rails (18)	Hardwood dowel	5⅞ x ¼in diameter (149 x 6mm diameter)

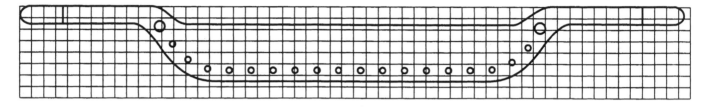

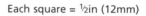
Each square = ½in (12mm)

Fig 23.1 Template for side shape and positions of rail holes.

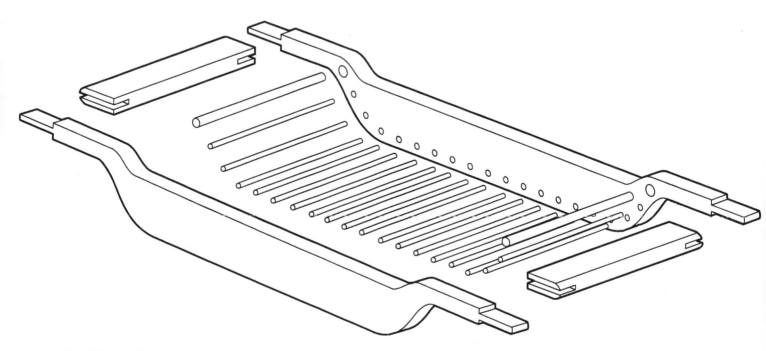

Fig 23.2 Rack construction.

CONSTRUCTION

SIDES

1 Make a template for the side shape by squaring up the shape in Fig 23.1 on to card (see the Note on page 61) and then mark it and the hole positions on to a suitable piece of pine. Try to avoid incorporating too many knots, as

they are potentially weak spots in the wood where the damp might penetrate.

2 Cut out the two side pieces with a bandsaw or any other saw suitable for curve cutting. Smooth the straight edges with a plane and use files or a rotary rasp for the acute corners and curves.

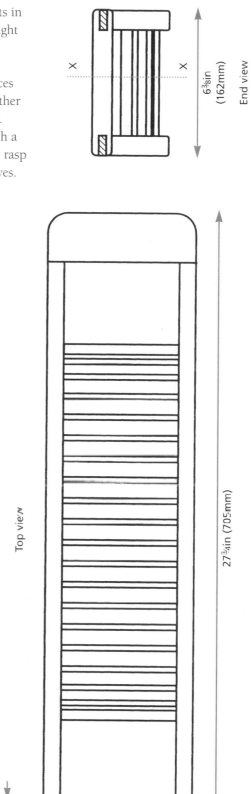

6⅜in (162mm)

End view

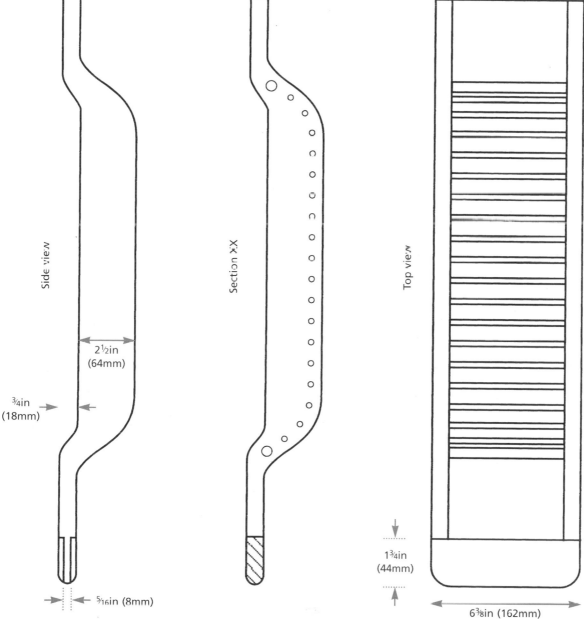

Side view

2½in (64mm)

¾in (18mm)

⁵⁄₁₆in (8mm)

Section XX

Top view

1¾in (44mm)

27¾in (705mm)

6⅜in (162mm)

Fig 23.3 Side view and section XX, top and end views, with dimensions.

A bull-nosed plane is useful for getting into the corners on the top edge of the central section.

3 Test that both sides are the same size and shape by placing them together. If they are not exactly the same, make any adjustments that are required.

ENDS

1 Mark out and cut the two end pieces, which are connected to the sides by corner bridle joints (see Fig 23.5). To make these joints, start by using a try square and pencil to draw a line around the end of each piece that is the same distance from the end as the width of the piece to which it will be joined. On the end pieces the line is drawn on all four sides ¾in (18mm) in from the end, and on the ends of the sides the line is drawn 1¾in (43mm) in from the end.

2 Use a mortise gauge to scribe lines around the ends of all four pieces to indicate where to cut the cheeks of the joint, and mark the waste wood areas with cross-hatching. On the sides, cut along these lines on the waste wood side of the scribed lines and then cut the shoulders, all with a tenon saw. To cut the joints on the two end pieces, use a tenon saw in the same way as for the cheeks but use a coping saw to cut across the bottom of the waste wood area, so that it can be removed. Use a ¼in (6mm) bevel-edged chisel to clean out any waste wood left at the base of the slot.

3 Test the joints for accuracy (see Fig 23.6) and make any adjustments that are required. The joints should be a tight fit that requires hand pressure to put them together. Do not glue at this stage.

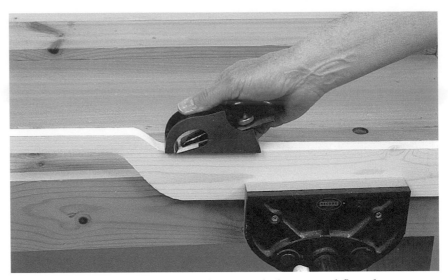

Fig 23.4 *A bull-nosed plane is used to smooth the recessed flat edges.*

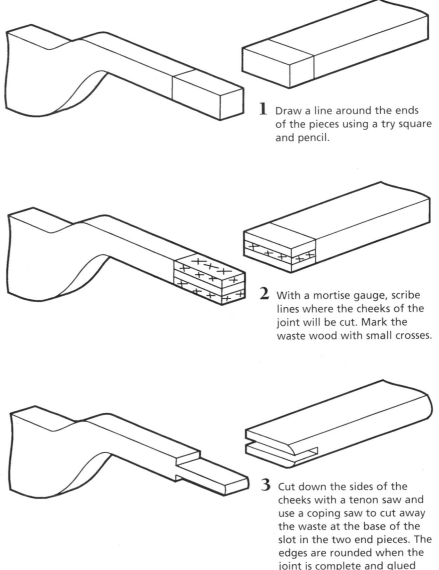

1 Draw a line around the ends of the pieces using a try square and pencil.

2 With a mortise gauge, scribe lines where the cheeks of the joint will be cut. Mark the waste wood with small crosses.

3 Cut down the sides of the cheeks with a tenon saw and use a coping saw to cut away the waste at the base of the slot in the two end pieces. The edges are rounded when the joint is complete and glued together.

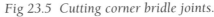

Fig 23.5 *Cutting corner bridle joints.*

RAILS

1 Lay the template back on to each side piece in turn and use a gimlet to pierce through it to indicate on the wood where the holes for the dowelling (rails) should be positioned. Note that the two end rails are ⅜in (9mm) in diameter and the other rails are ¼in (6mm). With the drill held in a vertical drill stand, fit a ⅛in (3mm) bit and make pilot holes where indicated by the gimlet. Put a depth stop on the bit so that it does not penetrate right through the wood (see the Note on page 82). Follow this by drilling the holes for all the rails with the appropriate-sized bits: drill to a depth of ⅜in (15mm).

2 Cut all the rails to length and chamfer the ends slightly with a pencil sharpener. To facilitate gluing the rails into the holes and fitting the two sides together, it helps if the rails do not fit into the holes too tightly. If they are a very tight fit, ease them slightly by using a craft knife to cut a flat on one side of each rail where it fits into its hole. This will allow any trapped glue to ooze out of the holes when the sides are assembled. If this is not done, it will be very difficult to fit the rails fully into the holes.

ASSEMBLY AND FINISHING

1 Apply glue to the holes in one of the sides and push the rails fully into them. Allow to dry.

2 Apply glue to all the joints and put glue into the holes in the other side before assembling the rack. This can be a bit tricky – it will help if the two sides are put into the vice and pressure is gradually applied. As the vice is tightened,

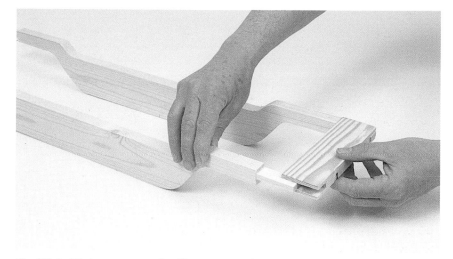

Fig 23.6 *Fitting a corner bridle joint together.*

check that all the rails are located in the holes, then keep tightening until they are all fully seated and the joints fit together without any gaps. Use a damp cloth to wipe off any surplus glue that is squeezed out before it dries.

3 To round the corners, turn the rack over and draw a quadrant of a circle with a radius of approximately 1¼in (32mm) on each corner – I drew around the base of a small paint can. Cut along

these lines with a coping saw (see Fig 23.7). Round all the outside edges carefully with a file and glasspaper.

4 Fill any holes or gaps with waterproof wood filler and glasspaper the entire surface.

5 Apply a single coat of clear waterproofing solution and leave for the time recommended on the can, before finishing with two coats of polyurethane varnish.

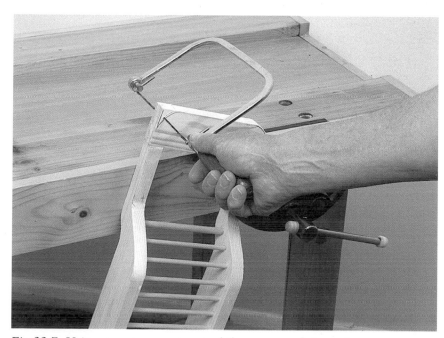

Fig 23.7 *Using a coping saw to round the corners of the rack.*

Bathroom Caddy

DEGREE OF DIFFICULTY: MEDIUM
TIME TO MAKE: 15 HOURS

Oₙₑ of life's small luxuries is soaking in a hot bath, up to the armpits in bubbles. A shower is great when you are in a hurry but when time permits a bath is wonderful. For people who, like myself, wish to read a book or drink a glass of wine at the same time, I have designed a bath caddy to facilitate these simple pleasures. The caddy is constructed from pre-jointed pine board (see the Note on page 76) and is on castors so that it can be moved up to the edge of the bath.

CUTTING LIST

Top (1)	Pre-jointed pine board	15 x 13¼ x ¾in (381 x 337 x 18mm)
Base (1)	Pre-jointed pine board	15 x 13¼ x ¾in (381 x 337 x 18mm)
Shelf (1)	Pre-jointed pine board	12½ x 11⅝ x ¾in (318 x 295 x 18mm)
Sides (2)	Pre-jointed pine board	16½ x 11¾ x ¾in (419 x 298 x 18mm)

ALSO REQUIRED:

40mm castors (4)

CONSTRUCTION
TOP AND BASE

1 On a wide board, mark out the top and base pieces using a large square, extending rule and pencil. It can be difficult to draw a rectangle with perfectly square corners, so test the diagonals to ensure that it is accurate (see the Note on page 136).

Cut out the pieces with a panel saw and plane the edges straight and square. Plane the end grain with a block plane and use one of the techniques shown in Fig 24.4 to ensure that the back edge does not split away.

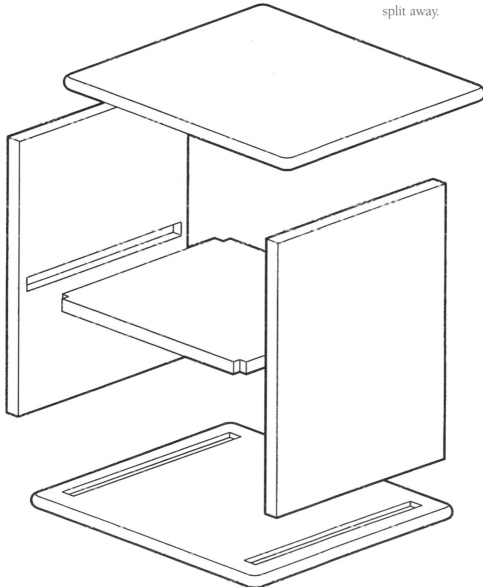

Fig 24.1 Caddy construction.

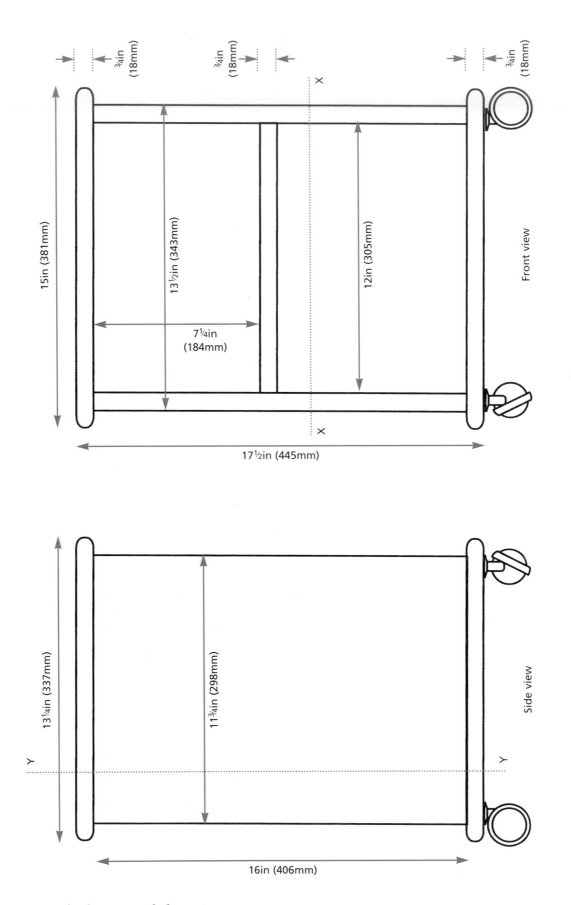

¾in
(18mm)

¾in
(18mm)

¾in
(18mm)

X

15in (381mm)

13½in (343mm)

12in (305mm)

7¼in
(184mm)

X

17½in (445mm)

Front view

13¼in (337mm)

11¾in (298mm)

Y

Y

Side view

16in (406mm)

Fig 24.2 *Front and side views with dimensions.*

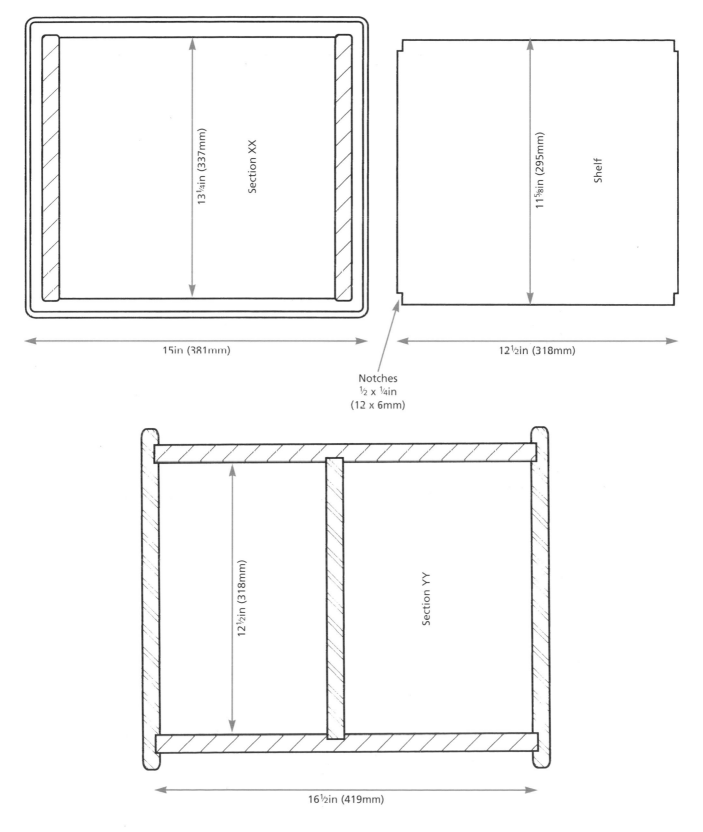

Fig 24.3 *Sections XX and YY, plus shelf, with dimensions.*

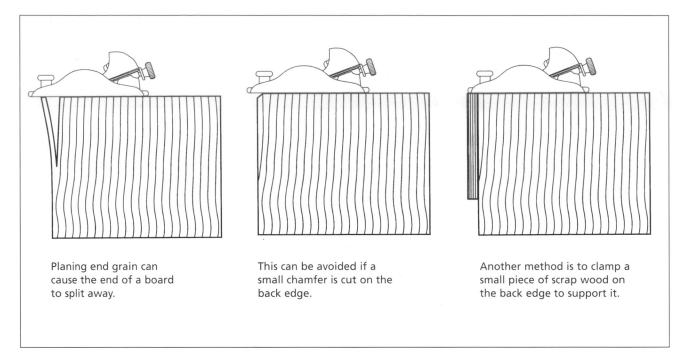

Fig 24.4 *Methods of preventing board ends splitting when planing end grain.*

Planing end grain can
cause the end of a board
to split away.

This can be avoided if a
small chamfer is cut on the
back edge.

Another method is to clamp a
small piece of scrap wood on
the back edge to support it.

2 On the underside of the top
and the top of the base, mark
out where the two recesses will be
cut to house the sides. To mark the
width to the correct size, use a scrap
piece of the same wood as that from
which the sides will be made as a
guide. Cut the recesses using a
router with a straight cutter. If you
use a $\frac{1}{4}$in (6mm) cutter, you will
need three passes for each recess,
which should all be made $\frac{1}{4}$in
(6mm) deep. When all four have
been cut, clean the ends of the
recesses with a bevel-edged chisel
(see Fig 24.5). To help make the
router cuts as accurate as possible,
particularly if the edge of the work
is not completely flat, it helps to
extend the metal fence supplied
with the router by adding a strip of
wood (see Fig 24.6).

When excavating the recesses, I
like to err on the side of making the
width slightly undersized. If the
sides do not fit into the recesses,
they are easily adjusted by planing
off a couple of thin shavings. This is
better than having a loose joint,

which will happen if the recesses are
slightly too wide.

Use a two pence piece as a guide
to draw a radius on each corner of
the top and base. Cut around this
with a coping saw and smooth with
a file. Round all the edges with a
plane, then use glasspaper to
smooth them.

SIDES AND SHELF

1 Mark out and cut the two sides
from a suitable piece of pine
board. Make the recesses for housing
the shelf in the same way as before.
Use a plane to round the edges of
the sides slightly – just enough to
take off the sharp corners. This is to
keep the visual appearance the same

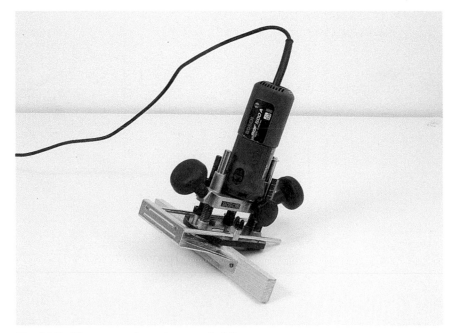

Fig 24.5 *The router fence is extended for greater accuracy.*

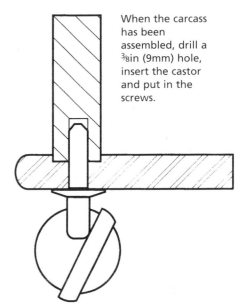

When the carcass
has been
assembled, drill a
³⁄₈in (9mm) hole,
insert the castor
and put in the
screws.

Fig 24.7 Fitting castors.

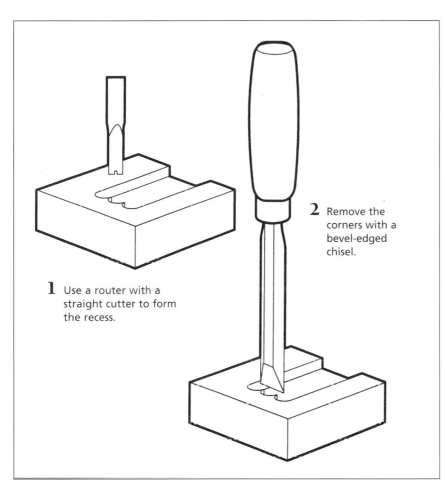

1 Use a router with a
straight cutter to form
the recess.

2 Remove the
corners with a
bevel-edged
chisel.

Fig 24.6 Cutting recesses.

throughout the design and reflects
the rounded edges for the top and
base, although the degree of
rounding is reduced.

2 Mark out and cut the shelf: this
is a rectangle with notches cut
in the four corners using a tenon
saw. Once again, round the sharp
edges slightly.

ASSEMBLY AND FINISHING

1 The whole caddy is glued and
assembled in one operation.
Glue the shelf into the two sides and
then the two sides into the top and
base. Use four sash cramps from the
top to the base. When the glue
oozes out, wipe off any surplus with
a damp cloth. Ensure that all the

joints are completely embedded and
that the assembly is square (see the
Note on page 136).

2 Once the glue is dry, drill four
³⁄₈in (9mm) holes to house the
40mm castors. Fit these into place
and secure with screws (see Fig
24.7).

3 Finish the entire surface with
fine glasspaper, paying
particular attention to the end grain
on the edges of the top and base.

4 As the caddy will be used in the
damp, steamy conditions of the
bathroom, apply three coats of
polyurethane varnish.

MISCELLANEOUS ITEMS

THE LAST TWO PROJECTS ARE NOT
INTENDED FOR USE IN ANY
PARTICULAR ROOM IN THE HOUSE.
THE PAINT BOX MIGHT BE USED
ALMOST ANYWHERE, EXCEPT POSSIBLY
IN THE BATHROOM, WHILE THE
GARAGE SHELF WOULD BE EQUALLY AT
HOME IN A GARDEN SHED OR AN
ENTRANCE PORCH.

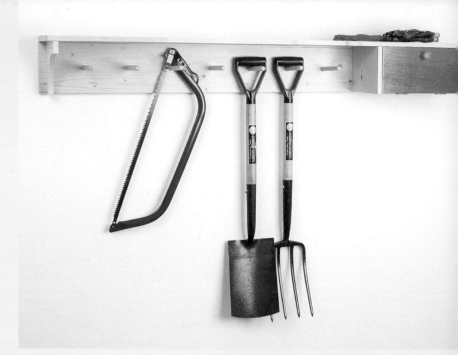

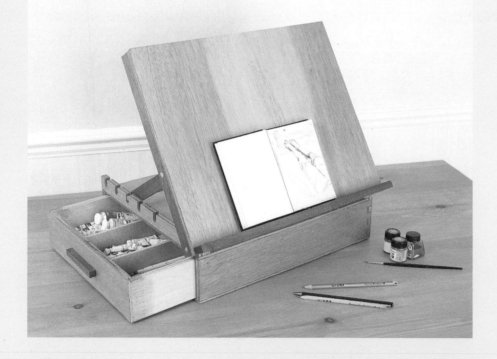

Paint Box with Drawing Board

DEGREE OF DIFFICULTY: ADVANCED
TIME TO MAKE: 25 HOURS

THIS paint box, designed for watercolour artists, consists of a box housing a drawer, and a drawing board. The drawing board adjusts for rake, and the drawer is subdivided to store tubes of paint and brushes. Watercolour paper can be stretched and taped to the board, or it can be held with thumb tacks; stiff artist's board can be propped on the ledge that also serves as a brush rest.

The box, drawer and drawing board are made mainly from plywood, with the prop for the board made from hardwood and hardwood dowelling (I recycled the hardwood from pieces of old window frame salvaged from a skip). The prop and notches arrangement used to adjust the rake of the drawing board was inspired by the type used for a deck chair. Appropriately, box comb joints are used for the corners of the box. There are simpler ways of doing the same job, but these joints are strong and look good if made accurately.

CUTTING LIST

BOX

A	Notched rail (1)	Plywood	13⅞ x 1 x ½in (353 x 25 x 12mm)
B	Side (1)	Plywood	13⅞ x 4¼ x ½in (353 x 108 x 12mm)
C	Swivel blocks (2)	Plywood	1 x 1 x ½in (25 x 25 x 12mm)
D	Front and back (2)	Plywood	16 x 3 x ½in (406 x 76 x 12mm)
E	Top support (1)	Softwood	12⅞ x 1 x ½in (327 x 25 x 12mm)
F	Top (1)	Plywood	15½ x 13⅞ x ¼in (393 x 353 x 6mm)
G	Base (1)	Plywood	16 x 13⅞ x ¼in (406 x 353 x 6mm)
H	Brush rest (1)	Hardwood	17⅛ x 1 x ½in (435 x 25 x 12mm)
J	Drawing board (1)	Plywood	17⅛ x 13⅞ x ½in (435 x 353 x 12mm)
K	Drawing board rails (2)	Hardwood	13⅞ x 1 x ½in (353 x 25 x 12mm)
L	Front pivot (1)	Hardwood dowel	17⅛ x ⅜in diameter (435 x 9mm diameter)
M	Prop sides (2)	Hardwood	8¾ x 1 x ½in (222 x 25 x 12mm)
N	Prop pivot (1)	Hardwood dowel	17⅛ x ⅜in diameter (435 x 9mm diameter)
O	Prop swivel blocks (2)	Hardwood	1 x 1 x ½in (25 x 25 x 12mm)
P	Prop catch (1)	Hardwood dowel	16 x ⅜in diameter (406 x 9mm diameter)
Q	Prop cross rail (1)	Hardwood	13⅞ x 1 x ½in (353 x 25 x 12mm)

ALSO REQUIRED:

Nylon washers to fit over ⅜in (9mm) dowel (2)

DRAWER

A	Front (1)	Plywood	12¹³⁄₁₆ x 2¹⁵⁄₁₆ x ½in (325 x 75 x 12mm)
B	Handle (1)	Plywood	4 x ½ x ½in (102 x 12 x 12mm)
C	Back (1)	Plywood	12⁵⁄₁₆ x 2¾ x ½in (313 x 70 x 12mm)
D	Sides (2)	Plywood	15⅛ x 2¹⁵⁄₁₆ x ½in (384 x 75 x 12mm)
E	Base (1)	Plywood	13¾ x 11¹³⁄₁₆ x ¼in (349 x 300 x 6mm)
F	Partitions (2)	Plywood	14 x 1¾ x ¼in (356 x 44 x 6mm)
G	Short base supports (2)	Softwood	11¹³⁄₁₆ x ⅜ x ⅜in (300 x 9 x 9mm)
H	Long base supports (2)	Softwood	13 x ⅜ x ⅜in (330 x 9 x 9mm)

CONSTRUCTION

BOX

1 Mark out and cut the front and back (parts D) and the side (part B) from a sheet of ½in (12mm) plywood. Plane all the edges flat with a jackplane and smooth with glasspaper.

2 To make the box comb joints on the ends of piece B, where the joints are to be made, draw a line around all four sides, ½in (12mm) from the end – this distance corresponds to the thickness of the wood. Set a pair of dividers to a gap of ½in (12mm) and mark along the drawn line with a pencil and straight-edge (see Fig 25.4). Draw the lines for the sides of the pins, parallel with the sides of the wood.

Cut across the base of the waste wood between the pins with a marking knife to prevent any splintering when it is cut away (see Fig 25.5). Put the piece in the vice and cut down the sides of the pins with a tenon saw, ensuring that you cut on the waste wood sides of the marked lines.

Remove the waste wood between the pins with a coping saw. Do not cut right up to the end line: stop short and remove the last small areas of waste by chopping down with a bevel-edged chisel on both sides of the wood. Make sure you hold the chisel perfectly upright, and give it a sharp rap with a mallet. Use the first set of pins to mark out the pins on the adjacent sides (see Fig 25.6).

The joints should fit together easily without too much pressure. If they do not, make small adjustments with a chisel until they do. Do not glue them at this stage.

3 Along the top edge of the side (part B), mark the series of notches that are used for adjusting the board. To make the notches, drill a row of ⅜in (9mm) holes. To prevent the plywood from splintering on the exit hole of the bit, drill from both sides of the wood and then saw down to the holes from the top edge with a tenon saw. This job is made easier and more accurate if pilot holes are drilled first with a ⅛in (3mm) drill bit. Smooth the inside of the notches with a ⅜in (9mm) round file and the sides with a flat file.

4 Cut a small block of plywood (part C), glue it to the front of the top edge of the side (part B) and drill a ⅜in (9mm) hole through the side and the block. This hole will house a hardwood dowel (part L). The dowel will swivel in the hole and act as a hinge for the drawing board; the block is to reinforce the hinge, as there will be a lot of wear at this point. Once the glue has set, use a coping saw, file and glasspaper to round the top corner of the side and block assembly.

5 Cut a strip of plywood for the notched rail (part A) on the

other side of the box and use the side (part B) as a template to draw the shape of the notches on to it. Cut the notches, attach a reinforcing swivel block (part C) and drill a pivot hole in the same way as before (see Fig 25.7).

6 Before gluing the front, back and side of the box together, cut a length of waste wood to hold the front and back apart at the opposite end to side B when the parts are clamped. The length of this piece corresponds to the inside measurement of the box, 12⅞in (327mm).

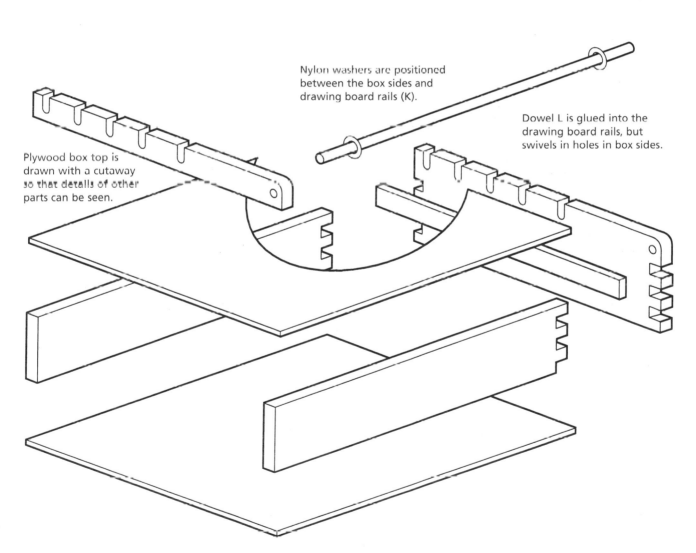

Nylon washers are positioned between the box sides and drawing board rails (K).

Dowel L is glued into the drawing board rails, but swivels in holes in box sides.

Plywood box top is drawn with a cutaway so that details of other parts can be seen.

Fig 25.1 Box construction.

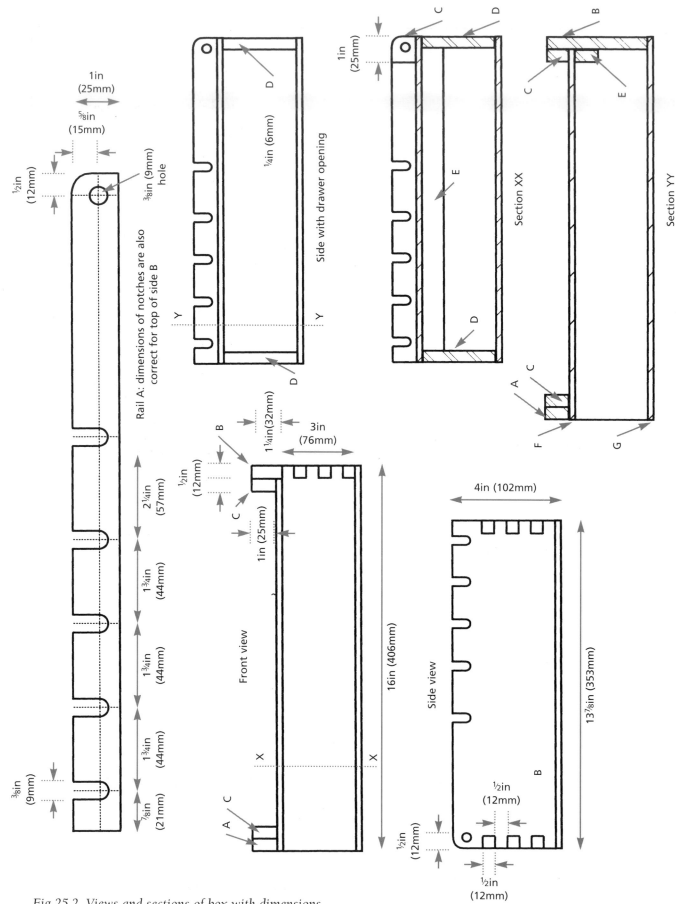

Fig 25.2 *Views and sections of box with dimensions.*

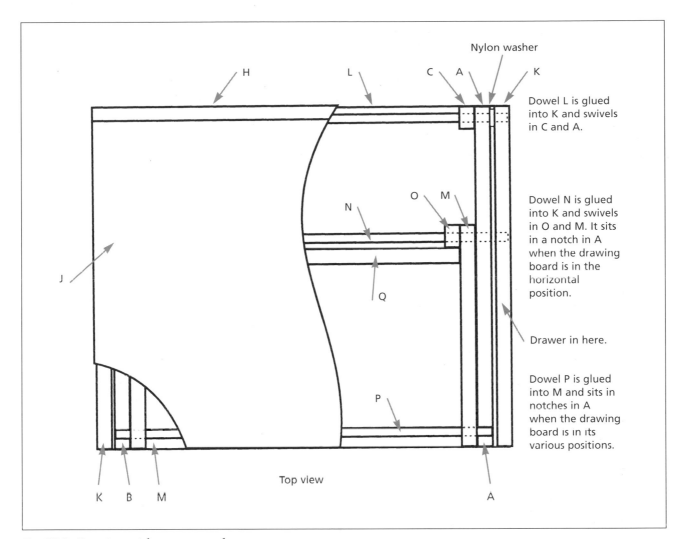

Nylon washer

H   L   C   A   K

Dowel L is glued
into K and swivels
in C and A.

O   M

N

Dowel N is glued
into K and swivels
in O and M. It sits
in a notch in A
when the drawing
board is in the
horizontal
position.

Q

J

Drawer in here.

Dowel P is glued
into M and sits in
notches in A
when the drawing
board is in its
various positions.

P

Top view

K   B   M   A

Fig 25.3 *Top view with parts named.*

Fig 25.4 *Using dividers to mark the position of the pins for the box comb joints.*

Fig 25.5 *Cutting across the grain at the base of the waste wood between pins.*

153

Fig 25.6 *Drawing the second set of pins using the first set as a guide.*

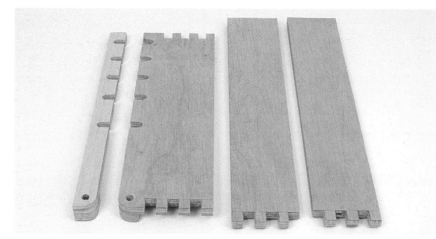

Fig 25.7 *The parts of the box before assembling.*

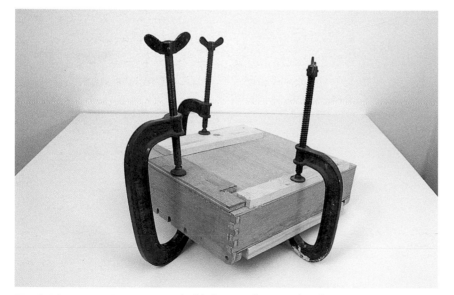

Fig 25.8 *Using 'G' cramps to hold the top, base, sides, front and back together while the glue sets.*

Apply plenty of glue to the joints so that it squeezes out when the box is clamped together. After clamping, but before the glue is set, wipe off any surplus glue with a damp cloth, check that the box is square and make any necessary adjustments.

When the glue is dry, cut a small softwood strip (part E) and fix it inside side B, near the top, with glue and pins. This will support the plywood top (part F).

7 Mark out the top and base (parts F and G) on a sheet of ¼in (6mm) plywood. Check that the corners are square by measuring the diagonals and then cut out the pieces. Smooth the edges with a plane and glasspaper.

On one end of the top (part F), glue and pin the notched rail (part A). When dry, glue the top and base (parts F and G) on to the side, front and back, and use 'G' clamps to hold them until the glue is dry (see Fig 25.8). However, before it is dry, wipe any surplus from the inside of the box with a damp rag, as this might hinder the smooth action of the drawer. Carefully clean up the box joints and the edges of the top and base with a plane and glasspaper. Use glasspaper to round all the edges of the box slightly to reduce any tendency for the plywood to chip. Fill any holes with suitably coloured filler and when dry, glasspaper it flush with the surface of the plywood.

8 Apply two coats of varnish, as it is easier to access all the surfaces before all the parts are joined together. One negative effect is that the varnish will fill in the pivot holes so that dowels cannot rotate freely; to overcome this, drill out the hole again using the original ⅜in (9mm) bit.

DRAWING BOARD

The drawing board has two rails (parts K) fixed to the back, which have holes in them to take the hardwood dowel that pivots on the front of the box (dowel L) and also to provide a pivot for the prop that is used to adjust the rake of the board (dowel N).

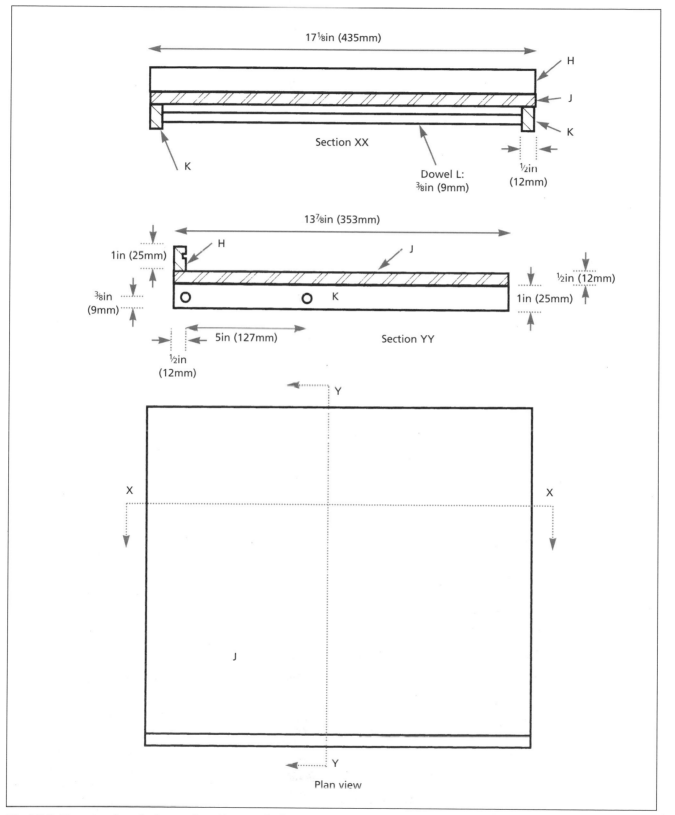

Fig 25.9 Drawing board plan and sections with dimensions.

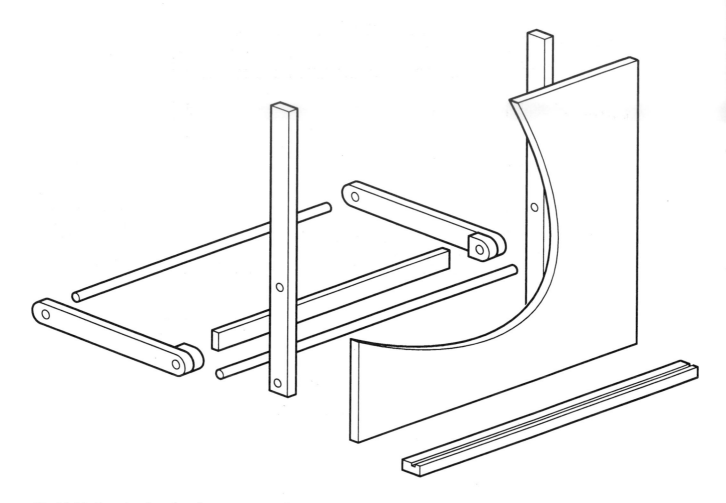

Fig 25.10 *Drawing board and prop construction.*

1 Cut the two hardwood rails
(parts K) to size and drill the
pivot holes with a ³⁄₈in (9mm) bit.

2 Cut the drawing board (part J)
to size, and fit the two rails to it
with glue and 1¼in (32mm) screws,
two per rail.

3 Cut out the brush rest (part H)
and use a router to make a ¼ x
³⁄₈in (6 x 9mm) groove in it to hold
the paintbrushes. Fix the brush rest
to the base of the board with glue
and pins. Varnish these parts.

PROP

1 Mark and cut the hardwood
prop sides (parts M) and the two
swivel blocks (parts O). Glue the
blocks on to the prop sides, drill
³⁄₈in (9mm) holes in the appropriate
positions and round the ends using
a coping saw and files. The holes
that pass through both the swivel
blocks and prop sides are for dowel
N, and the holes at the other end of
the sides are for dowel P, which fits
into the notches in the top of the
box when the drawing board is
being used.

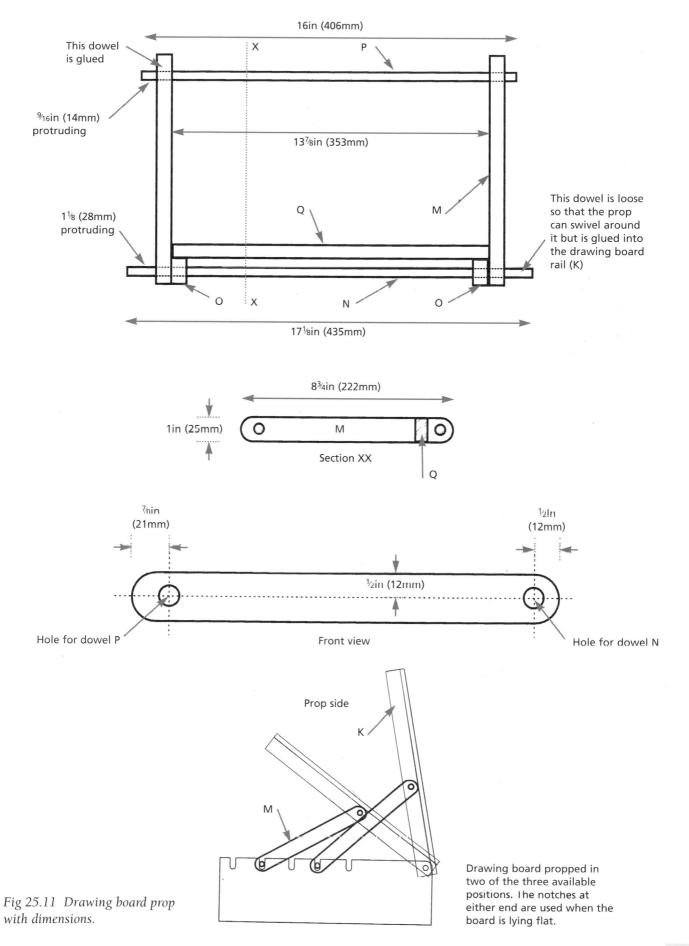

16in (406mm)

This dowel is glued

⁹⁄₁₆in (14mm) protruding

1⅛ (28mm) protruding

X

P

13⅞in (353mm)

Q

M

This dowel is loose so that the prop can swivel around it but is glued into the drawing board rail (K)

O

X

N

O

17⅛in (435mm)

8¾in (222mm)

1in (25mm)

M

Section XX

Q

⅞in (21mm)

½in (12mm)

½in (12mm)

Hole for dowel P

Front view

Hole for dowel N

Prop side

K

M

Drawing board propped in two of the three available positions. The notches at either end are used when the board is lying flat.

Fig 25.11 Drawing board prop with dimensions.

Fig 25.12 The assembled prop.

2 Cut out the prop cross rail (part Q) and fix it to the two prop sides (parts M) with glue and pins. Glue the dowel P into the prop sides (see Fig 25.12). Before the glue dries, check that the assembly is square, lies flat and fits into its allotted position in the top of the box.

ASSEMBLING BOX, PROP AND DRAWING BOARD

1 Cut lengths of dowel for parts N and L, both of which are as long as the width of the drawing board.

2 Fit dowel L first and place nylon washers between the drawing board rails and the sides of the box. Glue the dowel into the holes in the drawing board rails and apply candle wax to it where it rotates in the holes in the sides of the box.

3 Glue dowel N into the rails on the back of the drawing board and wax it where it rotates in the prop (see Fig 25.13).

DRAWER

1 On a piece of ½in (12mm) plywood, mark out the front (part A), back (part C) and two sides (parts D) of the drawer. Cut them out and smooth the edges. On the insides of the sides at the back, cut two housing joints with a router for the drawer back to fit into. In the inside of the back, cut two ¼in (6mm) through housings for the drawer partitions. On the back edge of the front, cut two rebates to house the sides and two stopped housings for the partitions.

2 Glue and pin the front, back and sides together, check that they are square and clamp until dry. Punch all the pins below the surface and fill the resulting holes.

3 Place this assembly on top of a piece of ¼in (6mm) plywood and draw around the inside of it to mark the size for the drawer base (part D). Cut it out with a panel saw and put to one side until required. Do the same with the partitions (parts F).

Fig 25.13 Pushing a dowel pivot into the back of the board.

4 Cut parts H and G to length from ⅜ x ⅜in (9 x 9mm) sectioned softwood. Glue and pin these pieces to the inside lower edge of the assembly to support the drawer base, then glue the base and partitions into place. You will need to bend the partitions as they are fitted so that they spring into place. They are glued along the bottom edge as well as at the ends.

5 Use a spare piece of hardwood to make a handle, and glue and screw it into the centre of the drawer front.

ASSEMBLY AND FINISHING

1 Varnish the drawer front and a little of the sides where they join the front. Use candle wax on the top and bottom edge of the sides so that they will run freely. Fit the drawer into the box to complete.

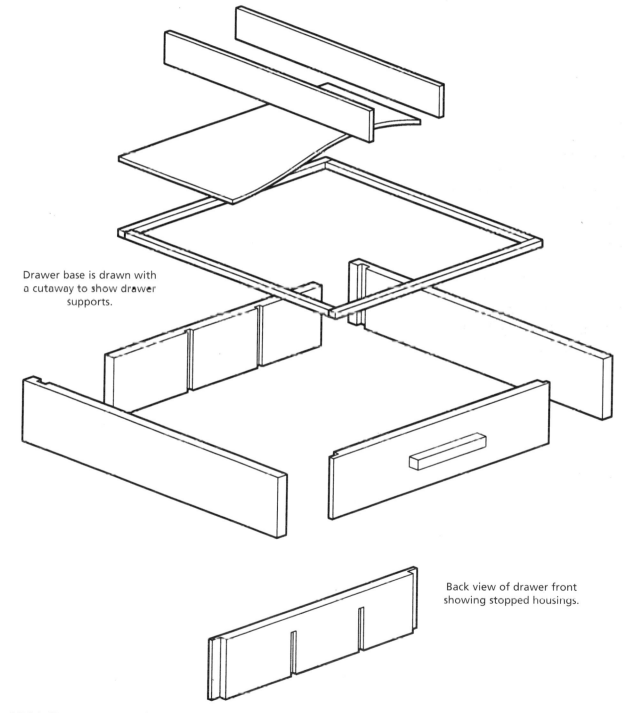

Drawer base is drawn with a cutaway to show drawer supports.

Back view of drawer front showing stopped housings.

Fig 25.14 Drawer construction.

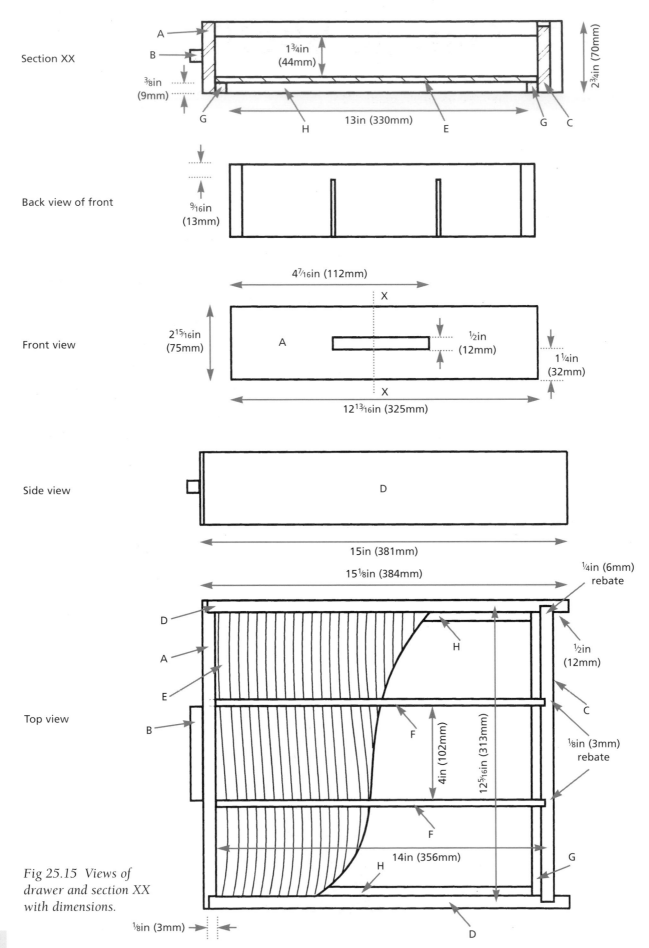

Section XX

A

B

$\frac{3}{8}$in (9mm)

G

H

13in (330mm)

E

G

C

$1\frac{3}{4}$in (44mm)

$2\frac{3}{4}$in (70mm)

Back view of front

$\frac{9}{16}$in (13mm)

Front view

$4\frac{7}{16}$in (112mm)

X

$2\frac{15}{16}$in (75mm)

A

$\frac{1}{2}$in (12mm)

$1\frac{1}{4}$in (32mm)

X

$12\frac{13}{16}$in (325mm)

Side view

D

15in (381mm)

Top view

$15\frac{1}{8}$in (384mm)

$\frac{1}{4}$in (6mm) rebate

D

A

E

B

H

$\frac{1}{2}$in (12mm)

C

F

$\frac{1}{8}$in (3mm) rebate

4in (102mm)

$12\frac{5}{16}$in (313mm)

F

14in (356mm)

G

H

D

$\frac{1}{8}$in (3mm)

Fig 25.15 Views of drawer and section XX with dimensions.

Garage Shelf

DEGREE OF DIFFICULTY: EASY
TIME TO MAKE: 15 HOURS

FOR most of us, the garage is not just for keeping the family car warm and snug but is also a combination of potting shed, workshop and extra storage facility. If this is your situation, you may like to make this useful garage shelf.

The shelf is wide and long, so that all those old cans of paint you are reluctant to throw out can be accommodated. Under the shelf there is a row of strong pegs that are ideal for hanging up garden tools. Underneath the end of the shelf there is a box with a door for storing small items such as garden chemicals, boxes of screws, nuts and bolts, small tools, gardening gloves and so on.

Because there is little call for furniture made in the Chippendale style for the garage, screws and glue are used for all the joints, and the wood is pine because it is cheap and readily available. The exception is the door on the box, which is a piece of hardwood-faced blockboard that makes a pleasant contrast to the rest of the shelf in both colour and texture.

CUTTING LIST		
Back (1)	Pine	64 x 8 x ¾in (1,626 x 203 x 18mm)
Top (1)	Pine	64 x 8 x ¾in (1,626 x 203 x 18mm)
Top support bracket (1)	Pine	8 x 7¼ x ¾in (203 x 184 x 18mm)
Box sides (2)	Pine	8 x 7¼ x ¾in (203 x 184 x 18mm)
Box base (1)	Pine	14 x 7¼ x ¾in (356 x 184 x 18mm)
Box door (1)	Hardwood-faced blockboard	14 x 7¼ x ¾in (356 x 184 x 18mm)
Pegs (7)	Pine dowel	6 x ¾in diameter (152 x 18mm diameter)

ALSO REQUIRED:

1in (25mm) pine knob (1)	
2in (51mm) easy-on hinges (2)	
10in (254mm) brass chain (1)	
Small screw eyes (2)	
Small magnetic catch (1)	

CONSTRUCTION

SHELF AND BOX

1 Cut two lengths of pine board for the top and back of the shelf. On the back edge of the top, drill a series of screw holes, using a drill in a drill stand to ensure they are vertical, and countersink them (see Fig 26.3). The holes should be wide enough for the screws to slide freely in them. Place the top in its final position on the back and, using it as a guide, drill

holes in the edge of the back – this time, the holes should be smaller than the diameter of the screws. Apply some glue and screw the two parts together (see Fig 26.4).

2 Mark out a piece of pine for the two box sides, cut them out and smooth the edges with a plane. Using a rule and try square, mark the position for these sides on the back and top. Drill holes for the screws and assemble the two box sides with the rest of the shelf. Follow the same procedure for the base of the box.

3 A bracket supports the shelf at the opposite end to the box. This is the same size as the sides of the box but has a decorative concave scallop cut from it. Draw around a paint tin or something similar to get the concave shape, cut it out with a jigsaw and smooth with a drum sander. Fix the bracket in place with screws and glue.

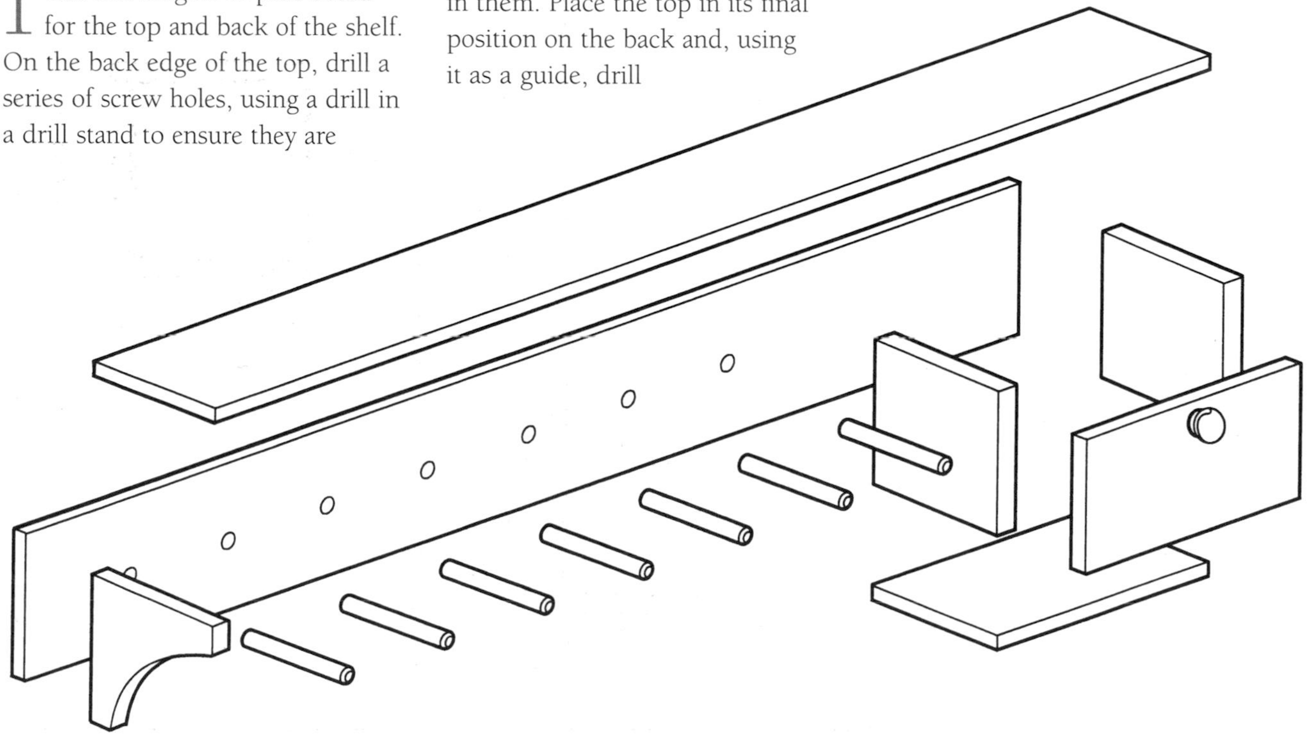

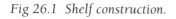

Fig 26.1 Shelf construction.

BOX DOOR AND PEGS

1 From a piece of hardwood-faced blockboard or other similar board, cut out the door for the box. Attach the wooden knob – this is done at this stage as it makes a convenient hand-hold when fitting and testing the hinges.

2 Although the hinges are relatively simple to fit, as a precaution fix them initially with a single screw and test to ensure that they fit accurately by opening and closing the door. Make any necessary adjustments and then fit the rest of the screws. Fix two small screw eyes and a length of chain to prevent the door opening excessively (see Fig 26.5).

3 Mark the positions of the pegs and then drill the holes for them to fit into with a ¾in (18mm) spade bit. Cut the pegs to size from a length of pine dowel and chamfer the ends.

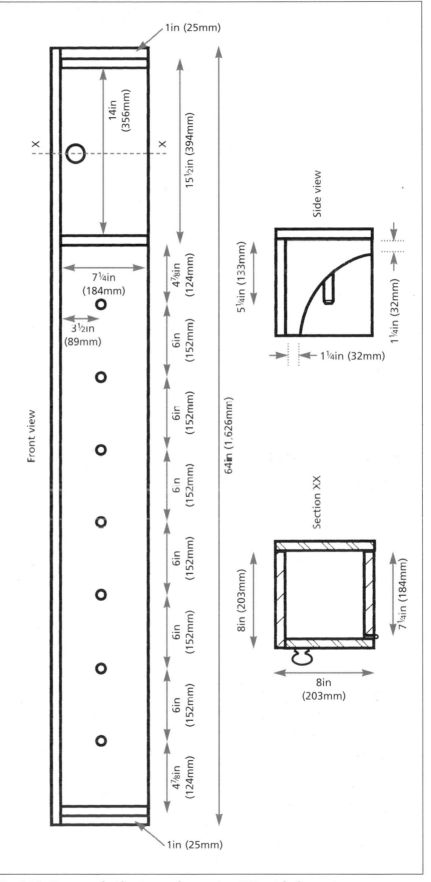

Fig 26.2 Front and side views, plus section XX, with dimensions.

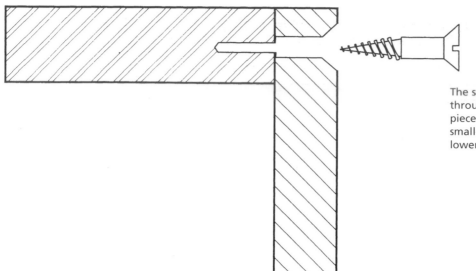

The screw should pass easily through the hole in the top piece and screw into the small-diameter hole in the lower piece.

Fig 26.3 Fixing screws.

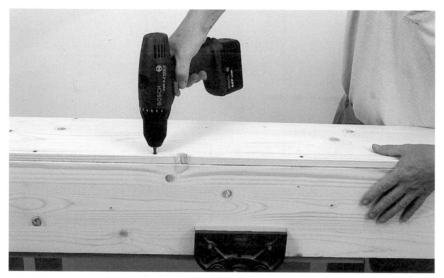

Fig 26.4 Fixing the back to the shelf with screws and glue.

Fig 26.5 Fixing the chain stay.

ASSEMBLY AND FINISHING

1 Knock the pegs into the holes with a mallet and glue into place. Drill three holes in the back for the screws or bolts that will fix the shelf to the wall.

2 Use neutral-coloured filler to make good any flaws in the wood and cover up the screw heads. When dry, clean off any excess with glasspaper. Finish with a coat of polyurethane varnish to help protect the wood against changes in humidity, insects, damp and so on.

METRIC CONVERSION TABLE

INCHES TO MILLIMETRES AND CENTIMETRES

in	mm	cm	in	cm	in	cm
1/8	3	0.3	9	22.9	30	76.2
1/4	6	0.6	10	25.4	31	78.7
3/8	10	1.0	11	27.9	32	81.3
1/2	13	1.3	12	30.5	33	83.8
5/8	16	1.6	13	33.0	34	86.4
3/4	19	1.9	14	35.6	35	88.9
7/8	22	2.2	15	38.1	36	91.4
1	25	2.5	16	40.6	37	94.0
1 1/4	32	3.2	17	43.2	38	96.5
1 1/2	38	3.8	18	45.7	39	99.1
1 3/4	44	4.4	19	48.3	40	101.6
2	51	5.1	20	50.8	41	104.1
2 1/2	64	6.4	21	53.3	42	106.7
3	76	7.6	22	55.9	43	109.2
3 1/2	89	8.9	23	58.4	44	111.8
4	102	10.2	24	61.0	45	114.3
4 1/2	114	11.4	25	63.5	46	116.8
5	127	12.7	26	66.0	47	119.4
6	152	15.2	27	68.6	48	121.9
7	178	17.8	28	71.1	49	124.5
8	203	20.3	29	73.7	50	127.0

About the Author

SINCE giving up his day job in the electronics pre-press industry, Dave Mackenzie now divides his time between lecturing – on graphic design, DTP and magazine journalism – and woodworking.

This is his third book, following a couple of hundred magazine articles on woodworking and DIY published over the last 20 years, ranging from furniture design to kite making and much else in between. His first two books, *Pine Furniture Projects* and *Bird Boxes and Feeders for the Garden*, are also published by Guild of Master Craftsman Publications.

Dave Mackenzie is married with two children and enjoys painting, walking and bird watching.

Index

Titles available from
GMC PUBLICATIONS

BOOKS

Woodworking

40 More Woodworking Plans & Projects	*GMC Publications*
Bird Boxes and Feeders for the Garden	*Dave Mackenzie*
Complete Woodfinishing	*Ian Hosker*
David Charlesworth's Furniture-making Techniques	*David Charlesworth*
Electric Woodwork	*Jeremy Broun*
Furniture & Cabinetmaking Projects	*GMC Publications*
Furniture Projects	*Rod Wales*
Furniture Restoration (Practical Crafts)	*Kevin Jan Bonner*
Furniture Restoration and Repair for Beginners	*Kevin Jan Bonner*
Furniture Restoration Workshop	*Kevin Jan Bonner*
Green Woodwork	*Mike Abbott*
Making & Modifying Woodworking Tools	*Jim Kingshott*
Making Chairs and Tables	*GMC Publications*
Making Fine Furniture	*Tom Darby*
Making Little Boxes from Wood	*John Bennett*
Making Shaker Furniture	*Barry Jackson*
Making Woodwork Aids and Devices	*Robert Wearing*
Pine Furniture Projects for the Home	*Dave Mackenzie*
Router Magic: Jigs, Fixtures and Tricks to	
Unleash your Router's Full Potential	*Bill Hylton*
Routing for Beginners	*Anthony Bailey*
The Scrollsaw: Twenty Projects	*John Everett*
Sharpening Pocket Reference Book	*Jim Kingshott*
Sharpening: The Complete Guide	*Jim Kingshott*
Space-Saving Furniture Projects	*Dave Mackenzie*
Stickmaking: A Complete Course	*Andrew Jones & Clive George*
Stickmaking Handbook	*Andrew Jones & Clive George*
Test Reports: *The Router* and	
Furniture & Cabinetmaking	*GMC Publications*
Veneering: A Complete Course	*Ian Hosker*
Woodfinishing Handbook (Practical Crafts)	*Ian Hosker*
Woodworking Plans and Projects	*GMC Publications*
Woodworking with the Router: Professional	
Router Techniques any Woodworker can Use	*Bill Hylton & Fred Matlack*
The Workshop	*Jim Kingshott*

Woodturning

Adventures in Woodturning	*David Springett*
Bert Marsh: Woodturner	*Bert Marsh*
Bill Jones' Notes from the Turning Shop	*Bill Jones*
Bill Jones' Further Notes from the Turning Shop	*Bill Jones*
Colouring Techniques for Woodturners	*Ian Sanders*
The Craftsman Woodturner	*Peter Child*
Decorative Techniques for Woodturners	*Hilary Bowen*
Essential Tips for Woodturners	*GMC Publications*
Faceplate Turning	*GMC Publications*
Fun at the Lathe	*R.C. Bell*
Illustrated Woodturning Techniques	*John Hunnex*
Intermediate Woodturning Projects	*GMC Publications*
Keith Rowley's Woodturning Projects	*Keith Rowley*
Make Money from Woodturning	*Ann & Bob Phillips*
Multi-Centre Woodturning	*Ray Hopper*
Pleasure and Profit from Woodturning	*Reg Sherwin*
Practical Tips for Turners & Carvers	*GMC Publications*
Practical Tips for Woodturners	*GMC Publications*
Spindle Turning	*GMC Publications*
Turning Miniatures in Wood	*John Sainsbury*
Turning Wooden Toys	*Terry Lawrence*
Understanding Woodturning	*Ann & Bob Phillips*
Useful Techniques for Woodturners	*GMC Publications*
Useful Woodturning Projects	*GMC Publications*
Woodturning: Bowls, Platters, Hollow Forms, Vases,	
Vessels, Bottles, Flasks, Tankards, Plates	*GMC Publications*
Woodturning: A Foundation Course	*Keith Rowley*
Woodturning: A Source Book of Shapes	*John Hunnex*
Woodturning Jewellery	*Hilary Bowen*
Woodturning Masterclass	*Tony Boase*
Woodturning Techniques	*GMC Publications*
Woodturning Tools & Equipment Test Reports	*GMC Publications*
Woodturning Wizardry	*David Springett*

Woodcarving

The Art of the Woodcarver	*GMC Publications*
Carving Birds & Beasts	*GMC Publications*
Carving on Turning	*Chris Pye*
Carving Realistic Birds	*David Tippey*
Decorative Woodcarving	*Jeremy Williams*
Essential Tips for Woodcarvers	*GMC Publications*
Essential Woodcarving Techniques	*Dick Onians*
Lettercarving in Wood: A Practical Course	*Chris Pye*
Power Tools for Woodcarving	*David Tippey*
Practical Tips for Turners & Carvers	*GMC Publications*
Relief Carving in Wood: A Practical Introduction	*Chris Pye*
Understanding Woodcarving	*GMC Publications*
Understanding Woodcarving in the Round	*GMC Publications*
Useful Techniques for Woodcarvers	*GMC Publications*
Wildfowl Carving - Volume 1	*Jim Pearce*
Wildfowl Carving - Volume 2	*Jim Pearce*
The Woodcarvers	*GMC Publications*
Woodcarving: A Complete Course	*Ron Butterfield*
Woodcarving: A Foundation Course	*Zoë Gertner*
Woodcarving for Beginners	*GMC Publications*
Woodcarving Tools & Equipment Test Reports	*GMC Publications*
Woodcarving Tools, Materials & Equipment	*Chris Pye*

Upholstery

Seat Weaving (Practical Crafts)	*Ricky Holdstock*
Upholsterer's Pocket Reference Book	*David James*
Upholstery: A Complete Course	*David James*
Upholstery Restoration	*David James*
Upholstery Techniques & Projects	*David James*

Toymaking

Designing & Making Wooden Toys	*Terry Kelly*	Restoring Rocking Horses	*Clive Green & Anthony Dew*
Fun to Make Wooden Toys & Games	*Jeff & Jennie Loader*	Scrollsaw Toy Projects	*Ivor Carlyle*
Making Board, Peg & Dice Games	*Jeff & Jennie Loader*	Wooden Toy Projects	*GMC Publications*
Making Wooden Toys & Games	*Jeff & Jennie Loader*		

Dolls' Houses & Miniatures

Architecture for Dolls' Houses	*Joyce Percival*	Making Miniature Gardens	*Freida Gray*
Beginners' Guide to the Dolls' House Hobby	*Jean Nisbett*	Making Miniature Oriental Rugs & Carpets	*Meik & Ian McNaughton*
The Complete Dolls' House Book	*Jean Nisbett*	Making Period Dolls' House Accessories	*Andrea Barham*
The Dolls' House 1/24 Scale: A Complete Introduction	*Jean Nisbett*	Making Period Dolls' House Furniture	*Derek & Sheila Rowbottom*
Dolls' House Accessories, Fixtures and Fittings	*Andrea Barham*	Making Tudor Dolls' Houses	*Derek Rowbottom*
Dolls' House Bathrooms: Lots of Little Loos	*Patricia King*	Making Unusual Miniatures	*Graham Spalding*
Dolls' House Fireplaces and Stoves	*Patricia King*	Making Victorian Dolls' House Furniture	*Patricia King*
Easy to Make Dolls' House Accessories	*Andrea Barham*	Miniature Bobbin Lace	*Roz Snowden*
Heraldic Miniature Knights	*Peter Greenhill*	Miniature Embroidery for the Victorian Dolls' House	*Pamela Warner*
Make Your Own Dolls' House Furniture	*Maurice Harper*	Miniature Needlepoint Carpets	*Janet Granger*
Making Dolls' House Furniture	*Patricia King*	The Secrets of the Dolls' House Makers	*Jean Nisbett*
Making Georgian Dolls' Houses	*Derek Rowbottom*		

Crafts

American Patchwork Designs in Needlepoint	*Melanie Tacon*	An Introduction to Crewel Embroidery	*Mave Glenny*
A Beginners' Guide to Rubber Stamping	*Brenda Hunt*	Making Character Bears	*Valerie Tyler*
Celtic Knotwork Designs	*Sheila Sturrock*	Making Greetings Cards for Beginners	*Pat Sutherland*
Celtic Knotwork Handbook	*Sheila Sturrock*	Making Hand-Sewn Boxes: Techniques and Projects	*Jackie Woolsey*
Collage from Seeds, Leaves and Flowers	*Joan Carver*	Making Knitwear Fit	*Pat Ashforth & Steve Plummer*
Complete Pyrography	*Stephen Poole*	Needlepoint: A Foundation Course	*Sandra Hardy*
Creating Knitwear Designs	*Pat Ashforth & Steve Plummer*	Pyrography Designs	*Norma Gregory*
Creative Doughcraft	*Patricia Hughes*	Pyrography Handbook (Practical Crafts)	*Stephen Poole*
Creative Embroidery Techniques		Ribbons and Roses	*Lee Lockheed*
Using Colour Through Gold	*Daphne J. Ashby & Jackie Woolsey*	Tassel Making for Beginners	*Enid Taylor*
Cross Stitch Kitchen Projects	*Janet Granger*	Tatting Collage	*Lindsay Rogers*
Cross Stitch on Colour	*Sheena Rogers*	Temari: A Traditional Japanese Embroidery Technique	*Margaret Ludlow*
Designing and Making Cards	*Glennis Gilruth*	Theatre Models in Paper and Card	*Robert Burgess*
Embroidery Tips & Hints	*Harold Hayes*	Wool Embroidery & Design	*Lee Lockheed*

The Home & Gardening

Home Ownership: Buying and Maintaining	*Nicholas Snelling*	Security for the Householder: Fitting Locks and Other Devices	*F Phillips*
The Living Tropical Greenhouse	*John and Maureen Tampion*	The Birdwatcher's Garden	*Hazel and Pamela Johnson*

VIDEOS

Drop-in and Pinstuffed Seats	*David James*	Twists and Advanced Turning	*Dennis White*
Stuffover Upholstery	*David James*	Sharpening the Professional Way	*Jim Kingshott*
Elliptical Turning	*David Springett*	Sharpening Turning & Carving Tools	*Jim Kingshott*
Woodturning Wizardry	*David Springett*	Bowl Turning	*John Jordan*
Turning Between Centres: The Basics	*Dennis White*	Hollow Turning	*John Jordan*
Turning Bowls	*Dennis White*	Woodturning: A Foundation Course	*Keith Rowley*
Boxes, Goblets and Screw Threads	*Dennis White*	Carving a Figure: The Female Form	*Ray Gonzalez*
Novelties and Projects	*Dennis White*	The Router: A Beginner's Guide	*Alan Goodsell*
Classic Profiles	*Dennis White*	The Scroll Saw: A Beginner's Guide	*John Burke*

MAGAZINES

Woodturning • Woodcarving • Furniture & Cabinetmaking • The Dolls' House Magazine
The Router • The ScrollSaw • Creative Crafts for the Home • BusinessMatters

---

The above represents a full list of all titles currently published or scheduled to be published.
All are available direct from the Publishers or through bookshops, newsagents and specialist retailers.
To place an order, or to obtain a complete catalogue, contact:

GMC Publications
Castle Place, 166 High Street, Lewes, East Sussex BN7 1XU, United Kingdom Tel: 01273 488005 Fax: 01273 478606
Orders by credit card are accepted